Praise for *Generation* j

'Dr. Peter Vogel's work on tackling youth unei
inspiring and gives hope to those who feel like
This book is an excellent read for anyone who   , _ ___ ____ __ ___
ate a better future for the generations to come. His mission is mine, to lay out
a blueprint for those with aspirations and great ideas, so that they can become
job creators, wealth creators, and in certain cases, go from unemployed to
self-employed.'
— **John Hope Bryant**, *Founder, Chairman and CEO, Operation HOPE*

'*Generation Jobless?* is a wonderful read and primer for anyone who cares to
make a difference. Truly the best work I have read on the youth labor market
crisis – and a personal invitation to each and every one of us to take part in
solving the crisis for our children.'
— **Carsten Sudhoff**, *Founder and CEO, Circular Society AG*

'How might we best prepare students for the world of work in the 21st century? This thorough and timely book about the youth unemployment crisis
describes interesting possibilities from around the world.'
— **Charles Fadel**, *Visiting Practitioner, Harvard University*; co-author of
21st Century Skills: Learning for Life in Our Times

'The world of work is transforming at a furious, unprecedented pace, and
young people are the ones that are hit hardest. This is a truly powerful book
that gives us hope that it is not too late to avoid a generation jobless.'
— **Mike Johnson**, *Chairman and Founder, the Futurework Forum*;
author of *The Worldwide Workplace: Solving the Global
Talent Equation*

'Unemployment is casting a shadow over the lives of millions of young people around the world. Yet it goes unchecked because the solutions are often
complex, opaque, and require aligned action by multiple stakeholders. In this
important and fascinating book, Peter Vogel takes a positive and uplifting view
of what it takes for a crisis to become an opportunity. Drawing on examples
from across the world, he shows how education, government, and employees
can each play their part. Most of the world's most complex challenges require
multi-stakeholder solutions – and this book shows the power of alignment.'
— **Lynda Gratton**, *Professor, London Business School*;
author of the book *The Shift*

'This is the best assessment and discussion of the current youth unemployment crisis that I have read. It is tremendously rich in content and insightful.

While most reports and media coverage focus on the crisis and its possible causes, Peter Vogel walks the extra mile to actually discuss the most essential part of all: solutions to youth unemployment! I highly recommend this book to anyone who cares about the future of our children.'

—**Melinda Emerson**, 'SmallBizLady'; *America's #1 Small Business Expert*; author of *Become Your Own Boss in 12 Months*

Turning the Youth Unemployment Crisis into Opportunity

Generation Jobless?

Peter Vogel

palgrave
macmillan

First published 2015 by
PALGRAVE MACMILLAN.

Palgrave Macmillan in the UK is an imprint of Macmillan Publishers Limited, registered in England, company number 785998, of Houndsmills, Basingstoke, Hampshire, RG21 6XS.

Palgrave Macmillan in the US is a division of St Martin's Press LLC, 175 Fifth Avenue, New York, NY 10010.

Palgrave is the global academic imprint of the above companies and has companies and representatives throughout the world.

Palgrave® and Macmillan® are registered trademarks in the United States, the United Kingdom, Europe and other countries.

ISBN 978-1-349-47754-8   ISBN 978-1-137-37594-0 (eBook)
DOI 10.1057/9781137375940

This book is printed on paper suitable for recycling and made from fully managed and sustained forest sources. Logging, pulping and manufacturing processes are expected to conform to the environmental regulations of the country of origin.

A catalogue record for this book is available from the British Library.

A catalog record for this book is available from the Library of Congress.

Typeset by MPS Limited, Chennai, India.

To my daughter Sophie Marie
Whose future will hopefully be full of opportunities!

This page intentionally left blank

Contents

Part II From Crisis to Opportunity

List of Figures and Tables

╱ Figures

/ Tables

List of Case Studies and Solution Ideas

Title & Initiator/ Proposer	Chapter	Title & Initiator/ Proposer	Chapter
4.0 Schools	5	Credit Suisse Apprenticeship System	6
Aiducation	5	D.schools	5
Apple Distinguished Educator	5	Dar Blanca Radio	4
Arab Stabilization Plan	7	DevEd	5
Arabreneur	4	Diageo Apprenticeship Program	6
AshokaU Changemaker Campus	5	Die Chance Foundation	6
Barclays Apprenticeship Program	6	DonorsChoose	5
Beyond the Classroom	6	Ecosofft	4
Build Your Own Business Curriculum	5	Education for Employment Foundation	6
Career Integrated Learning Project	5	Edupass	8
ccInspire	6	Elgazala Technopark	4
Cedefop	5	Empact	4
Ciett	7	Emzingo	5
CodeNow	5	enke: Make your Mark	8
Coderise	5	Enstitute	5
Coursera E-Learning Portal	5	Enternships	4

(continued)

Continued

Title & Initiator/ Proposer	Chapter	Title & Initiator/ Proposer	Chapter
EU Solutions to Youth Unemployment	7	Maker Education Initiative	5
Euforia	5	Makerbot Academy	5
Experience Institute	5	Manpower Programs	6
Fab Labs	5	Microglobal Age	8
Flexicurity Model	7	Mobile Schools	5
Generation Enterprise	4	MoneyThink	5
Generation Success	6	Monkeywrench	5
Global Economic Symposium Solutions	8	Nearpod	5
Google for Education	5	Nestlé needs YOUth	6
GUESSS Project	4	NFTE	4
Hackathons	5	Open University of West Africa	5
Hole in the Wall	5	Operation HOPE	4
ILO Solutions to Youth Unemployment	7	P21 Initiative	5
INJAZ-UAE	4	Peruvian Action Plan for Youth	7
Integration durch Austausch	7	Piggybackr	5
Job Sharing	6	Project H Design	5
Jobzippers	5	Project Leonhard	4
Jobzippers Speaker Series	4	Quest University	5
Junior Achievement	5	Reverse Mentoring	6
Khan Academy	5	Sanssi Card	7
Labster	5	School for Startups	4
Leadcap	5	ShowMe	5
Leaders of Tomorrow	8	Skillshare	5
LYNX	6	Skoll World Forum: Solutions	8

(continued)

Continued

Title & Initiator/ Proposer	Chapter	Title & Initiator/ Proposer	Chapter
Social Innovation Institute for Educators	5	Think Impact	5
Social Ventures Australia	5	Tradability of Tasks	8
Socionext	8	Treehouse	6
Socrative	5	UK "Youth Contract Program"	7
Souq.com	6	WEF Solutions	8
South African ALMPs	7	Work Inspiration	6
Spark Inside	8	Working for YOUth	6
The Big Issue	4	World of Warcraft in School	5
The Entrepreneurs' Ship	4	Worlds of Work (WOW)	6
The Fitzroy Academy	5	Young Enterprise Switzerland	4
The Future Project	5	ONEM: Self-Employment Scheme	7
The Prince's Trust	7	Ze-Ze	8

Foreword

I think we all know this intuitively: there is no shortage of work in today's world, there is a shortage of jobs. Look around the world and it is rarely the case that you will find idle people. Much more common is to find people busily engaged in economic activities that yield, at the end of the day, inadequate incomes. It is the case, and it has always been the case, that the majority of us are not in what we might call paid, regular jobs.

But, for young people, this is all the more the case. Many factors intervene here. There is the poor macroeconomic context in which we have lived now for many years. A rather sluggish recovery or no recovery at all in "advanced" countries from the Great Recession, a downward growth curve among the star performers of the emerging economies, the vagaries of technological change as it boosts some professions and seriously diminishes others—all these things add up to a global labor market facing quite stiff challenges.

And who bears the brunt of these stiff challenges? Predominantly, young people searching for a secure toehold in the labor market and not finding it. As this book makes compellingly clear, one issue is not the absence of information, but the contrary—its surfeit. I cite this from the book: "We are living in an era in which the enormous amount of information and experiences available makes us want to live at a frenetic pace, as we try to absorb everything and decide what is best for us." Many of us become "lost within this ocean of data" (Chapter 8).

We become lost as well in navigating the labor market. The assumption of a regular, secure, full-time job is increasingly questionable, as a variety of less secure contractual relations in the labor market has grown. Wage levels and income security are casualties of weak aggregate demand and the growing fragmentation of work experiences in the labor market.

That said, the message of this book is quite the opposite. It is not at all down-beat for the "millennials" and "digital natives" entering the modern labor market. There are solutions. There are opportunities. The need is for us to adapt our institutions—from basic education on up—to cope with change. For many young people, making your own work, rather than waiting for the magic door of employment to open more widely, is an enticing option. It is, moreover, an option increasingly open in a digital world of rapid technological change.

Just as there is no shortage of work, there is equally no shortage of ideas. This book is full of them. And Peter Vogel's display of them is impressive. The reader, at least this reader, left hopeful and solution-oriented, rather than wringing his hands, wondering whether anything could be done to turn "generation jobless" into "generation jobfull."

Duncan Campbell
Director Global Mega-Trends Team
International Labour Organization

Preface

⟋ The purpose of this book

Since the onset of the recent financial crisis and the associated increase in unemployment, in particular youth unemployment, there has been a strong increase in public attention on these issues; with leading labor market organizations such as the UN International Labour Organization (ILO) as well as policymakers devoting a lot of capacity to coming up with viable solutions. Likewise, some of the largest employers in the world have started implementing novel youth employment schemes. However, there are many more initiatives out there that are overlooked or not reported in the media despite suggesting promising solutions to the crisis. We are primarily exposed to sensational media releases that underscore the severity of the crisis, the hopelessness of young people in places such as Spain, Greece, the MENA region, or South Africa, and the threat of a "Generation Jobless" if we do not act quickly.

Moreover, the vast majority of debates do not go beyond a statement of the problem and an assessment of its causes. In failing to propose specific solutions, these debates leave us in a rather uncomfortable position and feeling helpless. The potential solutions that are being discussed behind the closed doors of policymakers rarely pass through to the public. I believe that by now we have all developed a pretty good sense of the drivers of the crisis but we still lack substantive suggestions about how to solve it. This is what I try to do in this book.

In my work as entrepreneur, researcher, and lecturer, I have come across a variety of outstanding initiatives that have given creative attention to solving the youth unemployment crisis. This book gives some of those ideas a wider audience. Moreover, it leverages the wisdom of the crowd and takes a multi-stakeholder approach to collect and discuss solutions from around the world. Following the description and assessment of these solutions we develop a better understanding of what it will take to replicate them elsewhere and to generate the greatest possible positive impact.

Given the magnitude and complexity of the issue of youth unemployment, the reader should not expect this book to contain a magic formula for tackling the problem. Instead, this book seeks to contribute in two ways: (1) it provides a broad yet deep insight into the crisis and the fundamental challenges we, as a society, are confronted with, and (2) it showcases best-practice examples from around the world; examples of individuals, companies, organizations, educators, or governments that have (or are planning to) address some of the underlying causes of youth unemployment.

How to read the book

This book is structured in two parts. Parts I (Chapters 1 to 3) assesses the current youth labor market crisis (Chapter 1), generational traits of today's youth (Chapter 2), and emerging trends in the labor market (Chapter 3). Part II (Chapters 4 to 8) takes a multi-stakeholder perspective to showcase proven solutions and outline creative and thought-provoking ideas for tackling youth unemployment, including the role of entrepreneurship (Chapter 4), insights into how to re-invent the education system (Chapter 5), the role of employers (Chapter 6), active labor market policies (Chapter 7), and a collection of many more creative ideas and projects that I have gathered over recent years (Chapter 8).

Each chapter can be read separately and the reader does not necessarily have to read through them in sequence. Yet, it might be advisable to read through Part I first as it provides the background information for Part II. If you are an employer, for example, you might be most interested in reading Part I and then move on to Chapter 6. Nonetheless, I would suggest that you also read the remaining chapters due to the interconnected nature of all the presented solutions.

Get involved and help me fight youth unemployment

Writing a book is one thing. But telling the world about it and making sure that one's ideas turn into reality is another thing. According to UNESCO, there are more than 1.5 million new books published each year. That is an awful lot of books in addition to the publisher's promotional activities, I decided to do more to ensure that this incredibly important topic is given sufficient attention.

First and foremost, I created the website www.generationjobless.eu which features case studies and creative ideas from all around the world. Visitors can submit their own experiences and solutions as well as discuss the submitted solutions. The goal is to build an interactive and community-driven collection of solutions and ideas to tackle youth unemployment. I encourage you to visit www.generationjobless.eu, to submit your ideas and to take part in the discussion on the topic.

Second, I engaged with various national and international organizations and enterprises that contributed to the book. Hopefully, this will also generate a multiplication effect to increase readership.

Third, I am inviting you, dear reader, to share the book with your friends, colleagues, and others. Here are a few suggestions to spread the word online. Thanks a lot for getting involved!

- Twitter: *"Can we avoid a #generationjobless? I just joined @pevogel's #movement to tackle #youthunemployment: www.generationjobless.eu."*
- Facebook: I have joined the movement to tackle youth unemployment. Are you going to join too? www.generationjobless.eu.
- Embed in your website/blog: Share the book cover page which you can find on www.generationjobless.eu/media and add a hyperlink to the page www.generationjobless.eu.
- Short Media/Blog Release: If you have your own blog I would be grateful if you published a short media release about *"Generation Jobless?"* I am happy to send you a customized template for a blog article. Contact me at info@ petervogel.org.

Acknowledgments

When I ventured into writing this book I thought it would be an easy job that would be completed in a few months. That was in April 2013. I soon realized that, given the complexity of the issue, it would be a much tougher job than I had first thought. So I decided to bring together the opinions and suggestions of experts from around the world. Without this joint effort it would not have been possible for me to write this book in this form. I am profoundly indebted to all of the contributors for their continuous support, input, feedback, and ideas throughout the process.

I would like to thank Mike Johnson who put me in touch with Palgrave Macmillan in the first place. Without his foresight and ability to connect the dots, this book would not exist.

I am also very thankful for the creative support that my sister, Susanna Vogel, has given to me during the preparation of this book. Having worked with her on various projects over previous years, I knew that Susanna would be the best person to get involved in this project. She has done a terrific job helping me with the design work for this book.

Another person I would like to thank is Dr. Duncan Campbell (Director Global Mega-Trends Research Department, ILO) who not only agreed to share some of his expert knowledge, but also agreed to write the foreword to the book. Duncan and I first met at a labor market conference in Greece in 2012, where we were both giving keynote speeches on how to tackle youth unemployment. Since then we bumped into each other over and over again at different events, clearly illustrating our common agendas.

A special thank you also goes to Michelle Blanchet who has taken the lead for Chapter 5 on changing the education system to improve youth labor market prospects. I first met Michelle at TEDxLausanne and since then I have had a lot of very fruitful conversations with her. Michelle is an educator and social entrepreneur who is passionate about inspiring innovation in the field of education. She has been working with young people for the past ten years and recently founded the Social Innovation Institute for Educators (SIIE), which aims to revolutionize teacher training and support educational innovation. She clearly was the right partner for this part of the book.

I would also like to express my gratitude to a few other individuals who have contributed to this book through co-writing a sub-chapter. I would like to thank Göran Hultin (Caden Corporation) for his contribution on workforce migration. Göran and I met through our joint work at the FutureWork Forum where we frequently give executive workshops on the future of talent management. Göran is also advisor to my organization The Entrepreneurs' Ship. Furthermore, I would like to thank Prof. Dr. Philipp Sieger (University of St. Gallen) for his contribution on entrepreneurial intentions, sharing insights from the GUESSS project. My gratitude also goes to Dr. Dennis Görlich (Kiel Institute for the World Economy) for his contribution on the tradability of tasks. I would also like to express my gratitude to Fungai Alexander Mapondera (CIYDA) and Farida Kamel (Flat6Labs) for their regional contributions on the SADC and the MENA regions. I am thankful for Dennis Pennel's and Michael Freytag's (CIETT) contributions on public-private partnerships (PPPs).

I would also like to thank the representatives of several companies and organizations for their case study contributions, including Laurent Freixe and Cédric Boehm (Nestlé), Sandra Elmer (Credit Suisse), Dr. Markus Rauh and Jean-Pierre Dällenbach (Foundation "Die Chance"), Dr. Abdul Malik Al-Jaber (Arabreneur), Daniel Ramamoorthy (Treehouse), Ian Choo (Socionext), Luis Sena (Global Shaper), Mohammad Nibras (Global Shaper), Milena Montesinos (Shape Europe), Vidyadhar Prabhudesai (Leadcap), Michele Baukens (Office National de l'Emploi), Pip Wheaton (enke), Rajeeb Dey (Enternships), John Hope Bryant (Operation HOPE), Kate Waters (The Prince's Trust), John Roberts (Open University of West Africa), Rohit Talwer (Fast Future), Simon Levy (Latinasia Group), Baillie Aaron (Spark Inside), Narkis Alon (Ze-Ze), Mpho Nosizinzo Pearl Mahanyele (Cabworld), Sheena Lindahl (Empact), Stanley Samuel (Ecosofft), Andrew Brough (FYA Australia), Dr. Robert Shea (Marine Institute), Andrea Gerosa (ThinkYoung) and Donnalee Bell (Canadian Career Development Foundation).

I would also like to thank several other people who helped me get in touch with some of the above mentioned people, namely Jim Pulcrano (IMD), Jeremy Liddle (G20 YEA), Viet anh Vu and Stéphanie Kergall (World Entrepreneurship

Forum), Dr. Denis Snower and Thierry Malleret (Global Economic Symposium) and Paul Smith (CACEE).

Further thanks go to my PhD supervisor Prof. Dr. Marc Gruber (EPFL) and my co-supervisor Prof. John Dencker, PhD (Northeastern University) for their support during my PhD and for an insightful research project on the active labor market policies that help unemployed transition to self-employment.

I am also thankful for the support of the publishing team at Palgrave Macmillan for their help in preparing this book and marketing it.

Last but not least, I would like to thank my family and in particular my wife, Dr. Stéphanie Vuillermot, for her support during the time when I was sitting and writing this book, granting me the freedom to do so.

About the Author

Dr. Peter Vogel is an entrepreneur, consultant, writer, and researcher. Over the past years he has built an expertise on the issue of youth employment. One of his companies, Jobzippers, addresses the gap between the education system and the labor market through smart and integrative technological solutions. Another organization he founded in the context of the youth unemployment crisis is The Entrepreneurs' Ship. He is also a partner of the FutureWork Forum, a global think-tank of HR and labor market experts. He received his PhD from the Ecole Polytechnique Fédérale de Lausanne, EPFL (Switzerland) where he investigated government programs that help unemployed transition to self-employment.

His company Peter Vogel Strategy Consulting works with companies on strategically building intra-organizational ecosystems of innovation and talent management, and also with governments on strengthening their regional or national entrepreneurship ecosystems.

Peter's background is in entrepreneurship, mechanical and biomedical engineering. He earned his degrees from institutions such as the Swiss Federal Institute of Technology in Zurich, the Georgia Institute of Technology as well as the EPFL. He has published several book chapters and journal articles on innovation, entrepreneurship, ecosystems, and the labor market. He frequently teaches executive classes on innovation strategies.

Peter is think-tank member of the World Entrepreneurship Forum and member of the World Economic Forum Global Shapers Community. He has spoken about entrepreneurship and innovation at TEDxLausanne, the Global Economic Symposium, the G20 Young Entrepreneurs' Alliance Summit, and the G20 Youth Forum, among other global conferences. Find him on www.petervogel.org.

This page intentionally left blank

Part I

Youth Unemployment— Background and Outlook

We are facing a great test of our time—an epidemic of youth unemployment. Half of the world's young people in the labor force are either working poor or unemployed. The global youth unemployment situation is intolerable, in particular for young women. In countries rich and poor, unemployment rates for young people are many times those of adults—and of course joblessness is the tip of the iceberg. Many are stuck in low wage work with no protection in the informal economy. Many others find that their schooling has not equipped them with the tools for today's job market … Work is far more than a source of income; it is a source of dignity! Ban Ki-Moon; ILO, 2014a

This page intentionally left blank

chapter 1

The Youth Unemployment Crisis and the Threat of a "Generation Jobless"

> I think it is probably the first time, at least since the Second World War, that a new generation faces the future with less confidence than the previous generation.
>
> *José Manuel Barroso; European Commission, 2011*

The recent economic crisis, the worst since the Great Depression in the 1930s, has led to a disproportionate increase in youth unemployment around the world. Young people in both developed and developing economies are facing harsh labor market conditions. In 2013, more than 70 million young people were unemployed with even greater numbers not even being considered in these statistics because they either dropped out of the system or because they never entered it.

In the developing world, where almost 90% of the world's youth is located, many young people are living in poverty with their only access to work being informal or under indecent employment conditions. However, as we have witnessed over the past years, youth joblessness is not only a problem of poor countries but a truly global problem with an equally grim picture being drawn in the developed world. In Europe, for example, youth unemployment rates have increased by 60% since 2008 (ILO, 2012a), leaving every fourth employable young person without a job. In many countries these numbers are even greater with Greece and Spain having passed 50% youth unemployment back in 2012. According to the ILO the overall youth unemployment is projected to further increase in the near future.

Other labor market indicators such as a widening gap between youth unemployment and adult unemployment and an increasing NEET (neither in employment, education or training) rate add up to an even bleaker outlook for youth. All these factors combined force us to take the initiative and come up with quick win solutions and at the same time sustainable ones for the future.

OFFICIAL STATISTICS BY THE ILO

The global youth unemployment rate, estimated at 12.6% in 2013, is close to its crisis peak. 73 million young people were estimated to be unemployed in 2013. At the same time, informal employment among young people remains pervasive and transitions to decent work are slow and difficult.

By 2018 the global youth unemployment rate is projected to rise to 12.8%, with growing regional disparities, as expected improvements in advanced economies will be offset by increases in youth unemployment in other regions, mainly in Asia.

Rising youth unemployment and falling labor force participation contributed to a decrease in the global youth employment-to-population ratio to 42.3% in 2013, compared with 44.8% in 2007. Part of this decrease is due to rising enrollment in education. The global youth employment-to-population ratio is projected to be 41.4% in 2018. Globally, the ratio of youth to adult unemployment rate hardly changed in recent years, and stands at 2.7 in 2013. Young people therefore continue to be almost three times more likely than adults to be unemployed, and the upward trend in global unemployment continues to hit them strongly.

Note: The ILO contribution was provided by Dr. Duncan Campbell, Director Global Mega-Trends Research Department, International Labour Organization (ILO) of the United Nations. It has been adopted from ILO (2013)

But why is youth in such a seemingly hopeless situation? Various complex and inter-connected issues have collectively caused this crisis and their resolution will also require a collective effort. One of the main reasons for why these past years have been particularly harsh for young people is that the economic crisis and the resulting drop in overall demand for employees has coincided with the occurrence of fundamental structural shifts in the way we live and work. This is best expressed by the fact that a quarter of all the job losses of young workers have occurred after the crisis was officially over (O'Sullivan et al., 2014).

Other reasons can be broadly classified as supply-side issues, demand-side issues, and supply-demand mismatch issues. On the supply side it is factors such as a rising youth population, lack of skills of young workers, the proportion of young people with tertiary but non-vocational degrees (mainly in developed world), and fundamentally different characteristics of today's young people compared to previous generations. Demand-side factors include poor macroeconomic performance, inflexible labor markets, a fundamentally different labor market and world of work and the rise of temporary employment of youth. Moreover, there is a mismatch between supply and demand including skills mismatch or an expectation mismatch.

Given the magnitude of these factors, the reduction of youth unemployment is one of the major challenges governments are currently facing and will be facing for decades to come (Schoof, 2006). If no suitable labor market solutions are identified, the result of the widespread and persisting youth unemployment will be economic waste, an undermined social stability and a marginalization of the local workforce, a valuable natural resource for any country.

In addition, this crisis could have long-term consequences for the unemployed youth. While unemployment is bad at any age, it is particularly harsh early in a person's professional life. A growing body of academic literature suggests that early unemployment has life-long "scarring" effects on an individual (decreased salaries, and affected mental and physical health), their families (increased financial burden and challenge of handling the situation), economies (waste of economic resources) as well as the entire country (threatened social stability, criminality, and loss of tax revenues). The economic and social costs resulting from a prolonged youth unemployment crisis continue to rise and undermine the growth potential of economies.

Everybody, from the protesters of the Arab Spring and those in front of the Greek parliament to policymakers, to international organizations, employers, entrepreneurs, media, parents, and young people, around the world are debating the youth labor market crisis, and coming to the conclusion that if we do not make this our priority number one and act, that today's youth will be scarred for life and branded as the "Generation Jobless," cursed to be marginalized at work and in society (Wallstreet Journal, 2011; The Economist, 2013).[1]

Youth unemployment does not have to end in a catastrophe. But if we want to avoid a Generation Jobless we need to act quickly and implement both short-term solutions for today's youth and long-term solutions to avoid repeating today's crisis. It is of critical importance that all involved stakeholders collectively work on these solutions to create decent employment conditions for young people around the world. Unfortunately, the short-term solutions that can be implemented on the spot are not necessarily sustainable and might even make things worse in the long run. Yet, do we have a choice?

What we know for sure is that there is no "one-size-fits-all" solution for youth unemployment. Instead, we need to build a plethora of customized solutions that each addresses one or more of the underlying issues. Tackling youth unemployment from different angles by implementing multi-stakeholder solutions that are well coordinated and orchestrated is the best bet we can make. The ultimate goal must be to create more and better employment opportunities for young people and associated with it a national and international framework to smoothen the transition from school to work. We need to rethink our education systems in order to improve the match between skill demand and supply; thus the issue of under-education or under-skilling (young people who do not have sufficient skills for the jobs that are available on the labor market) and that of over-education or over-skilling (young people's skills are not being used to the full potential). Furthermore, and linked to the previous point, we need to promote the attractiveness of vocational education and training (VET) to ensure that we achieve a more balanced set of profiles with academic and vocational competencies. Most importantly, industry partners need to be at the core of the solution to ensure that the proposed strategies are driven and fully supported by the labor market (ETUC, 2013).

By taking a global, multi-stakeholder perspective this book assesses the youth labor market crisis, including the drivers and outcomes, and showcases proven solutions. The goal is to give guidance to each of the involved stakeholders on how they can become part of the solution. This introductory chapter continues as follows: The next section will introduce a range of definitions and relevant youth labor market indicators. Thereafter, the main causes of the youth unemployment crisis are discussed, both from a supply and a demand perspective. This is followed by a regional analysis of the crisis pointing towards the major differentiators between developed and developing economies. The chapter concludes with an assessment of the situation in case we do not manage to get a hold of the crisis and the threat of a Generation Jobless.

1.1   Definitions and Indicators

The first thing to do before entering a more detailed discussion about youth unemployment is to define what I mean by "youth" and "unemployment."

While intuitively it seems quite obvious what these two words stand for, it actually becomes tremendously complex when employing a more holistic and global perspective that accounts for regional differences such as the education system (e.g., the differing levels of compulsory education and net enrolment rates across regions)[2] or the labor market (e.g., when do individuals in a specific country typically transition into the labor force? Are there any government programs that allow individuals to officially register as "unemployed"?). So to ensure that we are talking about the same things I will next discuss some core definitions that are being used in this book.

1.1.1 Youth

In the broadest sense youth can be considered the transition period from the dependence of childhood to the independence of adulthood and an awareness of that independence (UNESCO, 2014). Yet, as described above this is a somewhat relative measure and depends on a variety of factors such as the average age at which young people complete their education (or training) and the average age at which their communities would expect them to take on adult roles (e.g. enter employment). From a legal perspective the definition of youth also varies with respect to reasons such as marriage, voting rights, land rights, criminal offences, and military service, among others. Consequently, countries vary considerably in their definition of youth and policies need to be customized to the local conditions. While Uganda defines youth from 12–30 years, Nigeria and Bangladesh define youth from 18–35 years.

In this book I adopt the most widely used definition by the United Nations (ILO), which classifies youth as being between 15 and 24 years of age.[3]

1.1.2 Youth Unemployment and NEET

In preparing this book, I came across a variety of different conceptualizations with respect to the phenomenon we are talking about, and it is by far more complicated than simply putting it as "young people without a job." Most broadly speaking, a person is considered unemployed if he or she has not been working for a certain amount of time but would like to and therefore actively searches for a job. Yet, this definition is too vague and its interpretation varies across countries. For example, students who are looking for a job are considered to be part of the workforce in some countries whereas they are not counted as workforce in other countries. At the same time there is quite some variation across countries when it comes to young people who are not actively involved in the workforce but also not in education or training. Such variation makes cross-country comparison difficult if not impossible and, as a result, many of the reports, and in particular media reports, tend to compare apples and pears. As Assar Lindbeck stated at the global economic symposium:[4] "To facilitate relevant policy decisions, it would be useful [to have] more differentiated statistics on youth unemployment. For instance, in the case of my own country, Sweden, one can claim that the unemployment rate for young people is anything between 6 and 26 percent. The figure depends largely on the definition of unemployment, for instance on whether full-time high-school and university students in the age group 15–24 who wants to work a few hours a week beside their studies are classified as unemployed. Since about half of the individuals in this age group in developed countries are full-time students, the calculated unemployment rate depends also crucially on whether the rate is calculated with the entire population of the relevant age group, or only with those who do not study, in the denominator."

To take these issues into account, I will next provide a few basic definitions of the youth unemployment rate and ratio as well as the NEET rate (neither in employment, education or training). Moreover, I will briefly introduce the youth-to-adult unemployment ratio as an additional insightful metric to capture structural challenges on the youth labor market.

1.1.2.1 *Youth Unemployment Rate and Ratio*

The International Labour Organization (ILO) defines youth unemployment as follows: "The unemployed youth comprise all persons between the age of 15 and 24 who, during the reference period, were: (a) without work; i.e. had not worked for even one hour in any economic activity (paid employment, self-employment, or unpaid work for a family business or farm); (b) available for work; and (c) actively seeking work; i.e. had taken active steps to seek work during a specified recent period (usually the past four weeks)."[5]

Based on this definition, there are two specific measures that the ILO proposes: the youth unemployment rate and the youth unemployment ratio.

Youth unemployment rate

The youth unemployment rate is defined as the number of unemployed 15–24 year olds (i.e., youth) divided by the total number of 15–24 year olds active in the labor market, either being employed or unemployed.

A second and more specific youth unemployment rate is the long-term youth unemployment rate, which is defined as the number of young people who have been out of work for more than 12 months. An increase in long-term youth unemployment is particularly worrisome given that this indicates that it takes those young people that are actively looking for a job longer than before.

Youth unemployment ratio

Another interesting indicator is the youth unemployment ratio, which is the number of unemployed 15–24 year olds divided by the total population of 15–24 year olds. When comparing the youth unemployment ratio with the youth unemployment rate, one can see that as a result of the different denominator of the equation we consistently see smaller numbers for the youth unemployment ratio.

To illustrate the difference between the youth unemployment rate and the youth unemployment ratio, I will briefly explain Figure 1.1 (supplemented with values taken from Table 1.1). The youth unemployment rate for all EU28 countries is 23.3% (unemployed/labor force = 5.6 million/23.9 million). The youth unemployment ratio for all EU28 countries is 9.8% (unemployed/population = 5.6 million/56.6 million). The difference between these two values is entirely driven by the young people who are outside the labor force, a value that is particularly high for this age group because many of them are still in education. Of the 18.3 million employed individuals, 6.4 million were in education (including apprentices and students with side jobs) and 11.9 million were not in education. Of the 5.6 million unemployed, 1.3 million were in education and 4 million were not in education. Of the 32.7 million, 29 million were in education and 4 million were not in education.

1.1.2.2 Neither in Employment, Education or Training (NEET)

Traditional labor market indicators such as employment or unemployment rates are frequently criticized for their little relevance for young people, because they only look at those who either already have a job or are currently actively looking for one (Eurofound, 2012). These indicators, however, do not capture

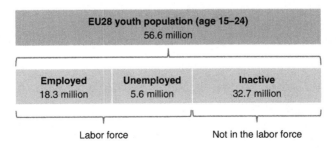

FIG 1.1 **Illustrative example of different measures of youth unemployment**

Data source: Table 1.1

the issue of young people, as those in education are classified as being "out of the labor force." The traditional linear transition models of "school-to-work" are being replaced by more complex views, with iterative cycles of moving in and out of the labor force as well as blending statuses. As a consequence, experts have urged the community to look for new and more youth-relevant indicators that go beyond the simple dichotomy of employment vs. unemployment. Various stakeholders including scholars, policymakers and international organizations are making increased use of the concept of NEETs when referring to the youth labor market crisis, a concept that has its origin in the 1980s in the UK (Istance et al., 1994; Furlong, 2007), where the term "Status Zero" was coined.

A young person (15–24) is considered a NEET if he or she is neither in employment (i.e., unemployed or economically inactive) nor has he or she received any education or training in the four weeks preceding the evaluation. While the overall issue of unemployed young people is worrisome, the NEETs deserve our greatest attention, given that they are not improving their future employability through investment in skills and at the same time they are not gaining any additional experience through employment. Figure 1.2 contrasts youth unemployment and NEET rates. NEETs are already in a disadvantaged position given that they are more likely to come from a low-income household and have lower levels of education in general (Eurofound, 2011). This group of young people is additionally exposed to a particularly high risk of long-term exclusion

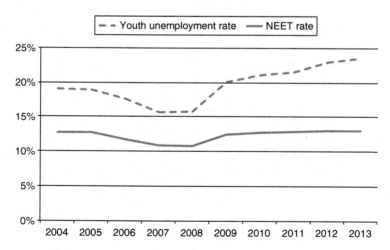

FIG 1.2   **Youth unemployment and NEET rate for EU28 countries (2004–2013)**

Data source: Eurostat

from the labor market and ultimately society. According to Eurofound, the cost of having 7.5 million unemployed young NEETs is more than EUR 153 billion per year (1.2% of the EU GDP).

However, as the UK government puts it: "It is slightly unfortunate that everybody collapses it into the word 'NEETs', because it is actually 'not in education, employment or training' and so, for example, someone who leaves university and might be waiting to take up a job is included in the NEET figures" (House of Lords, 2014).

Indeed, NEETs form a quite heterogeneous group of young people, which is why one needs to pay close attention when implementing policy measures for this group. As always, there is no one-size-fits-all approach when trying to re-engage NEETs with the labor market, education or training. More specifically, the NEET classification includes both vulnerable and non-vulnerable individuals and can be subdivided into five sub-groups (Eurofound, 2012):

1. Conventional unemployed (long-term and short-term)
2. Unavailable (young carers, young people with family responsibilities, or those who are sick or disabled)
3. Disengaged (not seeking jobs or education)
4. Opportunity-seekers (actively seeking work or training)
5. Voluntary NEETs (traveling or engaged in other activities such as art, music, self-learning).

1.1.2.3 NEET Rate vs. Youth Unemployment Rate

Clearly the concepts of NEET and youth unemployment are closely related. Yet, there are some fundamental differences between both which have quite strong influences on labor market policies. Youth unemployment captures the share of young people who are generally speaking economically active and looking for employment but cannot find a job. In contrast, NEET captures the share of young people who are currently disengaged from both the labor market and education, that is the unemployed and the inactive young people who are not in education or training (Eurofound, 2012). Figure 1.3 illustrates the differences.

1.1.3 Youth-to-Adult Unemployment Ratio

Another insightful indicator to explore the youth unemployment crisis is the youth-to-adult unemployment ratio. It is defined as the number of unemployed 15–24 year olds (i.e., youth) divided by the number of unemployed

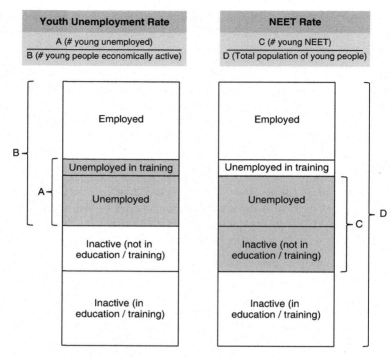

FIG 1.3   **Differences between the youth unemployment rate and the NEET rate**

25–74 year olds. This is an insightful characteristic of the labor market because it provides information beyond the absolute youth unemployment rate. More specifically, it offers insights into a second set of labor market problems related to the gap between the youth and adult populations.

While we are all familiar with the disproportionately high absolute rates of youth unemployment in many countries (e.g., Greece, Spain, South Africa, Portugal, among others), few people know that systematically different countries appear on the radar when we look at the youth-to-adult unemployment ratio. Across all OECD countries (as well as various other countries I have looked at for this analysis) there is not a single country with a youth unemployment rate that is equal or even lower than the adult unemployment rate. These findings are highly consistent over the past ten years, indicating that besides short-term and crisis-driven labor market fluctuations, we have a more fundamental and systemic problem.[6] While Germany, Austria and Switzerland consistently display the lowest youth-to-adult unemployment ratio (ranging between 1.3 and 2.0 over the past ten years), indicating a comparatively healthy labor market balance between young and old, other countries including Sweden, New Zealand or Italy have ratios of more than three, in certain years even four or higher, indicating massive structural problems at the level of the labor market as well as school-to-work-transition. The overall OECD and EU28 averages are consistently ranging between 2.4 and 3 (Eurostat, 2014; OECD, 2014). Figure 1.4 provides a detailed overview of the youth-to-adult unemployment ratios for various OECD countries.

In addition to taking this snapshot of the youth-to-adult unemployment ratio for the year of 2013, I analyzed the temporal development of this indicator for all OECD countries. From that list, I picked nine countries to illustrate some fundamental differences (Figure 1.5). While countries such as Sweden, Finland or the United Kingdom experienced the greatest absolute increase in youth-to-adult unemployment ratio (1.2, 0.9, and 0.9 respectively), there were other countries with very little or no increase or even a decline in the youth-to-adult unemployment ratio, including Germany, Switzerland, Austria, and, surprisingly, Greece. The fact that the Greek youth-to-adult unemployment ratio decreased from 2.7 to 2.3 over the same period of time during which the youth unemployment rate increased from 26% to almost 60% is an interesting insight that illustrates how important this indicator might be to uncover youth-specific labor market problems.

The question is why we see such discrepancies between youth and adult unemployment. There are several factors that are worth mentioning as they seem to be relevant explanations for the widening gap between youth unemployment and adult unemployment in some countries (Manpower, 2012).

First, today's youth has fundamentally different generational characteristics as compared to previous generations (see Chapter 2 for more details). These different characteristics can cause inter-generational tensions and misunderstandings (a concept that, *per se*, is not new to the world, yet is somewhat stronger in the context of the technological revolution). Consequently, employers are doubtful about the abilities of young people to apply their skills in a productive and meaningful manner, and at the same time they question youth's drive, clear career vision and commitment. Therefore, as long as there are unemployed adult workers available for hire, employers might be reluctant to make a hiring commitment with a young and inexperienced individual.

Second, we are facing a demographic shift that exerts significant pressure on the retirement and pension systems, forcing older generations to work longer

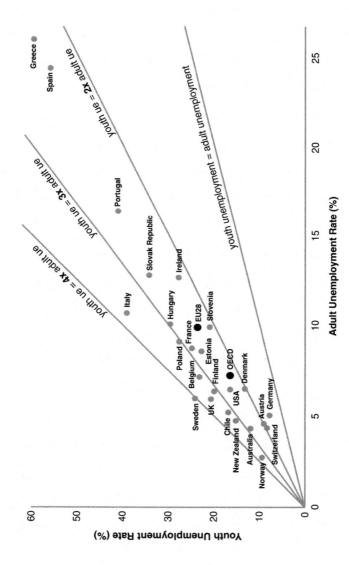

FIG 1.4 Youth-to-adult unemployment ratio in selected OECD countries

Data source: OECD (2013)

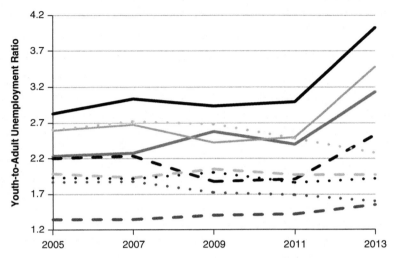

FIG 1.5   Temporal development of the youth-to-adult unemployment ratio in selected countries

Data source: OECD

in order to pay for their living. This, in return, reduces the amount of open positions for the influx of younger workers.

Third, national education systems are confronted with three major challenges. (1) We are experiencing an academic inflation ("academization") with more young people receiving a degree than ever before. (2) The national education systems typically prepare students in a rather theoretical and abstract manner, equipping them with skills that do not match those required on the labor market. "21st century skills" such as cooperation, communication, critical thinking, creativity and an entrepreneurial mindset are oftentimes missing (Trilling & Fadel, 2009; Rotherham & Willingham, 2010). (3) Education systems need to undergo a radical re-thinking instead of gradual reforms.

Fourth, and linked to the previous point on the education system, there are some structural differences between countries that partly explain the massive cross-country differences. Germany, Austria and Switzerland have low and stable youth-to-adult unemployment ratios whereas other countries (1) have highly fluctuating ratios and (2) much higher ratios. The success of Germany, Austria, and Switzerland in this regard is certainly linked to their successful dual education model with a healthy apprenticeship system (see Chapters 5.4 and 6.3 for more details). I will get to more drivers of youth unemployment later on in this chapter.

1.1.4   Low-to-High Skill Youth Unemployment Ratio

Another insightful metric is the distribution of youth unemployment across the spectrum of educational attainments. Based on data from Eurostat I created Figure 1.6, illustrating the low-to-high-education youth unemployment ratio across a range of selected European countries. The ratio was created by dividing the unemployment rates for those with low levels of education (highest attained education: upper secondary and post-secondary non-tertiary) by the rates for those with high levels of education (highest attained education: short-cycle tertiary, bachelor or equivalent, master or equivalent and doctorate or equivalent). Because among the youth (15–24) only a very small fraction will already have had the chance to achieve complete tertiary education, a lot of information was missing for that age group, which is why I decided to use a wider age-range for this plot, namely 15–39. By 39 one can assume that almost everyone in tertiary education will have completed it.

What we can see from Figure 1.6 is that higher education attainment leads to improved labor market prospects for young people and that lower education attainment leads to an increased risk of unemployment and inactivity. Across selected European countries the ratio of low-to-high-education youth unemployment ranges from about 1 in Macedonia to almost 4 in Lithuania. On average in the EU28 area in 2014, poorly educated youth have an unemployment rate that is 1.6 times higher than that of tertiary graduates.

When doing the same exercise for the same age group but replacing the numerator of the equation with the youth unemployment rate of those who do not have any degree, a primary degree or a lower secondary degree, the situation looks even worse, with the ratio going as high as 7.3 in the Czech Republic and an EU28 average of 3.1 (not visualized).

1.1.5   Further Selected Labor Market Indicators

Table 1.1 provides an overview of these different measures for the EU28 countries (2013 values taken from Eurostat), nicely illustrating the differences across countries as well as the major challenges that some countries face based

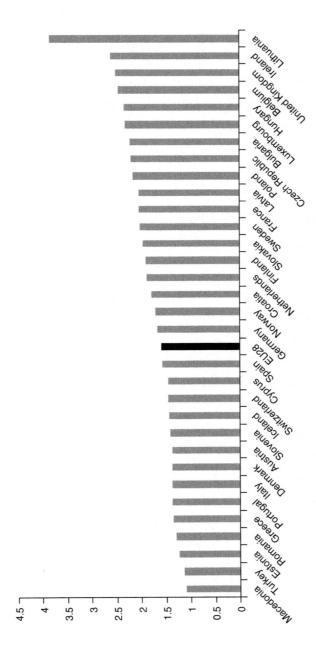

FIG 1.6   Low-to-high-education youth unemployment ratio

Data source: Eurostat for Q1 (2014)

TABLE 1.1   Various indicators related to youth unemployment: youth unemployment rate, adult unemployment rate, youth unemployment ratio, NEET rate and youth-to-adult unemployment ratio

Eurostat 2013 Data for youth (15-24 years)	Population in thousand	Employed in thousand	Unemployed in thousand	Inactive in thousand	Labor Force in thousand	Youth Unemployment Rate in %	Youth Unemployment Ratio in %	NEET Rate in %	Youth-to-Adult Unemployment Ratio
European Union (28 countries)	56,565.8	18,289.6	5,570.9	32,705.3	23,860.5	23.3%	9.8%	13.0%	2.5
Austria	989.3	532.7	53.7	402.9	586.4	9.2%	5.4%	7.1%	2.1
Belgium	1,325.5	313.4	97.4	914.7	410.8	23.7%	7.3%	12.7%	3.3
Bulgaria	774.5	164.5	65.1	544.9	229.6	28.4%	8.4%	21.6%	2.4
Croatia	515.1	74.8	73.9	366.4	148.7	49.7%	14.3%	18.6%	3.5
Cyprus	105.4	24.7	15.7	64.9	40.4	38.9%	14.9%	18.7%	2.9
Czech Republic	1,148.3	293.5	68.7	786.1	362.2	19.0%	6.0%	9.1%	3.1
Denmark	709.4	380.7	57.2	271.5	437.9	13.1%	8.1%	6.0%	2.2
Estonia	153.3	49.6	11.4	92.3	61.0	18.7%	7.4%	11.3%	2.5
Finland	638.2	264.9	65.9	307.4	330.8	19.9%	10.3%	9.3%	3.1
France	7,303.9	2,088.0	656.5	4,559.4	2,744.5	23.9%	9.0%	11.2%	2.7
Germany	8,850.6	4,145.5	356.2	4,348.9	4,501.7	7.9%	4.0%	6.3%	1.6
Greece	1,064.3	126.1	176.5	761.6	302.6	58.3%	16.6%	20.6%	2.3
Hungary	1,135.8	224.9	84.1	826.7	309.0	27.2%	7.4%	15.4%	3.1
Ireland	535.2	155.4	56.9	322.9	212.3	26.8%	10.6%	16.1%	2.3
Italy	6,020.4	983.1	655.4	4,382.0	1,638.5	40.0%	10.9%	22.2%	3.9
Latvia	235.5	71.2	21.5	142.8	92.7	23.2%	9.1%	13.0%	2.2
Lithuania	397.8	97.9	27.4	272.4	125.3	21.9%	6.9%	11.1%	2.0

Luxembourg	60.7	13.3	2.4	45.0	15.7	15.3%	4.0%	5.0%	3.0
Malta	54.5	25.1	3.7	25.7	28.8	12.8%	6.8%	10.0%	2.5
Netherlands	2,039.7	1,271.3	157.2	611.1	1,428.5	11.0%	7.7%	5.1%	1.9
Poland	4,481.2	1,084.7	407.3	2,989.2	1,492.0	27.3%	9.1%	12.2%	3.1
Portugal	1,095.2	243.7	147.6	703.8	391.3	37.7%	13.5%	14.2%	2.6
Romania	2,572.3	604.7	187.2	1,780.4	791.9	23.6%	7.3%	17.2%	4.0
Slovakia	704.7	143.9	73.0	487.8	216.9	33.7%	10.4%	13.7%	2.7
Slovenia	217.4	57.7	15.9	143.8	73.6	21.6%	7.3%	9.2%	2.3
Spain	4,538.4	763.3	951.1	2,824.0	1,714.4	55.5%	21.0%	18.6%	2.3
Sweden	1,225.0	510.4	157.2	557.4	667.6	23.5%	12.8%	7.5%	4.1
United Kingdom	7,674.2	3,580.7	924.5	3,168.9	4,505.2	20.5%	12.0%	13.3%	3.8

Data source: Eurostat

on one indicator but not so much based on another. While Greece and Spain have the highest youth unemployment rates (58.3% and 55.5% respectively), Bulgaria and Italy have the highest NEET rates (21.6% and 22.2% respectively), whereas Romania and Sweden have the highest youth-to-adult-unemployment ratios (4.0 and 4.1 respectively). These differences make clear that these different metrics all provide policymakers and other stakeholders with valuable insights and serve as a basis for the design and implementation of novel active labor market policies.

Figure 1.7 illustrates the education and employment distribution of European youth and the associated change from 15 to 34 years of age. At the age of 15, close to 100% of the population in the EU are still at school. The pace at which the proportion of young people in education decreases depends on the national system of education (e.g., the duration of compulsory education, the presence of apprenticeship and vocational education, etc.). At the same time, one can see the gradual increase of young people on the labor market, both employed and unemployed. However, the pace at which the share of young people in the education system decreases is not the same pace at which the share of young people on the labor market increases because there are some who are in education and on the labor market simultaneously (e.g., students

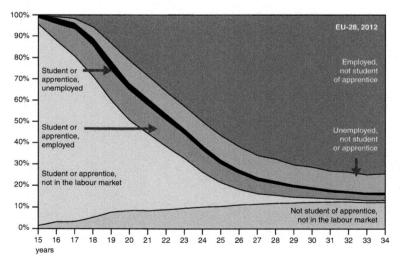

FIG 1.7   Structure of the EU28 youth population by education and labor market status

Source: Eurostat

who work during the semester breaks or apprentices) and others move out of education and stay outside the labor market. Having discussed several labor market indicators, I will now turn to the main causes of the crisis.

1.2   Causes of the Youth Unemployment Crisis

There are various factors that have collectively led to one of, if not the worst youth unemployment crisis in the history of mankind. These factors range from the structure of the labor market to generational characteristics and the education system. More broadly speaking we can classify the causes as either demand- or supply-side. Some of the major causes are briefly here.

1.2.1   Demand-side Factors

1.2.1.1   *Poor Macroeconomic Performance*

First and foremost, poor macroeconomic performance drives the high rates of youth unemployment. The fact that we are experiencing a lack of sufficient growth affects many people and some groups of individuals are disproportionately affected, including youth. It has been shown that youth unemployment fluctuates more strongly than does adult unemployment (Ryan, 2001). The reasons for this cyclical volatility are diverse, many of which are discussed further below in this chapter. However, there are additional factors I would like to highlight, including an increased voluntary resignation among youth given that they want to explore new opportunities and have reduced opportunity costs (O'Higgins, 2001). Another reason is that in times of economic downturn, companies will first stop hiring new people before they will lay off their employees. Given that young people are disproportionately represented among those searching for a job, they will also be disproportionately affected (O'Higgins, 2001). In sum, as long as we do not see a stronger overall economic growth rate, we will need to come up with more creative solutions to youth unemployment.

1.2.1.2   *Inflexible Labor Markets and Temporary Employment of Youth*

Youth is more likely to have temporary employment such as internships, seasonal jobs, or traineeships. "While temporary or fixed-term contracts can be a stepping stone in the transition from education to work, they can also trap young people in insecure jobs" (Eurofound, 2013: 1). Temporary employment is generally regulated (maximum duration and the number of times it can be renewed). However the restrictions vary considerably across countries and many countries have relaxed the regulations during the crisis hoping to stimulate job creation; notably Greece, Lithuania, the Netherlands, Poland, Romania, and Spain. Employment protection legislation (EPL) was generally introduced in the 1980s when the European economy suffered from high rates of unemployment. Many of these regulations have remained unchanged ever since (Görlich et al., 2013).

The option of hiring young people on a temporary basis is of course an attractive option for employers as it allows them to flexibly adjust their workforce to the market conditions and assess their junior employees' skills and capabilities prior to making them permanent employees. From the youths' perspective, however, these changes have led to increased job insecurity. During the crisis, employers would quickly let go of young people (as a short-term reaction to the crisis) and instead hold on to older employees who have been around longer (Martin, 2009; Demidova & Signorelli, 2011; Morsy, 2012). This leaves many young people in unemployment and, as a result, in a disadvantaged position when searching for a permanent job. Now, it appears as if there is a trend among employers to create even more temporary employment contracts for young people, indicative of the employers' reluctance to create permanent job opportunities for youth (Eurofound, 2013).

Furthermore, there is another problem with these temporary work opportunities for youth. While young people take on these positions—oftentimes unpaid—as a stepping-stone into a career and as an opportunity to gain necessary work experience, they are oftentimes trapped with unrelated basic grunt-work that will not help them in the learning process. However, as long as there are no alternatives to these largely unsatisfying temporary positions, youth have to cope with them in order to do something to improve their situation.

In addition, bogus self-employment among young people (quasi-independence although services are provided to only one client) is increasing, as employers are reluctant to pay social contributions for their employees. The number of young people who have made the transition from temporary to permanent jobs has been declining over the crisis period. One of the big challenges is to identify mechanisms to increase job security for young people.

1.2.1.3 Expectations from Graduates

Employers are expecting young people to be better educated/qualified for jobs than it was the case for previous generations. This spurs academization. Despite the fact that there is an awareness of the misalignment between the education system and the labor market, employers use credentials (such as diplomas and grades) as the primary way to evaluate applicants (Martin, 2009; Demidova & Signorelli, 2011). As a result of this rather limited approach to evaluating young people, young people are forced to remain in education longer in order to meet the employers' expectations (Martin, 2009). This decreases the time that young people can spend on gaining important work experience and increases the average age of job entrants. As I will discuss later in Chapter 3, today's education system is preparing a large proportion of young people for jobs that will no longer exist as they enter the world of work. The rising expectations towards job entrants also decrease the proportion of jobs that young people can realistically and successfully apply for.

1.2.2   Supply-side Factors

1.2.2.1   *Changing Demographics*

In many regions of the world, there is a growing proportion of young people, such as in the Middle East and Northern African (MENA) region as well as in Sub-Saharan Africa. These young people are faced with an overall low labor demand, which makes it disproportionately difficult for them for find jobs (Biavaschi et al., 2012). The situation is somewhat different in developed economies with an overall ageing population. Some advocate that the youth unemployment crisis will get resolved automatically over time, but the question remains whether it is not too late for today's youth if we simply wait for the older employees to retire? Another question is the role that global migration will play in counterbalancing this trend—with Asian workers, for example, filling void spaces (as elaborated in Chapter 3).

1.2.2.2   *Lack of Skills and Experience upon Graduation*

According to a study conducted by the FutureWork Forum (2010), less than one-third of young people believe that they were given the right/necessary skills during education. Moreover, 16% of young people believe that they were not given the right skills, with the vast majority being somewhat uncertain (see Figure 1.8). The pan-European study revealed strong regional differences with countries such as Italy or Greece having the lowest average score and Germany and the UK having the highest average score.

The same study (FutureWork Forum, 2010) also addressed the question of whether young people had been turned down from a job in the past and if so, why. Above all reasons, lack of work experience is the number one reason,

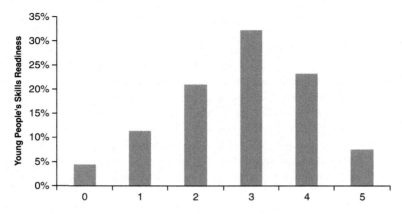

FIG 1.8   Skills readiness upon graduation (0 = not at all ready / 5 = absolutely ready)

Data source: FutureWork Forum (2010)

indicating that young people without any work experience during their education will have a harder time finding employment (no experience = no job) (see Figure 1.9).

Many young people do not know what the world of work actually looks like and therefore also do not really know what they want in their career. They did not spent enough time at school properly reflecting on their different career choices and then, shortly before or after graduation, they start looking for a job. This will, on average, lead to greater dissatisfaction of both the employer and the employee, as young people may be applying for less-than-ideal positions. The education system must assume more responsibilities at actually preparing students for the time after they leave school or university (see Chapter 5).

Moreover, youth have less experience in actually searching for employment making it more challenging for them compared to older individuals (Martin, 2009). Young people typically also have smaller social networks than older individuals, which is known to be one of the best sources of employment opportunities (Gough et al., 2013).

1.2.2.3   Family Support

As good as family support is in times when one really needs help (such as during unemployment), there are also negative effects of continued parental support. First of all, young people who never manage to "let go" from home

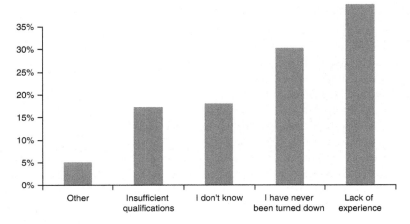

FIG 1.9 **Reasons for not getting a job**

Data source: FutureWork Forum (2010)

are less flexible and mobile and therefore will have lower chances of finding adequate employment. Second, young people who live at home and remain in a position of "comfort," might wait longer before they accept a job, which means that they will stay unemployed longer (Martin, 2009). In essence, it can slow down the process of growing up and assuming responsibility for oneself and possibly also a family.

1.2.2.4 Level of Academization

While the level of academization is largely a demand-side factor (given that employers want high qualified entrants), it is also a supply-side factor, given that people strive towards higher education. The level of academization is therefore another driving factor of youth unemployment. As I will discuss in Chapter 5.4, tertiary education is still regarded as the most popular outlet for students to succeed in their future career. This view has evolved over the past decades and earlier generations have longed for tertiary education (see Chapter 2), a mindset that is still being imprinted into young peoples' minds by their parents. This system causes significant pressure on the labor market and leads to a surplus of "theoretically-oriented" graduates as opposed to systems (such as those in Germany, Austria or Switzerland) with a strong prevalence of vocational training. Consequently, we need to critically assess the enthusiasm with which we want to foster tertiary education as the prime path into the world of work and to which extent we need a more balanced approach.

1.2.3   Mismatch between Supply and Demand

Just like a puzzle piece that does not fit, we are facing a major mismatch between youth as they leave education and the world of work. There exists a variety of mismatches between supply and demand that contribute to the youth labor market crisis. From a demand side, factors such as the level of economic development of a country, technological change or demographical change influence skill demand. From a supply side it is the generational traits, the degrees of education, career development plans, among many other factors that shape skill supply. The extent to which the supply of skills and the demand for skills match is therefore a major factor influencing the economy as a whole, productivity, and competitiveness, among many other factors. In our ever-changing world the education system and labor market need to consistently interact to implement strategies that effectively tackle the mismatch. In the following I will briefly discuss a few forms of mismatch that are believed to play a role in the youth labor market crisis.

Firstly, as a result of the massive reduction in jobs that triggered a concentration of available jobs in a small number of sectors (ILO, 2013), many young people are forced into considering jobs for which they do not possess the necessary skills (under-qualification) or possess too many skills (over-qualification). In both cases this may directly affect the satisfaction of employers and employees alike, having a long-term impact on whether employers will consider young people for these jobs in the future or whether they will instead turn to more experienced senior individuals.

Second, and linked to the first argument, there is a more systemic mismatch between the skills and capabilities that young people bring along when entering the world of work and the expectations and needs of the employers (Manaconda & Petrongolo, 1999; Coenjaerts et al., 2009). A "skills mismatch in the labour market describes the fact that levels or types of skills of individuals are inadequate in view of particular job requirements" (Wolbers, 2003). A perfect match is never possible and the labor market responds to mismatches through salary adjustments. The skills mismatch is, in part, the result of an outdated education system that has not yet arrived in the 21st century (see Chapter 5 for a discussion about how to address different types of mismatch on the educational level). Moreover, there is a lack of communication between the labor market and the education institutions. Each year, the Canadian

Association of Career Educators and Employers (CACEE) surveys nearly one thousand Canadian employers to understand their hiring practices and needs as well as the skills they seek when recruiting. What they find is astonishing. While the five most desired skills may not be surprising, the five least desired skills are very surprising (Figure 1.10), given that entrepreneurship and creativity are regarded as critical 21st century skills. However, their findings are relatively constant over the past few years.

Third, there is a mismatch between what the next generation of employees expects from work and what employers expect from their future employees. This is most pronounced when it comes to topics such as salary, flexibility at work, promotions, among many other factors. As I will discuss in the next chapter, the next generation of employees is much more demanding than previous generations and at the same time less loyal to their employer, thus putting companies in a rather challenging situation.

Fourth, the types of skill mismatches vary considerably between developed and developing economies. While developed economies typically face rather high levels of formal education and, as such, experience over-education, developing countries have much lower levels of education and, as such, suffer from widespread under-education. Both mismatches require close attention and a systematic implementation of change.

The skills (and expectations) mismatch has become a growing problem for both the young population and the labor market. Over-education (over-skilling) coexists with under-education (under-skilling). Due to the complexity of the situation, the skills mismatch makes solutions to the youth unemployment crisis much more difficult and time consuming. Moreover, in the case of over-education, society is losing people's valuable skills and forfeiting the greater

5 Most Favored Skills				
Communication Skills	Analytical Skills	Teamwork Skills	Strong Work Ethic	Problem Solving Skills
5 Least Favored Skills				
Creativity	Entrepreneurial Skills	Tactfulness	Strategic Planning Skills	Sense of Humor

FIG 1.10   Most and least favored skills of job entrants

Source: CACEE (2014)

productivity that could have been achieved if people were utilized according to their skills. (ILO, 2013).

A THINK PIECE: WHAT SKILLS AND WHERE?

– Göran Hultin, Founder and CEO of Caden Corporation –

Currently one in three employers experience difficulties in finding the right skills for their job vacancies. The rise of the emerging economies and their growing ranks of middle class consumers provide the makings for boosting global investment, economic growth, and employment. We need to see beyond the current crisis. Labor and skills are set to be in even shorter supply.

While national training policies differ from country to country, they share a number of common challenges. The list is long and on top of it is how to create a closer link between education, training, and the world of work. There is an increasing awareness among governments of the importance of skills and employability, and there is also an openness to work with the private sector to get their training and skill development right. The spinoffs of such a positive public-private partnership agenda would be mutually beneficial.

Meeting future skills requirements needs a rethink in many ways: How we define the skills, how we train the workforce and for what, how we make use of the skills and how they are developed and maintained. But not all of it is about what the skills are; some of it is where they are. We need to add talent and skill mobility to the overall agenda of meeting future labor market needs.

1.3   A Regional Analysis

OFFICIAL STATEMENT BY THE INTERNATIONAL LABOUR ORGANIZATION (ILO)

Numbers from around the world

Since 2009, little progress has been made in reducing youth unemployment in the Developed Economies and European Union as a whole. The youth unemployment rate in 2012 is estimated at 18.1 per cent, the same rate as in 2010 and the highest level in this region in the past two decades. If the 3.1% discouragement rate is taken into account, the discouragement-adjusted youth unemployment rate becomes 21.2%. The youth unemployment rate is projected to remain above 17% until 2015, and to decrease to 15.9% by 2018.

Between 2008 and 2012, the number of unemployed young people increased by more than 2 million in advanced economies, growing by almost 25%. In the second quarter of 2012 the youth unemployment rate exceeded 15% in two thirds of advanced countries. However, there are significant variations across countries and some countries are showing positive results. The youth unemployment rate was below 10% in six countries in the Developed Economies and the European Union in the second quarter of 2012, and in three countries, youth unemployment rates are currently below the level in the same quarter of 2008 (Germany, Israel, and Switzerland). From 2008 to 2010, the proportion of young people not in employment, education or training in the youth population, the "NEET" rate, increased by 2.1 percentage points to reach 15.8% as an average of OECD countries. This means one in six young people were without a job and not in education or training.

The youth unemployment crisis in advanced economies is also reflected in longer job search periods and lower job quality. In the majority of OECD countries, one third or more of young jobseekers are unemployed for at least 6 months. In Europe, an increasing proportion of employed youth are involved in non-standard jobs, including temporary employment and part-time work, and evidence shows that a significant part of the increase is involuntary rather than by choice. Youth part-time employment as a share of total youth employment in Europe was 25.0% in 2011. Another 40.5% of employed youth in the region worked on temporary contracts.

Regional youth unemployment rates show large variations. In 2012, youth unemployment rates were highest in the Middle East and North Africa, at 28.3% and 23.7%, respectively, and lowest in East Asia (9.5%) and South Asia (9.3%). Between 2011 and 2012, regional youth unemployment rates increased in all regions except in Central and South-Eastern Europe (non-EU) and

Commonwealth of Independent States (CIS), Latin America and the Caribbean, and South-East Asia and the Pacific. Encouraging trends of youth employment are observed in, for example, Azerbaijan, Indonesia and the Philippines.

In developing regions where 90% of the global youth population lives, stable, quality employment is especially lacking

Developing regions face major challenges regarding the quality of available work for young people. ILO confirms that in developing economies where labor market institutions, including social protection, are weak, large numbers of young people continue to face a future of irregular employment and informality. Young workers often receive below average wages and are engaged in work for which they are either over-qualified or under-qualified. As much as two-thirds of the young population is underutilized in some developing economies, meaning they are unemployed, in irregular employment, most likely in the informal sector, or neither in the labor force nor in education or training.

In advanced economies long-term unemployment has arrived as an unexpected tax on the current generation of youth

Youth unemployment and its scarring effects are particularly prevalent in three regions: Developed Economies and European Union, the Middle East, and North Africa. In these regions youth unemployment rates have continued to soar since 2008. Youth unemployment increased by as much as 24.9% in the Developed Economies and European Union between 2008 and 2012, and the youth unemployment rate was at a decades-long high of 18.1% in 2012. On current projections, the youth unemployment rate in the Developed Economies and European Union will not drop below 17% before 2016.

As was discussed in the 2010 edition of the ILO's *Global Employment Trends for Youth*, there is a price to be paid for entering the labor market during hard economic times. As mentioned above, much has been learned about "scarring" in terms of future earning power and labor market transition paths. Perhaps the

most important scarring is in terms of the current youth generation's distrust in the socio-economic and political systems. Some
of this distrust has been expressed in political protests such as
anti-austerity movements in Greece and Spain.

Note: The ILO contribution was provided by Dr. Duncan Campbell,
Director Global Mega-Trends Research Department, International Labour
Organization (ILO). It has been adopted from ILO (2013a)

Figure 1.11 visualizes the youth unemployment rates around the world
indicating major regional differences.

While it might seem surprising at first that youth unemployment rates are
much lower in, for example, South Asia and many African countries as compared to many European countries, it is less surprising when considering the
working poor in the developing countries. The overall high levels of poverty
in those regions do not allow young people to enter a state of "not working,"
hence they enter vulnerable employment, living on less than two dollars a day
(ILO, 2014b). They therefore do not officially count in the youth unemployment category, but in fact their standard of living is hardly any better than
that of their unemployed peers. Consequently, policy measures need to take
into account the full range of indicators and select those that appear most
relevant for an individual country or region. While in developed economies
the youth unemployment rate appears to be a useful indicator (next to the
NEET rate), developing economies should be regarded in a more differentiated manner.

In most regions of the world, youth unemployment is projected to stay at a
high level or even increase (Figure 1.12), with the global youth unemployment rate being estimated to stand at 12.8% by 2018 (ILO, 2013). However,
as illustrated in Figure 1.12, there are major regional differences. While the
developed economies (including the EU) are projected to see decreasing youth
unemployment rates until 2018, the majority of other regions around the
world are projected to see growing youth unemployment rates.

In the following I will discuss the youth unemployment situation in the
EU28, the Middle East and Northern Africa (MENA), the South African
Development Community (SADC) as well as Latin America as selected
regional examples.

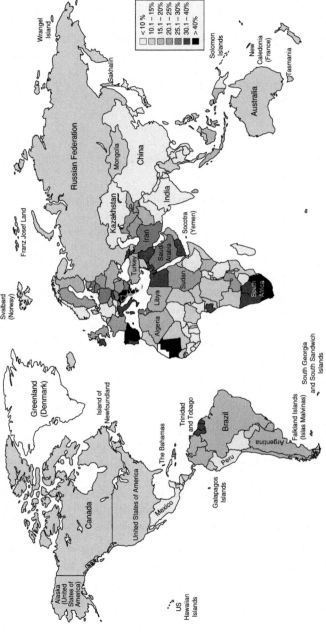

FIG 1.11 World map of youth unemployment rates

Data Source: World Bank, 2012

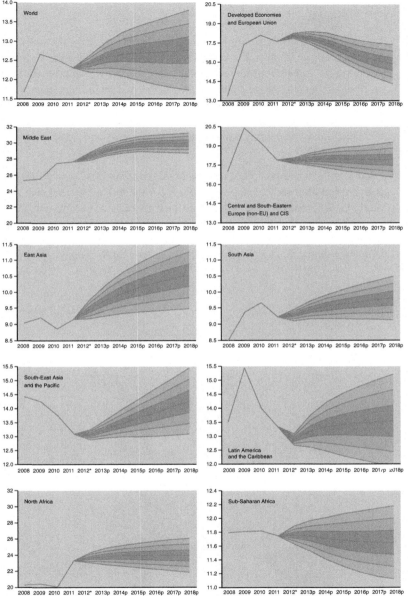

FIG 1.12 Overview of regional youth unemployment rates and projections

Source: ILO (2013)

1.3.1   Europe

The youth unemployment rate in Europe is disturbingly high. However, the national youth unemployment rates are just as diverse as are the countries (Figure 1.13).[7] While countries such as Austria, Germany, Norway, Switzerland, and The Netherlands have youth unemployment rates of less than 10%, countries such as Bosnia and Herzegovina, Croatia, Greece, Macedonia, Montenegro, Serbia, Spain have youth unemployment rates of greater than 40% (in Bosnia and Herzegovina, Greece, Macedonia, and Spain it is even greater than 50%).

Similar to other developed countries, the recent economic crisis has hit European youth disproportionately hard, leaving roughly one in four without a job in 2012 (World Bank database). In addition, there is a growing issue of long-term youth unemployment with one in three unemployed youth having been unemployed for at least six months (ILO, 2013). The combination of high youth unemployment rates with longer periods of job search have been shown to result in

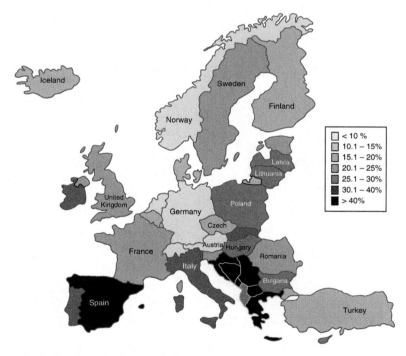

FIG 1.13   **Youth unemployment in Europe**

Data Source: World Bank data for the year 2012

increased discouragement and a state of resignation (Bell & Blanchflower, 2011), as expressed in a growing NEET rate. In Estonia, Iceland, Ireland, and Spain the NEET rate increased by more than five percentage points between 2008 and 2010, an alarming indicator of a major youth labor market crisis (ILO, 2013). Chapter 7.2 discusses a variety of EU Active Labor Market Policies (ALMPs) that have been implemented trying to avoid a Generation Jobless in the EU.

1.3.2 Middle East and Northern Africa (MENA)

– This section is written in collaboration with Farida Kamel, Program Manager at Flat6Labs Cairo –

As the euphoria of the Arab Spring subsided, newly appointed governments in the Middle East and North Africa (MENA) region soon discovered that they cannot, as previously done by the former regimes, ignore the voices on the streets (largely composed of youth) calling for more inclusive and sustainable economic reform. Much to the disappointment of the many who had fallen for the romanticism of the Arab Spring, the success of the latter is fundamentally dependent on the emancipation of the awakened force for regional change— frustrated unemployed youth. Newly appointed governments can no longer afford to ignore them. The Arab Spring has been much politicized as a purely political reformist phenomenon. However, to categorize it as solely so, would be simplistic, naïve, and bluntly offensive to the 15 million unemployed individuals in the region, with youth unemployment rates alone as high as 25% (ILO, 2013). Of all regions, the MENA region has the highest youth unemployment rates. In the Middle East, the youth unemployment rate is projected to increase to 30% by 2018 and is projected to increase to 24% in Northern Africa (Figure 1.14). Hence, it is clearly an alarming situation that requires massive structural reforms.

The MENA region is home to 21 different countries, with contrasting economic structures including oil-rich economies in the Gulf, and other countries facing daunting economic trials such as the Yemen. Although economically diverse, the region is in dire need of bold and aggressive economic reform strategies aiming to materialize the aspirations of Arab youth. The success of the Arab Spring will depend on it.

With the highest youth unemployment rate in the world, a new type of development strategy, driven by entrepreneurship and innovation, is an imperative to sustain high economic growth rates in the region. Such a strategy needs to tackle the multifaceted challenges of bringing down the staggering youth unemployment rate in the region, a rate attributable to poor education systems, inadequate development of an entrepreneurial ecosystem supporting aspiring entrepreneurs, and many other broader macroeconomic challenges.

FIG 1.14   Youth unemployment in the MENA region

Data Source: World Bank data for the year 2012

Solution-driven and dynamic interactions amongst local, regional and international private and public stakeholders are fundamental to sustain, renew, and diversify the sources of economic growth to create the millions of job opportunities needed in the region.

1.3.3   Sub-Saharan Africa

While the youth unemployment rate in Sub-Saharan Africa is lower than in most other regions of the world (Figure 1.12), it is still considerably higher than the adult unemployment rate. Across the region, the youth-to-adult unemployment ratio is 2 (ILO, 2013). Yet, within the region there are significant differences between countries, with Mauritania, South Africa, and Swaziland having youth unemployment rates of greater than 40% and Botswana, Gabon, Lesotho, Namibia between 30–40%. Similar to South Asia, the relatively low youth unemployment rates are linked to the overall high levels of poverty. The vast majority of employable young people cannot afford not to work. Yet, the employment they get is certainly far from being decent, with 70% of the youth population living on less than two dollars a day (ILO, 2014b). Overall, the Sub-Saharan region has the highest proportion of working poor population. While the absolute youth unemployment rates do not look more shocking on the map (Figure 1.11) than they do in Europe or the Middle East, the numbers should not be confused given that there are major differences with respect to the working poor which is why youth unemployment in this region is as much a quantitative problem as it is a qualitative one (see Figure 1.15).

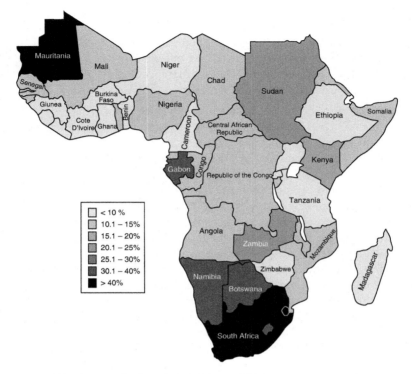

FIG 1.15   Youth unemployment in Sub-Saharan Africa

Data Source: World Bank data for the year 2012

- provided by Fungai Alexander Mapondera, CIYDA -

REGIONAL SNAPSHOT: SOUTH AFRICAN DEVELOPMENT COMMUNITY (SADC)

Youth unemployment has always been a source of concern and remains a problem to grapple with in the Southern African Development Community (SADC). While overall youth unemployment across Africa is generally just over 25%, figures in SADC show an uneven dispersion. To compound the situation, in countries like South Africa and Zimbabwe, the youth unemployment rate is considered to constitute at least 60% of the overall unemployment rate.

Arguably, South Africa as the economic anchor of SADC has always been alluring thus taking on most of the unemployed youths from across the region in particular, Lesotho, Swaziland, and Zimbabwe. Needless to point out, like in the OECD countries, youth unemployment in SADC is observed to be a substantial threat to socio-economic development, regional integration, as well as peace and security (Wentworth & Bertelsmann-Scott, 2013).

With youth accounting for the majority of the mainstream population in SADC (76% under the age of 35 years), they have to contend with a range of challenges that cause them to seem inconsequential in the region's development. In particular rural unemployed youths tend to bear the brunt of the situation and their plight is exacerbated by their seeming marginalization. For those youths at the cusp of the labor market, there seems to be a continued struggle to gain the requisite experience and know-how needed to integrate effectively into the labor market. Furthermore, challenged with inadequate experience and know-how, the basic fact of unemployment further hinders young people from supplementing their education by acquiring practical skills, which are required for the labor market. The political and social frameworks that are characterized by consolidated public services and debilitated service delivery at local levels aggravate these challenges. This, combined with challenging legal structures and unnecessary bureaucracy, among other issues within SADC countries, generates an environment that undermines the opportunities for youths to establish themselves, to progress, and to contribute to socio-economic development initiatives.

UNICEF estimates that there are approximately 100,000 child-headed households in SADC countries such as Zimbabwe. When these children reach the recognized working age to enter the labor market, providing for their households, constantly battling the threat of diseases and starvation and safeguarding their own career development becomes a challenge, with the majority being unemployed or lacking the requisite entrepreneurial skills.

1.3.4   Latin America

Overall youth unemployment in Latin America decreased from 17.6% in 2003 to 13.5% in 2008 and 12.9% in 2012 (despite the global economic crisis) (Figure 1.16). However, the ILO expects that the regional youth unemployment rate will rise again (ILO, 2013). In response to strong economic growth in the region, this trend is generally much more positive than in most other regions of the world. Yet, the youth labor market issues are nonetheless omnipresent with a youth-to-adult unemployment ratio that has increased from 2.5 to 2.8 and many countries experiencing ratios of greater than 3.0 (e.g. in Argentina it stood at 3.6 in 2011). Another concern is the NEET rate, which stood at 19.8% in 2010 (ILO, 2010).

FIG 1.16   **Youth unemployment in Latin America**

Data Source: World Bank data for the year 2012

1.3.5   Indigenous Communities

While we consistently speak about different regions of the world, we automatically focus on countries as we see them from our Western perspective. But what about all the young people of indigenous communities—those young people who have grown up under disadvantaged conditions from the beginning? In Australia, for example, the indigenous population makes up a total of 3% of the overall population, of which more than 50% are below the age of 25 (AIHW, 2012). As Dr. Shamshad Akhtar Detho, former Assistant Secretary-General for Economic Affairs of the UN Department of Economic and Social Affairs (DESA) said: Indigenous youth "face higher rates of illiteracy and school drop out rates and they tend to experience lower enrollment ratios, higher unemployment rates and lower incomes. Indigenous youth struggle to develop and define their identities, maintain their cultures and preserve and revitalize their languages" (United Nations, 2013b).

In most countries with indigenous communities, a long history of failed policies with respect to indigenous communities has led to major inequalities in health, wellbeing, education and employment leaving many young indigenous in poverty (cf. Center for Native American Youth, 2014)). Solid statistics are difficult to find.

Among most indigenous communities, youth make up a large proportion of the population. Consequently, tackling youth unemployment must be priority number one if we want to make sure that the world does not accelerate towards a monoculture but maintains its cultural and lingual diversity despite the contrary pressures on indigenous communities around the world.

1.4   What if We Don't Act? Threat of a Generation Jobless

The situation described earlier is shocking and it does not seem to improve, unless we collectively manage to implement creative solutions with an immediate effect.

While the second part of this book features many solutions from around the world, the question remains what might happen if we do not succeed? Not that I am saying that we won't but we should certainly be prepared for the worst. That brings us to the question of what this "worst case" actually looks like. What will the world look like when the majority of the population belongs to a Generation Jobless? Did we already reach that point?

Is it too late? Can things become even worse for the generations to come? Unemployment has detrimental effects on an individual, an economy, and an entire country.

Unemployment has a wide range of negative effects on an individual, an economy, and on society and these effects are particularly grave if they concern young people. In the following I wish to outline a few of these effects.

1.4.1   Effects on Society and the Economy

Unemployment not only leads to the waste of an enormous amount of unused economic potential, but it also threatens to undermine the social stability of entire societies through the marginalization of large groups of people from the working population, particularly youth. In developing countries, the wasted economic potential is particularly grave given that youth makes up the majority of the population and thus limits the input for urgently needed growth. In developed countries the effect is a different one with a lack of qualified young workers creating a bottleneck in the labor market as well as the old-age pension system (Manpower, 2012). While the psychological distress experienced by unemployed youth is less severe than that experienced by older people (Rowley & Feather, 1987; Broomhall & Winefield, 1990), there are other factors making youth unemployment a major social problem (Winefield, 1997). Moreover, the disproportionately high rate of youth unemployment compared to adult unemployment illustrates a major imbalance and consequently an unsatisfactory situation for young people.

Particularly in countries where the family plays a central role (collectivist countries, but increasingly also individualist countries), young people will find it even more difficult to jump out of the nest and start flying on their own. This will have major long-term implications for entire societies, possibly ending in a downward spiral. Parents may have to take care of their children for much longer than, say, 50 years ago, and as a consequence will have to work longer past their retirement age. In turn, this might again block potential positions for young people, and so on.

Youth unemployment leads many young people to leave their home countries in search of better employment opportunities. This might lead to a long-term brain drain from some countries to others, having major societal and economic impacts on the home country. Moreover, many young people need to take job opportunities for which they are either over-skilled or sometimes also under-skilled (if the employer cannot find appropriate talents), leading to an inefficient use of a country's human resources (Hussainat et al., 2012).

Likewise, high rates of youth unemployment lead to social unrest and political revolutions, as proven by the Arab Spring as well as protest movements in Greece.

Youth unemployment affects the economy and society as a whole. It is estimated that joblessness in the United States alone will account for a total of USD 20 billion in lost earnings over the next ten years (Jacobs, 2014). Young people are earning less during times of recession (Ayers, 2013) resulting in a major loss of tax revenues (O'Sullivan et al., 2014).

Lastly, social alienation may lead to increased incidences of criminal and other antisocial behavior, including the formation of gangs as well as the abuse of drugs and alcohol (Thornberry & Christenson, 1984; Ehighebolo & Ogie-Aitsabokhai, 2014). This, in turn, requires greater safety net expenditures. As these young people grow old and have their own families, their lifestyle, attitudes towards work and society, and their failure to accumulate economic and social capital will perpetuate the same negative spiral for their children, thus creating long-term downside effects for both the economy and society.

1.4.2 Effects on the Individual

Besides the negative economic and societal effects, youth unemployment also has negative effects on the individual, ranging from financial disadvantage to increased criminality, social alienation to physical and mental health issues.

First, there is a scarring effect on the individual's human and social capital (O'Higgins, 2001). An individual's stock of knowledge and experience depreciates over time if not used regularly. Likewise, social connections get lost, leading to a long-term loss of important networks. Unemployed individuals are at a disadvantage when it comes to building the necessary industry ties, which are known to be a prime source of employment opportunities.

Second, it has been shown that unemployment during the first years of a person's professional life has life-long effects on the person's earnings (Gregg & Tominey, 2004; Morsy, 2012)—and the longer the wait, the bigger the negative effect. That is mainly because people could not build the necessary skills, experiences and professional networks in the early years of work and hence will always lag behind their peers. It has been estimated that the earnings penalty is 20% for up to 20 years after unemployment, until they can ultimately "catch up" with their peers again (Morsy, 2012). This will, collectively, contribute to a widening gap between rich and poor and force many young people into poverty. Spain, for example, witnessed an 18% increase in income inequality over the past years (Morsy, 2012). Moreover, young people with an unemployment history could have more difficulties accessing financial credit and mortgages, again adding to a widening gap between rich and poor.

Third, based on life span development theory (Erikson, 1959), scientists have made the assumption that unemployment during young years may retard healthy psychosocial development (Gurney, 1980) and negatively impact the individuals' well-being (McKee-Ryan et al., 2005). In fact, youth unemployment is a major public health issue and has many effects that go way beyond the idleness of the individual. Unemployment during youth has been correlated with decreased happiness, job satisfaction, overall well-being as well as other mental health issues (Morsy, 2012). "Research reveals that long-term unemployed young people are more than twice as likely as their peers to have been prescribed anti-depressants" (The Prince's Trust, 2014).

Fourth, there is a potentially increased risk of suicide (Platt, 1984), because young people feel that they are a failure in life and that they do not add any value to their community (in particular if they continue living with their parents) (Hussainat et al., 2012). "Unemployment is proven to cause devastating, long-lasting mental health problems among young people. Thousands wake up every day believing that life isn't worth living, after struggling for years in the dole queue. One in three have contemplated suicide, while one in four have self-harmed" (The Prince's Trust, 2014).

Fifth, linked to the previous point, youth are increasingly remaining in the family home or returning to live with their parents again (say, after university), and remaining there into their late twenties (Martin, 2009). This phenomenon has been nicknamed the "full-nest syndrome." This not only adds strain on the family (financially and emotionally) but it also has mental effects on youth as they feel useless and become more and more disconnected from society. Moreover, it may lead the individual and the family to slip into poverty (ETUC, 2013). In addition, it will prevent young people from thinking about having children themselves, pushing them well into their 30s or 40s before they start building a family. The prevalence of full-nest syndrome is particularly pronounced in collectivist countries such as Spain, where more than 50% of all 25–29-year-olds live at home with their parents (BBC, 2013a).

Sixth, if young people enter unemployment directly out of school, they do not have a chance to develop the necessary work values and ethics, making it even more difficult for them to enter the world of work. This effect is less severe for individuals who have been employed before, given that they have already had some exposure to the labor market, but it is extremely bad for graduates.

Seventh, the current jobs crisis forces many young people to be less selective about the type of work they accept. More young people are turning to part-time or temporary employment or employment in domains where they lack any experience or training just to do something. Secure employment—once the norm for previous generations—is becoming much less accessible to young people (ILO, 2013).

Last but not least, early unemployment leads to an increased chance of a subsequent period of unemployment (Arulampalam, 2001; Nordström Skans, 2004). Moreover, there may be long-term generational effects because the children of Generation Jobless would be raised by individuals who suffer from all these different problems, thus passing on their values, ethics and lifestyle to their children. There is also a threat that if we cannot help today's young unemployed enter the world of work, employers will skip this generation once the economy picks up again and will hire young (and "fresh") graduates who do not suffer from all the negative effects of unemployment.

1.5   Conclusion

Taken together, we must do everything that is in our power to avoid a Generation Jobless. We can only imagine what the world would look like in 20 years from now if we do not find adequate solutions to help more young people find decent employment. The complexity of a world characterized by ever-increasing efficiency paired with a rapidly growing global population causes enormous societal strain.

Before I talk about specific solutions to tackle youth unemployment in Part II, I would like to discuss the topic of generational emergence and more specifically the characteristics of today's youth—the Digital Natives (Chapter 2). This is essential knowledge as a basis for any solution because if we do not understand the way today's young people live, work, and think, we cannot build suitable solutions to foster their employability. I will also provide an outlook on and some insights into the future of the global labor market (Chapter 3).

Millennials and Digital Natives

chapter **2**

These kids are different. They study, work, write, and interact
with each other in ways that are very different from the ways
that you did growing up.

Palfrey & Gasser, 2008

With the introduction of the World Wide Web in 1991, the world began to
change. Blogs started to pop up, the first search engines emerged, e-commerce
sites and email services were established and, of course, the social networks
and messaging services came into existence. Paired with the introduction of
smartphones, the world would change for good. This technological revolution
has transformed how people live, how they relate to one another, how they
work, and even how they think and process information. Figure 2.1 summarizes some of the major technological inventions that have followed since
the introduction of the World Wide Web and that have contributed to the
characteristics of today's youth—the Digital Natives.

The companies and services displayed in the timeline of Figure 2.1 were all
invented by Digital Settlers—those that have helped shape the digital world
we live in today (Palfrey & Gasser, 2008). These pioneers of the digital world
are equally immersed in the digital world as are the majority of the Digital
Natives In contrast, the vast majority of earlier generations (i.e., those born
between 1991) are not Digital Settlers but instead Digital Immigrants (Prensky,
2001)—those who adopted email and other computer-based technologies
later on in their life without pioneering them themselves.

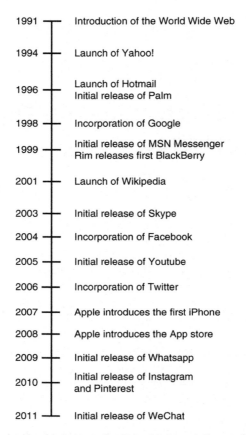

FIG 2.1   Selected technological introductions that have influenced today's youth

The Digital Natives and the Digital Immigrants live radically differ-ent lives. While Digital Natives see the virtual space as an equally important part of life—thus blurring their virtual and their real-life identities—the Digital Immigrants keep these two clearly separate from one another. This has major implications for intergenerational communication and collaboration in the 21st century workplace (cf. Part II).

However, from a global perspective, we must not fool ourselves. There is still a large proportion of young people around the world who do not even have access to these technologies and therefore cannot really be called Digital Natives by any means. They still live a life that is very similar to that of previous generations, but it is only a matter of time until we can also call a majority of youth in those places Digital Natives.

Consequently, the following assessments of generational emergence and the generational traits of previous generations as well as today's youth are clearly focused on more developed, and in particular Western, societies. Understanding today's youth—the way they think, live, and work—will help contextualize the youth unemployment crisis and consequently design adequate solutions. The next section will outline the generational emergence over the past century and discuss generational traits that distinguish the different generations.

2.1   Generational Emergence

Just like individuals, generations have specific traits and characteristics that are shaped by the political, social, and economic setting within which the individuals are embedded. Although it is difficult to put chronological boundaries between generations (Taylor & Keeter, 2010: 5), there are certainly some patterns (periodic effects, cohort effects, and life cycle events), which allow us to describe a specific generation and to draw the line between generations. Take for example the end of World War II. While those born prior to that date lived through some of the toughest times of history, those born right after the end of World War II were exposed to a completely different world which will have a different imprinting effect on the lives of young people. Moreover, while those generations born between 1945 and the introduction of the Internet in 1991 experienced an evolutionary generational development with economic ups and downs and upcoming globalization, the introduction of the Internet, computers, and mobile phones marks a distinctive and revolutionary change in the way people live, work, and think. Hence, generations born after this "shock" are markedly different from previous generations.

Figure 2.2 depicts the generational emergence over the past century, from the Silent Generation to the Digital Natives. The latest generations, those that I am concerned with in this book, carry many titles: Generation Y (or also referred to as Millennials) and Generation Z (also referred to as Digital Natives, Internet Generation, Net Generation or iGeneration).

However, researching generations is somewhat challenging given the complexity of influencing factors and the variety of individuals within a society. On top

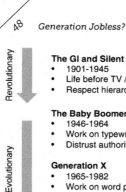

Revolutionary

The GI and Silent Generations
- 1901-1945
- Life before TV / WW I and WW II
- Respect hierarchy

The Baby Boomers
- 1946-1964
- Work on typewriter / revolutions
- Distrust authority

Evolutionary

Generation X
- 1965-1982
- Work on word processor / tough economic times
- Don't trust anyone

Generation Y (Millenials)
- 1982-1990
- Work on computer / growing up in stability
- Environmentally conscious / Dual-income parents

Revolutionary

Generation Z (Digital Natives)
- 1991-present
- Virtually connected / exposed to a global competition
- Worried about future / seek security / reduced loyalty

FIG 2.2   **Generational emergence in Western societies**

Source: Vogel (2013a)

of that you have the full spectrum of individuals within one generation. As discussed in the previous example on the introduction of the Internet and the resulting web and mobile companies, the Digital Settlers were the avant-garde of their time and consequently more similar to the average Digital Natives than most of their fellow Baby Boomers or Generation X-ers. However, certain events such as the end of World War II or the introduction of the Internet had a pronounced effect on the individuals.

Having said that there is no 100% right or wrong answer about generational traits and that it is difficult to ascribe one behavioral trait to one generation but not another, there are indeed certain patterns and trends. Table 2.1 describes various factors related to the generations of the last hundred years, including the key influencing events of that period and novel technologies (i.e., periodic effects), the generation's core values and traits, the attitude towards education, their work style and their attitude towards work (cohort effects). These details will be important when discussing solutions in Part II, given that multi-generational workforce management (Chapter 6) or the process of changing the education system to be ready for the 21st century (Chapter 5), depend on these generational characteristics.

TABLE 2.1 Generational characteristics

	Traditionalists	Baby boomers	Generation X	Generation Y	Generation Z
Other names (or included sub-generations)	Silent, Greatest Generation, GI, Forgotten Generation, Veterans, Lost Generation	"Me" Generation	Gen X, Xers, Post Boomers, 13th Generation, Latchkey generation, MTV generation	Gen Y, Millennials	Digital Natives, Internet Generation, Net Generation, iGeneration
Years of birth	1901–1945	1946–1964	1965–1981	1982–1990	1991– to date
Key events of that period	• WW I & WW II • The Great Depression	• Post-WWII economic growth and prosperity • Vietnam • Cold War • Space exploration • Atomic age	• Vietnam • Watergate • Cold War • Rise of mass media	• End of Cold War	• Worst youth unemployment crisis in history • Technological revolution: introduction of the WWW • War on Terror(ism)
Other influencers & markers	• Grew up in very difficult times • First commercial flight in 1914	• Grew up to become the "radicals" of the 70s and 80s. • Highest divorce rates and 2nd marriages in history	• Dual income parents • Single parents • Thinking they have to take care of themselves • First generation to financially do worse than their parents	• First cell phones • First computers at home	• Academization • Global competition for jobs • Global opportunities • Low-cost airlines • Social media
New communication technologies	• Telefax • Telephone	• Picture phones • Touch tone phones	• Mobile phones	• Text messaging • Email • MSN Messenger	• Facebook & Twitter • Whatsapp & WeChat • Instagram & Pinterest
Core values & characteristics	• Adhere to rules • Age=seniority • Command and control • Conformity • Discipline • Hard working • Hierarchy • Honor	• Anti-policymaking • Anti-war • Challenge & distrust authorities • Competitive • Dislike laziness • Entrepreneurial • Ethical	• Adaptable • Anti-establishment • Confident • Competent • Distrust • Diversity • Flexible • Global thinking	• Achievement • Confidence (maybe too confident) • Entrepreneurial • Flex-time/part-time work • It's all about fun • Job hopping • Global community • Highly educated	

(continued)

TABLE 2.1 Continued

	Traditionalists	Baby boomers	Generation X	Generation Y	Generation Z
	• Life before TV • Loyalty • Trust authorities • Patriotism • Saving money • Self-sacrifice • Strong work ethics • Work hard to maintain job	• Everything is possible • Imbalance of family and work • Loyalty • Optimistic • Strong work ethics • Work very hard	• Highly educated • Dislike hypes • Independence • Loyalty • Skeptical • Self-reliance • Seek life-balance (in response to workaholic parents) • Self-sufficient • Work to live	• Hopeful • Independent • Loyal to peers, but less towards employers • "Me first" attitude • Multi-lingual • Multi-tasking • Respect given for competence, not title • Sabbaticals • Seek for life-contribution to world • Tech-savvy • Virtual connections • Worried about future	
Role of/attitude towards education	A dream/a privilege	Birthright	It is a necessary means to reach the goal	Expensive but necessary	Academization, self-paced e-learning
Working style & ethics	• Conservative • Hierarchical • Linear • Loyal • Rules • Top-down • Work is an obligation	• Advancement • Democracy • Equal opportunity • Flat hierarchy • Humane • Process oriented • Warm environment • Work is an adventure	• Access to information • Care less about advancement • Efficient • Flexible • Output focused • Work-life-balance • Work is just a job	• Achievement • Collaborative • Creative • Diverse • Goal oriented • Less loyal • Work is a means to an end (fulfillment)	
What they expect from work	• Clear rules • Recognition • Respect • Security	• Ability to shine • Contribution • Overall "fit" with company • Team	• Ability to have an input • Flexibility • Modern • Work-life balance	• Flexibility and home office • Great people • High salaries • International opportunities • Learning • On-site access to social media • Opportunity to "leave a dent in the system" • Work-life balance	

Source: Vogel (2013a) and WMFC (2013)

2.2   Millennials and Digital Natives

Today's youth have not only changed incrementally as compared to previous generations but instead radically. It is not just about changing music taste, slang or clothes. Instead, we are witnessing a true discontinuity as a result of the digital revolution that has emerged since the introduction of the WWW in 1991. As we saw earlier, this first generation to be fully immersed in this novel virtual world (Generation Z, Digital Natives, Internet Generation, iGeneration, Net Generation) has distinctly different characteristics, values, and attitudes as compared to the previous generations (the Digital Immigrants who have grown up in an analogous world and immigrated into a digital era) (Prensky, 2001). This is a result of the fact that they have spent their entire life surrounded by computers, videogames, cell phones, digital music players, digital cameras, emailing, instant messaging, or social networking all of which have become an integral part of their lives. Today we know that the way young people "think and process information [is] fundamentally different from their predecessors" (Prensky, 2001: 1). As Prensky argues: While the Digital Natives speak the digital language from the beginning (it is one of their native languages), the Digital Immigrants had to learn it, always maintaining their "accent."

These characteristic differences between the Digital Natives and the digital Immigrants cause major challenges in education and the labor market. While in education, those who "teach" the Digital Natives are speaking an outdated language, the world of work is facing major challenges to set up multigenerational workplaces and prepare the workplace for this new generation of employees (cf. Chapter 6).

THINK PIECE ON TODAY'S YOUTH

– Andrea Gerosa, Founder and CEO of ThinkYoung –

Working with and for young people since 2002, there is one thing we have seen dramatically increase in the last years, and no, it is not youth unemployment. What has dramatically increased is a new attitude of young people towards the job market, especially towards career: salary is not on top of the agenda anymore. Instead, what young people are looking for is the opportunity to make an impact. If salary is not considered a priority in times of economic crisis, probably, things are really changing.

In 2011, when we started our first *"Skills Mismatch"* study, we were confronted with a striking gap. On the one hand, European employers frequently pointed to the lack of skilled workers able to fill specialized positions, claiming that the university system was detached from the job market and that young workers tended to be short-term oriented. On the other hand, the same young workers perceived themselves to be rather skilled both for their ideal job and their actual job, meanwhile lamenting about the limited entry-level opportunities, the omnipresent requirement of "past experience" and lack of a corporate long-term vision. How to address such disconnect?

The skyrocketing youth unemployment figures have attracted most of media's attention and have forced policymakers to take immediate and strong decisions. For example, measures like the "Youth Guarantee" initiated by the European Commission or Italy's simplified fiscal regime to start a company for under 35 year olds are just two examples of how the Generation Y and the Generation Z got to the center of policymakers' attention. Nonetheless, we argue that this simplified view does not reveal the underlying factors and the deeper cultural differences constraining the full potential of European youth.

Over the past years, ThinkYoung has conducted various research projects related to the skills mismatch, entrepreneurship, mobile communication and young people's attitude toward the future of the work place. The collage of these projects has allowed us to draw a picture of a European youth as very mobile, optimistic despite the current dire challenges, extremely adaptable but, above all, no longer attached to the idea of "a job for life." The job market has been facing a structural reform since the recent technological revolution. Against this backdrop, Europe's young workers have been reshaping the concept of a job, mainly in three areas: (1) the collapse of the sense of authority, at least in the traditional patriarchal meaning, (2) the quest for the meaning behind a job and (3) a shift from strong top-down leadership to mentoring and entrepreneurship:

- Authority: Today's European youth grew up in a much less authoritarian system than did their parents. For example, only four of the EU member states still have mandatory military service. Authority is increasingly technocratic or meritocratic, and even in the domestic setting rights and duties are commonly recognized equally among members by the legislation. This has systematically changed over the past 40 years (see for example the right to divorce). Moreover, technology grants to any member of an organization access to most of the information, regardless of the person's rank, which means that there are less natural knowledge barriers. On the job, youngsters tend to attribute power and authority to leaders who are open to confrontation/challenge, which back their own decisions with convincing arguments and master skills reinforcing their legitimacy for the role they cover.

- Quest for meaning: Another characteristic factor to describe today's European youth is that they want to find an employer with whom they can clearly identify and where their values are well aligned. In one of the ThinkYoung studies, young people indicated their long-term goals within a job are to become an expert in a field they are passionate about (ca. 50%) and to improve the life of others and to improve the society (42%), whereas the goal to afford a luxurious life was indicated by only 12% of European young people. In 2013, young people also indicated that environmental sustainability is an essential factor when choosing an employer.

- Shift from vertical to horizontal leadership: In another study, ThinkYoung identified a growing desire for mentoring, first-hand experience and the ability to fulfill entrepreneurial needs. Entrepreneurship and intrapreneurship are gaining importance in European economic development. This is becoming an increasing issue, as employers do not necessarily seek entrepreneurially minded job entrants. Young job entrants do not want vertical top-down leadership but instead seek project-based intergenerational teams where they can also bring in core competencies to teach older employees.

Concluding, young Europeans are anything but a "Generation Jobless." However, it is important that we understand their core capabilities in order to build employment opportunities that are well aligned with their goals in life. Steve Jobs' 2005 commencement speech is illustrative of today's youth: *"Keep looking, don't settle... Stay hungry, stay foolish"* (Stanford, 2005).

2.3   Influence on the World of Work

Today's youths—the Digital Natives—are the first generation to have been fully immersed in this novel virtual world resulting in quite distinct characteristics, values, and attitudes as compared to previous generations. As outlined in Chapter 1, these generational differences massively impact the world of work and are part of the drivers of the current youth labor market crisis.

Digital Natives are always connected, communicating in real-time via email, Facebook, Whatsapp, Twitter (etc.) expect the same in their professional life. There is relatively little reflection prior to sending out an application. While historically, one would have to prepare a 1-page handwritten letter, this is now being replaced with an informal email. I get emails like the following on a daily basis (without any attachment!):

> *Dear Mr. Vogel,*
>
> *I came across your open position and am greatly interested in it. Please let me know when you are available for an interview.*
>
> *Best regards,*
> *Applicant*

The poorly reflected application process illustrates the aforementioned generational changes. But this attitude towards speed and convenience not only affects communication but also a person's approach to planning a career. Young people are becoming less interested in 10-year career projections. Instead they expect 1–2 year incremental promotions and will quickly switch employer if their promotion does not move sufficiently fast. Digital Natives are used to receiving and processing information very fast, doing things in parallel and multi-tasking. The world of work will have to adapt to this.

On top of that, young people's attitudes and loyalty towards their employers have changed fundamentally. Increasing workforce turnover rates exert major administrative and financial strain on organizations.

Moreover, the digital revolution and the introduction of social networks has led young people to lose their sensitivity towards what should be shared on the web (or mobile) with their "friends" and what not. The divide between private and public information has been blurred. From an employer's perspective this may have downside effects with regards to openly sharing sensitive information about the company on the web.

The loss of distinction between the virtual world and reality is influencing the work style, both within a company as well as with external stakeholders. Companies must adapt to this changing world and create a setting that embraces the upside potential of this change—by introducing a 21st century workplace (cf. Chapter 6).

There is a major shift of skills—both among young people and among the employers—causing the biggest skills mismatch to date (cf. Chapter 5). Young people are losing basic skills such as reading or writing cursively; Digital Natives think and communicate in 160-character messages instead of 20–30 word sentences. The ability to store and recall information from the brain is also massively impacted by digital storage, online calendars, etc. "Common sense" intelligence is being replaced with a human-computer hybrid intelligence.

Digital Natives think and act in short 160-character messages instead of 20–30 word sentences

However, there are also many benefits of hiring youth. By getting young people on board, companies can greatly benefit from their digital literacy. They can help the Digital Immigrants learn about the most recent technological advancements (Prensky, 2001). They can join reverse mentoring programs where they closely work with an older colleague (cf. Chapter 6.4). Moreover, they are very enthusiastic and express a great willingness to learn about how they can make a difference in the world. They want to see the big picture and understand how they fit in. They are more flexible than their older counterparts, a clear advantage for employers when it comes to working over hours or relocating for the job. Today's youth has a global attitude and is more willing to move than previous generations. Young people are also less driven by money, which means that they will be, on average, less costly than their older counterparts would have been.

2.4 Conclusion

Overall, today's youth is markedly different from previous generations. This brings with it both challenges and opportunities for the labor market in general and for employers in particular. The technological revolution has led to new ways of living and working which will influence the workplace of the future. Understanding those generational characteristics of today's youth that are contributing to the high rates of youth unemployment will allow the different stakeholders—policymakers, educators, companies, organizations, parents, among others—to better adapt to this changing world and implement programs and workplace strategies that accommodate these changing patterns. Part II focuses on these strategies and solutions. But before going to the solutions section, I want to give a brief outlook of the future of the labor market including migration patterns, emerging industries and jobs of the future.

chapter 3

Trends and Outlook

> We are currently preparing students for jobs that don't yet exist, using technologies that haven't been invented, in order to solve problems we don't even know are problems yet.
>
> *Richard Riley; Gunderson et al., 2004*

What will the world of work look like in 2030? We are living through very dynamic times with important changes taking place in the world economy— changes that will have long-term consequences for the world of work. Among the ten patterns of change that we will be facing in the next 15 years, some are particularly relevant to the context of the youth labor market, including the demographic shift, economic turbulence, business 3.0, technology, generational crossroads, and rethinking talent, education, and training (Fast Future, 2008; Johnson Controls, 2009). The technological revolution, including ubiquitous technologies or 3D printing, will further accelerate the process that has been initiated with the development of personal computers, the Internet, email, social media, and smartphones. The labor markets of both developed and developing economies will be heavily impacted by these trends, particularly when accounting for them in the context of the global challenge of creating 470 million jobs between 2015 and 2030—the amount of jobs needed simply to keep up with the predicted growth of the world's working age population (United Nations, 2013a).

It will require visionary leaders and the great collective effort of multiple stakeholders to anticipate the skills that will be necessary for future employment opportunities and to prepare future generations for the world of work, particularly to avoid repeating what we are currently experiencing with respect to youth employment. The United Nations expect that for the decades ahead, policymakers need to cope with both structural changes (i.e., the 21st century challenges) and still unresolved 19th century problems such as underemployment, working poor, forced and child labor or a lack of respect for rights at work. Moreover, problems with respect to lifetime employment and pension models might emerge triggering social inequalities due to a widening gap between skilled and unskilled workers. Likewise, older employees will be forced to work longer beyond their expected retirement age due to a pension crisis.

The world to come will undergo major demographic changes. Some countries will be faced with the challenge of adapting their labor markets to an ageing work force. Others will have to cope with a large group of youth that seeks employment. In addition, the workplace is becoming increasingly complex with up to five generations working at the same time, causing major strain on both the employers and the employees. This becomes even trickier given the generational shifts that I described in the previous chapter and the different traits of Digital Natives and Digital Immigrants (Prensky, 2001). Moreover, we will experience intensified and changing migration patterns (rural-urban national migration paired with international migration) that will also pose additional challenges and opportunities.

Our personal and professional life is becoming increasingly virtual in nature. Many young people spend just as much time online as they do offline with the majority of interaction with their peers happening through Facebook or Whatsapp. Social norms and ways of communication and collaboration are fundamentally shifting.

We are faced with rising globalization. Countries are becoming more diverse in terms of nationalities, cultures, and languages, causing additional administrative challenges for on the employer. Moreover, the type of work being done in one country depends on the type of work being done in others. It is no longer the case that China, India, Taiwan, and other Asian countries are only suppliers for Western companies. Instead, they are now entering the global market with their own products, openly competing with Western companies. This obviously affects the types of jobs that are available across the globe.

Employment itself, including the jobs, the workplace, and the ways of working are changing as well. Job sharing, virtual team structures, flexible employment contracts are just a few of the 21st century buzzwords. International travel has been made, in part, obsolete through the introduction of video conferencing. The permanent connectivity and availability of individuals has led to a blending of work and personal life with a 24/7 mentality.

In addition, the majority of tomorrow's youth will end up with jobs that have not been invented yet (US Department of Labor, 1999). The biggest concern is the time lag between the skills being required on the labor market and the skills that are being provided by the education system, calling for a much closer collaboration between educators and employers.

In the next two sections I will discuss some of the consequences that we are expected to see from these changes—global work migration including brain drain and the emergence of new industries and jobs.

3.1   Global Mobility and Work Migration

– This section is written in collaboration with Göran Hultin, Founder and CEO Caden Corporation –

> For thousands of years, human beings have migrated in search of a better life. Migration is the result of numerous factors; many migrate in search of greater opportunities—to earn a better living, to live in a more agreeable environment or to join family or friends abroad. (IOM, 2013)

Migration is among the most natural things. While the fundamental phenomenon remains, motivations and patterns of migration, just like the departure and destination countries, vary over time (Figure 3.1 and Figure 3.2).

The US, often referred to as being built by immigrants, continues to attract masses from around the world. With over 40 million immigrants, top source countries include Mexico, China, the Philippines, and India. Germany, Europe's economic powerhouse, witnesses some of the largest share of immigrants in the region with individuals from Turkey, Italy, Poland, and Greece forming the bulk of incomers. Very much in line with the US, Canada receives the largest share of immigrants from the UK, China, India, and the Philippines. The UK on the other hand, in addition to historically strong immigration from India and Pakistan, receives significant immigration from Poland and Ireland (see Figure 3.3) (World Bank, 2011).

The well-established decade-long migration patterns continue to dominate the global migration landscape. However, global migration patterns are becoming far more nuanced and new trends are emerging. With less

FIG 3.1 Early human global migration

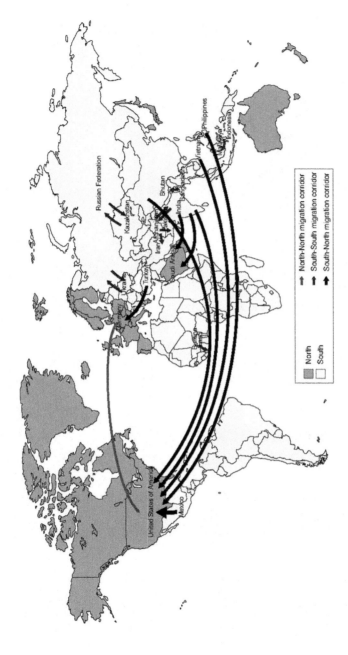

FIG 3.2   Global migration in 2010

Data Source: IOM (2013)

FIG 3.3   Migration in Europe in 2010

Source: European Commission (2012a)

favorable prospects in many industrialized countries combined with strong and sustained economic growth in major emerging economies, return migration is starting to break the traditional migration patterns.

L E A R N   M O R E

Here are two useful and insightful visualization tools for global migration patterns:

- The IOM tool: www.iom.int/cms/en/sites/iom/home/about-migration/world-migration.html
- Migration Map: http://migrationsmap.net/

3.1.1   Drivers of Work Migration

So which factors drive these migration patterns? In addition to a growing gap in living standards and wage differentials between countries or employment opportunities followed by greater economic growth, a number of "pull-factors" can be identified when examining global migration patterns. Geographical proximity certainly has a strong influence, as can be witnessed in the strong migration flows between India, Bangladesh, and Pakistan. This also applies for the strong movement of people within the former Soviet Union and the Mexico-United States corridor. Ex-Soviet states also benefit from cultural proximity and a low language threshold. The lingual (and colonial) aspect has also played a role in the strong movement of Indians and Pakistanis to the UK as well as North Africans to France. Migration flows have led to an established presence of diasporas in many countries, forming yet another pull-factor for continued migration. Turks in Germany, Mexicans in the US or Indians in the UK have become an enrooted phenomena and a part of society in the destination countries.

Among the above-discussed factors, the radical differences in employment outlook levels between the industrialized world and the emerging economies can be identified as the key factor contributing to the migration phenomena (and more specifically also to the phenomena of brain drain as well as return migration). Emerging economies, China, India, Mexico, and Brazil, continue to show high levels of hiring activity whereas the industrialized countries lag far behind in employment outlook levels. This current situation is highlighted in Figure 3.4, providing a fairly strong message regarding the level of hiring in respective countries, indicating the percentage of employers with hiring intentions.

When looking at European youth, for example, the question arises where they should go provided that the hiring intentions of companies in their countries might not be changing quickly enough. This question forms one of the fundamental issues of the entire youth unemployment debate and policymakers are worrying that their best talents will flee the country in search for better opportunities elsewhere; a trend that will have devastating long-term effects on the society and economy of their home country.

Strong emerging economies with positive employment outlooks have led to a fundamental disruption of the global work migration behavior, with many of the traditionally strong emigration countries facing increased return migration.

- Brazil, for example, has witnessed strong return migration during the past decade with an increase of almost 100% between the 2000 and 2010. Japan, the United States and Portugal were the top source countries in terms of returning Brazilians, with over 75% of individuals coming from these countries being Brazil-born (IOM, 2013).
- In the case of China, proactive programs try to foster return migration of highly skilled Chinese workers in order to tackle prevailing skill shortages on

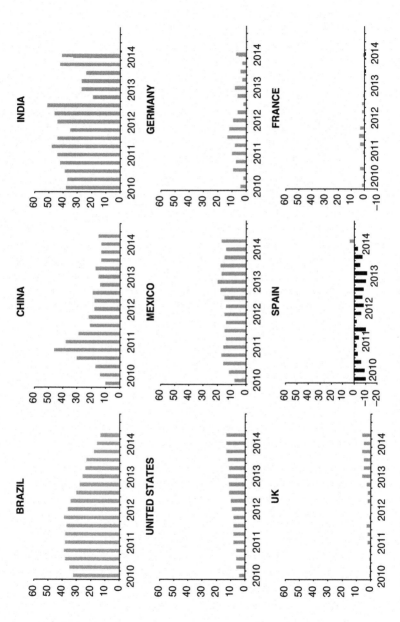

FIG 3.4 Employers' hiring intentions (as % employers planning to increase staff)

Source: ManPower (2013)

the Chinese labor market. These targeted municipal- and government-level programs have been launched to attract overseas Chinese to return to China and contribute to the domestic economy (Shanghai Bureau of Human Resources and Social Security, 2014).

- The Mexico-US-Mexico corridor has historically been labeled by a massive flow of individuals heading north. Today, due to return migration, the southbound flow equals the amount of people heading for the US (NY Times, 2013).
- In the case of India economic growth and fast emerging skill shortages have stimulated return migration and estimates indicate an annual 75,000 professionals heading back home (ILO, 2011).

The favorable employment outlook in major emerging economies, whilst the majority of European economies simultaneously face a negative employment outlook, certainly increases the likelihood of an era of more significant return migration. A comparison between the pre-2010 and post-2010 hiring levels provides a grim picture regarding the shift in Europe and the US towards a declining hiring trend whereas the emerging economies continue to show an upward trend in employment levels (cf. Figure 3.5).

3.1.2   Brain Drain or just Mobility?

In addition to this overall negative employment outlook of European economies, drastic rates of youth unemployment shed a grim light on these labor markets and confront young educated European talent with a very uncertain future. At the same time, opportunities continue to arise in the parts of the world showing strong and sustained economic growth. While the above-described return migration to emerging economies is associated with something positive (i.e., stronger home economies that pull their citizens back home), the global youth unemployment crisis leads to an involuntary or necessity-based migration away from the home country in search for better employment opportunities. Prevailing labor market conditions allow for a careful estimation of increased flows of young educated European talent heading for the emerging economies to pursue their professional careers.

The fundamental question is to what extent we can speak of regular opportunity-based work migration—that is voluntary movement as a result of some attractive employment opportunity elsewhere—as opposed to forced emigration. In a recent article, a young Spaniard was interviewed and he stated the following that seems to be somewhat illustrative for a whole generation of young Spaniards (and Greek alike): I "never believed [I] would be forced

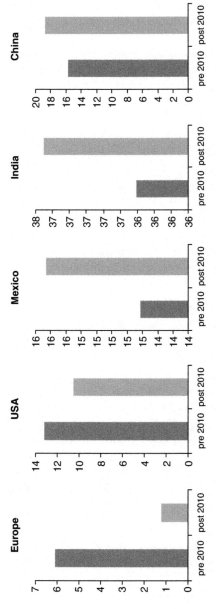

FIG 3.5 Comparison of employers' hiring intentions (pre- and post-2010) (as % employers planning to increase staff)

Source: ManPower (2013)

to migrate to Europe to begin an independent life … [I] was always dreaming about learning more languages than just Catalan and Spanish, but [I] was not expecting to be forced to learn English so quickly to get a job" (Green European Journal, 2013). So the degree to which this mobility is voluntary or involuntary—necessity-driven or opportunity-driven—is uncertain. Yet, as Johnson (2014) states, the majority of young people do not want to work abroad. They would rather stay close to home. This statement is backed by empirical evidence from a recent study performed by the FutureWork Forum and the Generation Europe Foundation (FutureWork Forum, 2010). They asked 7,000 young people across Europe where they are looking for employ-ment. Figure 3.6 illustrates the responses.

the majority of young people do not want to work abroad

Taken together, these statements illustrate that we can speak of an involuntary youth migration rather than a voluntary one. However, the long-term effects on the country's society and economy are uncertain. Many more questions arise when digging a bit deeper.

we can speak of an involuntary youth migration rather than a voluntary one

Is it necessarily negative that young people are "forced out of the nest" to gain professional experience elsewhere? Wasn't the search for better opportunities also one of the main drivers of immigration to the US? Isn't that what today's global workplace requires? Could it be that those countries that are currently experiencing a youth brain drain will benefit from return migration at some point, similar to the Mexican case outlined above? If yes, could the benefits of

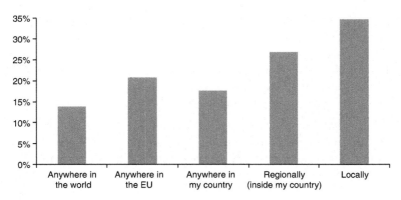

FIG 3.6 Geographic work preferences of Europe's youth

Source: FutureWork Forum (2010)

that youth having been abroad outweigh the negative effects of them staying at home? What are some of the measures to be taken by policymakers, by employers, by educators or the Next Generation itself to counteract a brain drain? Should we let this brain drain continue and observe what will happen or do we need to act now to avoid long-term scarring? What are the effects of the Bologna reform, Erasmus programs, etc.? Do they need some modification in the face of the current youth unemployment crisis? Does the net benefit of sending youth abroad for education (and most likely also employment) outweigh the net negative effects on the country of origin? Should programs instead rather focus on providing defined return programs with guaranteed job opportunities to ensure that young talents are not leaving for good? The majority of these questions will remain unanswered for a while until we find definite answers. What is clear, however, is that globalization has altered the global migration map for good.

Most respondents of the FutureWork Forum survey who supported the idea of cross-border working felt that it needed to be backed up by some sort of national or EU support. The creation of a Europe-wide clearing-house for jobs was a popular concept. However there were few takers for the idea that job seekers should just "go" and find out what opportunities were like in other countries.

3.2   Industries and Job Profiles of the Future

Just as global migration patterns and national employment outlooks are dynamic in nature, so are industries and associated job profiles. The regional and global emergence of new industries (e.g., the ICT industry and associated ICT hot spots such as Silicon Valley as a major hub for job opportunities) and the disappearance of others (e.g., record stores or video rental) influence the face of national and regional employment. In a recent study[1] on the shape of future jobs, Talwar and Hancock (2010) analyze the labor market of the future, describing the driving forces of change and potentially resulting future jobs.

We can observe that, on a global agenda, we are facing major economic, political, and societal shifts. The current economic turbulence might carry on for another few years with growth remaining the biggest driver of economic recovery. The role of Asia (in particular China) has already (and will further) change, taking on a global leadership position. Global interconnectivity and globalization of businesses is further on the rise with novel industrial sectors emerging as a result of the fast-paced technological advancements that are being made. A growing (and in many regions ageing) population will cause major strain on the labor market, the pension system, the healthcare system and make the achievement of many UN Millennium Development Goals (MDG)—such as the alleviation of poverty and hunger—difficult if not impossible. At the same time, we are facing major environmental challenges related to the need for energy, access to fresh water and food and of course climate change. Table 3.1 summarizes the ten key patterns that will drive (individually and in combination) change in the coming 15 years as well as resulting possible future jobs (Fast Future, 2008).

TABLE 3.1   Key patterns of change

Key patterns of change	Potentially emerging future jobs
Demographic shift • Population growth • Ageing societies • Urbanization • Increased life expectancy • Ethnical diversity	• Genomics Developer/Architect/Baby Designer • Body Part Maker • Farmer of Genetically Engineered Crops and Livestock • Old Age Wellness Manager/Consultant Specialist • Personal Body Weight/Obesity Consultant • Longevity Provider • Cryonics Technician • Insect-Based Food Developer, Chef, Nutritionist • Population Status Manager • Socialization/Culturalization Therapist • End-of-Life Planner
Economic turbulence • Legacy of the economic crisis • Emergence of new economic powers • Redistribution of wealth around the world	• Bioinformationist • Genetic Hacker • Weather Modification Police • Knowledge Broker • Virtual Police • Holographer • Teleportation Specialist • Water Traders • Desert Land Rights Trader • Currency Designer
Politics get complex • Increasingly complex issues demand coordinated solutions • Asia rising in political influence • Pressure on public funding	• Quarantine Enforcer • Climate Change Compliance Auditor • Business Consultant for Climate Change Compliance • In-House Simplicity Expert • Complex Security Integrator • Mind Reading Specialist • Virtual Police • Infrastructure Specialist • Societal Systems Designer • Currency Designer • Non-military Defense Specialist • Privacy Protection Consultants

(continued)

TABLE 3.1 Continued

Key patterns of change	Potentially emerging future jobs
Business 3.0 • Increasingly global • Widening technological choice • Innovative business models	• Complexity Analyst/Gaiantologist • Chief In-Company Health Enhancement Officer • In-Company Gene Screener • In-Company Sustainability Coordinator • Recycling Analyst • Social Network Analyst • Global Work Process Coordinator • Chief Networking Officer • Spaceline Pilot • Spaceport Designer • Space Tour Guide • Terraformer of the Moon and Other Planets • Space Architect • Astrogeologist, Astrophysiologist and Astrobiologist • Director of Responsible Investment • Executive VP Foresight, Oversight, and Governance
Science and technology go mainstream • Countries compete on innovation • Technology is essential in our everyday lives	• Personal Enhancement Advisor • Nano-Medic • Telemedicine Technician • Biometric Identification Specialist Experimental Petrologist • Machine Linguist • Quantum Computing specialist • Professional VR Citizen • Robot Designer/Trainer • Robot Mechanic • Robot Counselor • Synthetic Life Designer/Scientist/Engineer
Generational crossroads (see Chapter 2) • Increasing life expectancy forces people to work past retirement age • Five generations in the workforce • Massive differences across generations • Challenges of managing multi-generational workforces • Talent gap resulting from the retirement of Baby Boomers	• Personal Enhancement Advisor • Memory Augmentation Surgeon • Mind Reading Specialist • Intelligent Agent Designers and Manager • Virtual Personal Shopper/Shopping Assistant • Social "Networking" Worker • Socialization/Culturalization Therapist
Rethinking talent, education and training • Widening talent gap • Education is critical in developing countries	• Avatar Manager/Devotee • Human to Machine Interface Controller • iKnowledge Guide • Cybrarian • Personal Learning Programmer

(continued)

TABLE 3.1 Continued

Key patterns of change	Potentially emerging future jobs
• Growing concerns about the quality/relevance of education in some countries (see Chapter 5) • Importance of lifelong learning • Growing importance of online learning	• Enhanced Games Specialist • Memetics Manager/Analyst/Trader/Generator
Global expansion of electronic media • Increased connectivity • More devices • More functionalities • Smart phones as "personal assistant"	• Personal Entertainment Programmer • Psycho-Customizer • Human to Machine Interface Controller • Narrowcaster • Data Miner • Waste Data Handler • Privacy Protection Consultant • Virtual Clutter Organizer • Off-the-Grid/Off-the-Net Facilitator • Designer of Advanced Interfaces for Ambient Intelligence Systems • Network Relationship Counselor • Virtual-Reality Actor
A society in transition • Increased global responsibility and accountability • Societal norms and global monitoring (through technology) • Pressure to serve the greater good • Lack of trust in key institutions	• New Science Ethicist • Experimental Therapy Experts • Resource Use Consultant • Virtual Property/Home Owners' Association Manager • Vertical Farmer • Media Ethicist • Computer Sex Worker/Therapist/Designer • Time Broker/Time Bank Trader • Black Swan Life Advisory • Authorized Narcotics Salesman • Personal Branders • Intelligent Clothing Designer/Engineers
Natural resource challenges • Growing resource pressure • Growing energy demand • Climate change • Increasing commodity prices	• Wind Farmer • pharmer of Genetically Engineered Crops and Livestock • Climate Change Reversal Specialist • Drowned City Specialist • Consumer Energy Analyst • Battery Technician • Chlorophyll Technician • Fusion Engineer • Vertical Farmer • Water Trader • Desert Land Rights Trader • Hydrogen Fuel Station Manager • Alternative Vehicle Developer • Scarce Metal Tracer • Solar Flight Specialist

Source: Adopted from Fast Future (2008)

From this long list of different potential future jobs, Fast Future in collaboration with their partners selected a representative list of twenty jobs. These were shared in an online survey whereby popularity, job impact, environmental impact, educational benefits, developing country benefits, financial rewards and attractiveness of each job was assessed. The top five jobs that respondents would most like to see are: (1) Old age wellness manager/consultant; (2) vertical farmer; (3) non-medic; (4) Climate change reversal specialist; and (5) new scientist ethicist.

3.3 Conclusion

What does the future hold? We know that the world is rapidly changing and with it the labor market. A plethora of changes are happening, including a major demographic shift with an ageing population in some countries and an increasingly young population in other countries, ongoing economic and political turbulence in many regions of the world, a global rebalancing of political and economic power, global migration patterns with a decrease in population in some countries and a massive increase in others, growing diversity of countries with more nationalities, cultures, religions, and languages jammed into urban areas, the introduction of novel technology that is changing our everyday life (both private and professional), the changing generational traits that will dictate the way future generations will live, think and work, new industries and jobs that are emerging, the virtual space is partly replacing real life, just to name a few.

The current youth unemployment crisis does not take place in a vacuum but instead is embedded in a complex and rapidly changing global labor market, one where we can only speculate what it will exactly look like in 20 or 30 years time. Nonetheless we will need to make sure that today's and tomorrow's youth is better prepared for this uncertain future, both in terms of skills and experience. With the portfolio of jobs that are becoming more and more demanding we must be careful to maintain jobs that are youth-compatible; jobs in which youth can enter the world of work and gain credibility and experience on the job.

To find short-term and long-term solutions to the current youth unemployment crisis it is of critical importance that we take into account both the complexity of the issue and the dynamism of the world to come. Global challenges of the magnitude of the current youth unemployment crisis cannot be solved by individual attempts by one stakeholder; instead it requires the collaborative, orchestrated effort of different stakeholders. In Part II, I will take a multi-stakeholder approach and assess the role of entrepreneurship in tackling youth unemployment, the changes needed in the education sector to solve the skills mismatch equation, the role that employers play, the duties of policymakers to provide a platform for solutions, and an overall aggregated insight into dozens of viable solutions from around the world.

This page intentionally left blank

Part II

From Crisis to Opportunity

Around the world, there is growing recognition of the need to strengthen policies and investments involving young people … Youth can determine whether this era moves toward greater peril or more positive change. Let us support them developing into productive and powerful leaders. Ban Ki-Moon; United Nations, 2012

This page intentionally left blank

chapter **4**

Entrepreneurship: Turning Job Seekers into Job Creators

Sail away from the safe harbor. Catch the trade winds in your sails. Explore. Dream. Discover.

Mark Twain

Our view on the role of entrepreneurship in society and the economy has drastically changed over the last half century. While the common belief of the past was that established companies and not new ventures are the sole drivers of innovation, economic and societal prosperity, and job creation, we now know that this is not true and that entrepreneurship actually plays a central role (Audretsch, 2002; Acs, 2006; Van Praag & Versloot, 2007; Carree & Thurik, 2010).

Recent statistics indicate that the average net employment growth rate in the United States between 1980 and 2005 would have been negative, if not for the jobs created by new ventures (Haltiwanger et al., 2009). Along the same lines, there is evidence that jobs created from new ventures are much less volatile or sensitive to economic turbulence compared to jobs created in the entire economy (Stangler, 2009). Moreover, research points out that the creation of new firms has an important effect on a nation's political and societal stability, as it promotes social cohesion by offering the opportunity of self-employment to everyone (e.g., facilitating the integration of immigrant and marginal communities) and allows broad participation in the economy regardless of a person's background (Monitor Company Group, 2009). Given these important functions of entrepreneurship, it thus may not be surprising that economists such as Edward Lazear (Stanford University, and former Chairman of the

President's Council of Economic Advisors) conclude that the entrepreneur is the single most important player in modern economies (Lazear, 2005).

As a consequence, governments, international organizations, educational institutions, among other stakeholders around the world have shown increasing interest in entrepreneurship as a phenomenon in general and as an active labor market policy (ALMP) in particular (Fayolle et al., 2006). Policies and programs are being initiated to foster entrepreneurship and self-employment. Educational institutions are seeking to include entrepreneurship into their curriculum (cf. Chapter 5). In the period from 1979 to 2001, the number of entrepreneurship courses offered in the United States increased tenfold (Katz, 2008). Similar trends are observable in Europe (European Commission, 2008) and more recently anywhere around the world. An incredible pace of global transformation and the shattering youth job crisis has spurred this increased interest in entrepreneurship.

In recent years in the context of the current youth unemployment crisis different stakeholders have started creating an armamentarium of youth entrepreneurship policies and initiatives. But does it make economic sense to foster youth entrepreneurship? Is this really the best option for young people who have difficulties entering the labor market? Or is it just the next best thing that people can come up with in the wake of the current crisis with a sword of Damocles hanging over us, threatening that today's youth will enter history books as the Generation Jobless?

This is a very fundamental question that hitherto remains unanswered. I still have not seen any study that provides solid empirical evidence that overall youth entrepreneurship is a viable solution to youth unemployment. There is a clear lack of in-depth empirical research on youth entrepreneurship and any "evidence with regards to the impact of youth entrepreneurship on economic growth and employment creation is largely anecdotal in nature" (Simpson & Christensen, 2009: 6).

However, the most intuitive answer is yes, given that it cannot be harmful to help young people turn into job creators rather than job seekers. Nonetheless, one also needs to factor in the jobs that are being destroyed by entrepreneurs—those jobs inside the incumbent firms that are being replaced by the new firms, because their products are better, faster or cheaper. Yet, I do not seek to engage in this kind of debate right now, as this would require an entire book in itself to analyze this in greater detail. Nonetheless, I would like to outline a few pros and cons of youth entrepreneurship in the context of the current crisis.

Among other ALMPs, youth entrepreneurship is becoming increasingly accepted as a means and critical alternative for income generation among young people (Simpson & Christensen, 2009) and a mechanism to unleash the economic potential of young people. Blanchflower & Oswald (1998) and Chigunta (2002) summarize several reasons for the importance of promoting youth entrepreneurship: It (1) creates employment opportunities for those who start the businesses as well as those whom they employ (Curtain, 2000), particularly because young entrepreneurs are prone to hiring other young people (Meager et al., 2003); (2) brings back alienated and marginalized youth into the labor market (Curtain, 2000; White & Kenyon, 2001); (3) helps address socio-psychological issues arising from unemployment; (4) helps youth develop new skills and professional experience that, in turn, could enhance their general employability (ETUC, 2013); (5) revitalizes local communities through new products and services (OECD, 2001); (6) capitalizes on the youth's particular responsiveness to new trends and opportunities; and (7) at least keeps otherwise idle young people occupied, which is always better than them not having anything to do and feeling useless (cf. Chapter 1).

Although there is an increased global awareness that entrepreneurship is a viable career option for young people (as reflected in the increased interest of young people in this career path as well as several international initiatives such as the G20 Young Entrepreneurs Alliance or the ILO Youth Entrepreneurship Program), the majority of entrepreneurship promotion programs do not account for the specific characteristics and needs of young would-be-entrepreneurs and treat them as part of the general adult population (Lewis & Massey, 2003; Schoof, 2006). There is empirical evidence that experience positively influences the chances of new venture survival (Cooper et al., 1994). Given that young people typically lack professional experience, they might be more likely to fail, which brings with it substantial costs on an individual, economic and societal level (e.g., Shepherd et al., 2009). Moreover, with regards to employability if they then seek regular employment at a later stage, such entrepreneurial experience is not particularly beneficial given that employers have a hard time estimating the particular value of the young person's experience and also do not specifically look for entrepreneurial traits in young applicants (see Chapter 1).

Whether or not it is beneficial to foster youth entrepreneurship is also a function of the region or country. Entrepreneurship is a highly regional phenomenon with major differences across regions and countries, for example when it comes to entrepreneurial culture, the regulatory environment, societal attitudes towards failure, the financial system, among many other factors. The Global Entrepreneurship Monitor (GEM) studies as well as the World Bank *Doing Business* reports provide useful insights into where it might make more sense to engage in entrepreneurship—as compared to a different career path—and where it might make less sense.

This chapter focuses on a small subset of the complex and inter-related elements to address the question of whether entrepreneurship is a viable solution to youth unemployment or not. The next section features some of the findings of the GUESSS project (Global University Entrepreneurial Spirit Students' Survey) on young people's entrepreneurial intentions, followed by the pros and cons of raising kids to become entrepreneurs, the myth of college dropout billionaires, the benefits of glimpsing into entrepreneurship, entrepreneurship promotion for marginalized communities as a whole, how to build entrepreneurship ecosystems and a selection of case studies from around the world.

4.1   Students' Entrepreneurial Intentions

– Content for this section is provided by Prof. Dr. Philipp Sieger, University of St. Gallen –

Young people represent the entrepreneurs of tomorrow, and their entrepreneurial plans and activities will shape tomorrow's societies and overall economic and societal well-being. In addition, becoming an entrepreneur is a meaningful way to escape the unemployment trap. Hence, it is of great interest for numerous stakeholders such as academics, practitioners, educators, policymakers, and last but not least young people themselves to investigate how many of them intend to create their own firm in the future. As entrepreneurship is a truly global phenomenon, an investigation across many different countries is of particular value.

The GUESSS project investigates entrepreneurial intentions and activities of students using a geographical and temporal comparison. Data is gathered using an on-line survey. Since its inception in 2003, six data collection waves have taken place. In 2011, the fifth wave was conducted, followed by the sixth wave between October 2013 and March 2014 that took place in 34 countries at more than 700 universities, resulting in more than 109,000 complete student responses.

In the following, a few main findings will be presented. As the main focus, students' entrepreneurial intentions in 2001 (Figure 4.1) are compared to those in 2013/2014 (Figure 4.2). This is done by comparing data from the 21

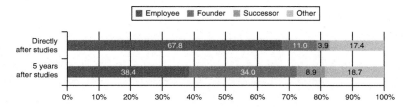

FIG 4.1   Career choice groups in GUESSS 2011 (Wave 5)

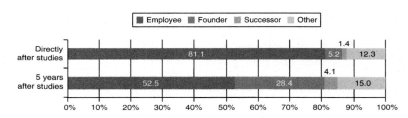

FIG 4.2   Career choice groups in GUESSS 2013/2014 (Wave 6)

countries that took part in both data collections. From the 2013/2014 dataset we could rely on 71,051 answers; from the 2011 dataset, 89,803 responses could be used. To capture students' entrepreneurial intentions, they were asked which career path they intend to pursue directly after completion of their studies and which one 5 years later. Among several options, one career path was being "a founder (entrepreneur) working in my own firm." On the aggregated global level, we see that for 2013/2014, 5.2% of all students intend to become an entrepreneur directly after studies, compared to 28.4% 5 years after studies. The 2011 data reveals higher numbers: there, 11.0% of all students are classified as intentional entrepreneurs directly after studies, and 34.0% related to 5 years after studies.

To delve deeper into this issue and to reveal country-specific differences, the share of intentional founders in the 21 countries is analyzed separately. The focus is on intentional founders five years after completion of studies as this provides a more reliable picture (see Figure 4.3). Viewing the absolute levels of the share of intentional entrepreneurs, an interesting pattern emerges: on the one hand, many developing and emerging economies can be found among those countries with the highest share of intentional entrepreneurs. Examples are Mexico, Argentina, Russia, Estonia, Hungary, and Brazil. On the other hand, many developed countries can be found in the lower half of the table

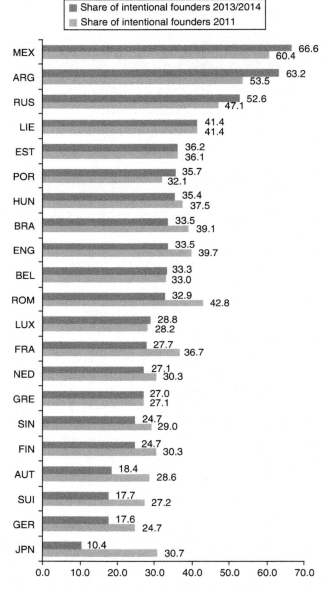

FIG 4.3   Share of intentional founders across time/countries (5 years after studies)

Data Source: GUESSS

(which means with lower absolute shares of intentional founders among their students), such as Japan, Germany, Switzerland, and Austria.

Viewing the changes across time, Figure 4.4 shows that the share of intentional founders has been increasing in six countries, decreasing in 13 countries, and stable in two countries; out of those 21 countries, five exhibit differences smaller than 1 percent. Again, the countries that report higher numbers in 2013/2014 compared to 2011 are developing or emerging countries (Argentina, Mexico, Russia, Portugal). Among the countries with the strongest decline in entrepreneurial intentions are many industrialized countries such as Japan, Austria, Switzerland, France, and Germany.

It has to be noted that the samples of the two GUESSS editions are not identical. More specifically, the number and types of universities participating in each country vary between 2011 and 2013/2014, as does the number of

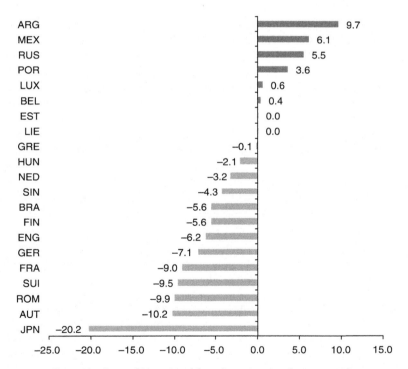

FIG 4.4   Change in share of intentional founders over time by country (5 years after studies)

Data Source: GUESSS

responding students per university and per country. Moreover, the relevance of entrepreneurial intentions varies considerably depending on the field of study. For instance, previous studies have shown that students in the business and economics field are more likely to intend to create an own firm than students in the natural sciences or social sciences (Sieger et al. 2011). The share of students in the respective fields also varies between the two samples. However, numerous tests taking issues such as study field into account have shown that the results reported above are stable and reliable.

Based on these results, three main conclusions can be derived.

- Students' entrepreneurial intentions are stronger in less developed countries. This is in line with previous findings that creating an own firm is a desired career option particularly when other options are not that numerous. In developing or transition countries, job markets and financial markets are less developed than in industrialized countries, and unemployment is mostly higher. Hence, students might increasingly see creating an own firm as a way to start their professional career.
- On global average, entrepreneurial intentions have been declining from Spring 2011 to Autumn/Winter 2013/2014. One possible explanation is the overall economic environment. In many countries, the economic situation in Autumn/Winter 2013/2014 was better than in Spring 2011. In 2011, the effects of the global economic crisis that started in 2008/2009 were more prevalent than in 2013/2014. This means that the students surveyed in the 2013/2014 wave find more and better job opportunities in the regular job market, which reduces the share of so-called "necessity entrepreneurs" who enter self-employment because they cannot find a good job elsewhere.
- Related to the second main finding, entrepreneurial intentions have been declining more strongly in more developed countries than in less developed countries; in some of the latter, even increasing shares of intentional entrepreneurs are reported. A possible reason might be that when the immediate effects of an economic crisis wane, the number of attractive alternative job opportunities increases more rapidly in developed countries.

To conclude, students' entrepreneurial intentions are an intriguing phenomenon that needs to be looked at on the global level. The relevance of entrepreneurial intentions varies considerably across countries, and external factors such as an economic crisis have important consequences in that regard. This may show that the option to create an own firm is indeed an appropriate "counteraction" to unemployment. Both researchers and practitioners are encouraged to further investigate this interesting and relevant topic in the future.

4.2 Raising the Next Generation of Entrepreneurs

Tomorrow's entrepreneurs are today's young children—children who have been raised by their parents in an entrepreneurial spirit. Mary Mazzio produced a documentary movie called *Lemonade Stories* in which she interviewed entrepreneurs like Richard Branson and Arthur Blank alongside their moms. From that she learned that entrepreneurship can be taught and it made her change the way she raises her own children (*Lemonade Stories*, 2004). Likewise, Cameron Herold's TEDx talk addresses this point in a very illustrative manner, discussing arguments why we should raise our children to become entrepreneurs and how this can be done (TEDx, 2010). In my TEDx talk I concluded by saying that we need to help young people realize their entrepreneurial potential to re-define the labor market for themselves and for their peers—a duty that we have as parents as educators and as society (TEDx, 2013).

So why exactly should we raise our children to become entrepreneurs and why should educators contribute in this process by teaching them entrepreneurship? There are various arguments that speak for it and simple tricks that can be applied to teach children entrepreneurship in everyday life. Gaining entrepreneurial experience and exposure early on in life …

- …is essential as entrepreneurship is one of the big things in the 21st century skills framework (see Chapter 5). Despite that fact that employers are not necessarily keen on to entrepreneurially minded new entrants, it is nonetheless becoming increasingly important and valued in different aspects of life.
- …teaches children the different aspects of business in a playful way (ideally in a "learning by doing" approach).
- …allows them to gain hands-on skills that are incredibly important in the world of work, including negotiation skills, financial literacy, presentation skills, and problem-solving, among many more.
- …helps children to figure out where their passion lies and develop something off of it. Ultimately, the reflection process about what they want to do with their life is incredibly important and it will give the children an advantage over those who do not go through this reflective process as they can navigate their entire career in a pre-determined direction.
- …helps young people go back to school and contextualize what they are learning there, be it math to build a financial statement, written languages to write a business plan, participating in theatre to learn presenting and pitching, etc. Once they can connect the dots between what is needed in the real world and what is taught in school, they can better absorb knowledge.

...teaches them everything they need to know about failure, given that entrepreneurship—just like life itself—is a constant up and down with successes and failures. This is oftentimes forgotten when raising a child, leaving them with a harsh lesson as they are thrown out of the nest just to learn how to fly on the way down. Ultimately, it is "only those who dare to fail greatly that can ever achieve greatly" (Robert Kennedy). We must teach our children the valuable lesson that they need to stand up once more than they fall down in order to be successful.

We need to:

- ...make room for creativity and inspiration so that our children can learn how they can solve their own problems in a creative way. Micromanaging our children and trying to "shut them off" by putting them in front of a TV will not do them any good on their way to becoming an entrepreneur. Give them their free space to explore their creativity and learn to entertain themselves. Cameron, for example, illustrates that he does not read his children bedtime stories every night but instead they take turns in coming up with stories. This can be facilitated by using simple objects from the room—pick three things and ask your child to come up with a story that builds off of these three things.
- ...give our children the opportunity to develop financial literacy in a fun and playful manner, be it the lemonade stand around the corner, selling old stuff at a flea market or a garage sale, or starting a tech company. While the money they make through these activities is secondary, the process of earning money gives them a better sense of the value of money they make as well as a feeling of freedom and responsibility.
- ...help our children jump over their own shadows and pro-actively engage in conversations with adults as this will help them overcome their shyness and ultimately help them in various ways for their entrepreneurial career.
- ...expose our children with situations where they are on stage for performance, either through music, dance or theatre. Competitive settings (e.g., sports) are also helpful.
- ...foster their problem-solving skills by brainstorming solutions with them, doing formal evaluations of different solutions and ultimately pick the best one. Formalizing this process spurs creativity and at the same time develops analytical skills and the ability to properly reflect on things prior to taking a decision.
- ...turn the regular learning process that every young person is going through—including the "no you are not supposed to do this and that..."—into a playful game in which you and your children brainstorm on how they could do things better next time. This will not only help the learning but at the same time also be rather constructive and less harsh of a criticism towards your child.

- …let our children take responsibility and make decisions. It is critical that our children learn to feel confident in the decisions they make. When they are small you can let them choose their clothes or between two types of vegetables. This will help them build confidence in their own decision-making ability.
- …help our children in experiencing risk and their own boundaries by supporting them with incrementally more challenging tasks, be it in sports, crafts or whatever else. This will again help them build confidence and empower them.
- …allow our children to be critical about the status quo and come up with better ideas. The traditional world in which we live (and the majority of people who live in it) are conformist with very limited questioning about the usefulness of specific solutions or processes. The education system is set up in a way that our children must not question the teacher's perspective. Likewise, the world of work is set up in a way that the superior's opinion is not to be questioned. By asking children their opinion on what needs to be changed, why, and how, will greatly foster their entrepreneurial mindset.

In addition to all these small things that can be done to expose our kids to entrepreneurship, there are many organizations that promote early-on exposure with entrepreneurship. One of these examples is Empact—the following case study.

CASE STUDY: EMPACT

– Sheena Lindahl, Founder –

"Empact celebrates the many different faces of entrepreneurship, breaking down stereotypes and creating entrepreneurial communities based on authenticity, humility & generosity."

Sheena Lindahl

How does your organization tackle youth unemployment?

Empact's programs and services focus on facilitating a culture of entrepreneurship in communities around the world through exposure and celebration. Empact holds an annual showcase and celebration of young entrepreneurs age 35 and under as part of its Empact Showcase & Empact100 List. Entrepreneurs are connected to each other and receive recognition through an award ceremony and mastermind event that in the past has taken place at the White House, United Nations and US Chamber of Commerce. Within this community we have created space for authentic sharing among entrepreneurs around the ups and downs of entrepreneurship and the challenging journey it can present.

Over the past six years, Empact has held a program called the Extreme Entrepreneurship Tour, which taps into this network to further spread the message of entrepreneurship as a viable career path. The idea behind this is that by showing the many different types of entrepreneurship and the variety of personalities of entrepreneurs more individuals will be able to see themselves as entrepreneurs. Each event introduces individuals to the various types of entrepreneurship, increases entrepreneurial self-identification, and then feeds into programs and resources available.

The key performance indicators (KPIs)

The Empact Showcase demonstrates how much young entrepreneurs impact the economy. For example, the 2013 Empact Showcase community consisted of 306 companies run by founders under age 36. These companies contributed a combined USD 1.3 billion and almost 9,000 jobs to the economy. The Extreme Entrepreneurship Tour events are inspirational exposure events. Empact organized 1,000 speeches and 500 events at colleges and universities, workforce development organizations, associations, corporations, Small Business Development Centers, and governmental organizations. By catalyzing individuals to self-identify as entrepreneurs, Empact leads them to take advantage of the numerous programs and resources that support entrepreneurs which are available to them in their communities.

Empact has:

- Changed the lives of more than 17,980 people inspiring them to pursue their passions, set goals and change the world
- Increased the proportion of participants who see entrepreneurship as a realistic career for a young person under the age of 30 from 73% before the event to 92%
- Encouraged 80% of participants to say they are likely to pursue an entrepreneurial venture one day
- Inspired 90% of participants to consider entrepreneurship as a respectable career after the events as opposed to 82% before

- Helped 90% of participants decide to take the next step as an entrepreneur.

Learnings and recommendations

If someone does not self-identify as an entrepreneur, they will not seek out the resources to become one. This has direct implications for how entrepreneurial a world we are today and how entrepreneurial we'll become in the future.

The first key point is that everyone has the potential to become an entrepreneur. For individuals who otherwise would not consider an entrepreneurial path, one of the first steps could be exposing them to the different approaches to entrepreneurship and the characteristics of each. With this support, individuals could determine if there is some type of entrepreneurship that fits their goals and personality. All types of entrepreneurs add value to our society in unique and important ways. We have found that it is exceedingly important to expand the celebration of entrepreneurs beyond venture-backed, high-growth entities. By expanding our respect and exposure to entrepreneurs who might be franchisees, freelancers, or social entrepreneurs, more individuals would see the appeal of starting a business. Further, by exposing individuals to entrepreneurs from a variety of backgrounds (i.e. different genders, ethnicities, socioeconomic groups) and who have different personality types (i.e. introspective as well as gregarious), the likelihood that an individual will self-identify as an entrepreneur drastically increases. By helping would-be entrepreneurs see whether and how some type of entrepreneurship is right for them, we can boost diversity among startups and catalyze the value they have to offer to society.

The second key point is to ensure that the entrepreneurs who we are exposing potential entrepreneurs to are willing to be vulnerable and open about their experience—and to talk not only about the challenges they have faced, but also the emotions and internal struggles that those challenges have caused them to experience. The reason this is important is that it humanizes the experience of entrepreneurship. Entrepreneurial success stories are often recounted in such a way that an individual faced insurmountable odds and overcame. The entrepreneur is placed in the role of the hero, who despite the challenges always knows what to do and has complete faith that they will ultimately succeed. Yet, rarely is this truly what is going on in the entrepreneur's mind. The roller-coaster experience of entrepreneurship is filled with moments of self-doubt. Certainly, there is a vision and the entrepreneur is unwaveringly persistent. Still, this does not mean they do not question themselves and their ability among other things. They must learn to be comfortable with the uncertainty and to push through the self-doubts. For new entrepreneurs, knowing that uncertainty and self-doubt are a normal experience and not something that makes them weak or not cut-out for the path can be extremely empowering and can help them stick in the game.

LEARN MORE

- Network for Teaching Entrepreneurship (NFTE): Founded in 1987 by Steve Mariotti, NFTE is an international non-profit organization whose mission is to engage and inspire young people in low-income countries and help them acquire the necessary skills to start their own businesses. NFTE brings entrepreneurship into the classroom, teaching the kids financial literacy, among many other subjects. History has shown that these programs have a long-term successful impact on the young people's employability. To date, more than half a million young people benefited from the programs offered by NFTE and more than 5,000 individuals have participated in their train-the-trainer programs.
- School for Startups: Launched in 2008, School for Startups runs entrepreneurship programs all around the world. It combines educational programs, events, online and offline support for budding entrepreneurs.
- INJAZ-UAE: INJAZ-UAE was started in 2005 and it is part of Junior Achievement (JA). It is a partnership between the business community, educators and volunteers—all working together to inspire young people to dream big and reach their full potential. This program focuses on teaching kids in the Arab world key concepts of work readiness, entrepreneurship, and financial

literacy, among many other useful skills. Since 2005, INJAZ-UAE has reached more than 20,000 students with the help of more than 2,500 volunteers at over 50 schools and universities.

- Young Enterprise Switzerland (part of Junior Achievement): An organization that helps high school students work on business projects and take an initial idea to the market.
- Jobzippers: Entrepreneurship speaker series; events held at different universities to sensitize students for an entrepreneurial career—comparing it and discussing the advantages and disadvantages as compared to other career paths.
- Shanghai New Business Starter program (NBS): The Shanghai government has made substantial investment in promoting new venture creation among young people. According to Mr. Arkless, Manpower Group's President of Global Corporate and Government Affiars,[1] the program assesses millions of young people on entrepreneurial capabilities, selects the top few percent and helps them start their own ventures.
- Dar Blanca Radio: A radio station in Morocco that provides career and particularly entrepreneurial advice to young people over the radio.

4.3   The Myth of Entrepreneurial College Dropouts

Who hasn't read one of those idealized stories of college dropout billionaires Bill Gates, Larry Ellison, Michael Dell, or Mark Zuckerberg, just to name a few? It is one of the biggest debates surrounding the topic of youth entrepreneurship, predominantly steered by US entrepreneurs. Should you spend your time getting an education that, as we will see in Chapter 5, is to some extent useless for the world of work, or should you instead focus on building a company, making money, and learning the necessary skills hands-on by simply executing the tasks you need to take care of as an entrepreneur? Should we support young people in building their own companies instead of attending tertiary education? This is, in fact, exactly what initiatives such as the Thiel Fellowship are doing—financially supporting young entrepreneurs to drop out of college and focus on their businesses.

As with most things in life there is no single best answer to this question because it largely depends on (1) what the young person is planning to do as an entrepreneur (what is the business about and which capabilities and resources are needed, in which sector the business is operating, etc.) and (2) on the person him- or herself (personality, skills, knowledge, ability to learn, etc.). However, what is clear is that we should never make generalizations based on a few outliers such as those highlighted above. Making a causal link between dropping out of college and entrepreneurial success is challenging and so far also not supported by any scientific study I am aware of. Particularly when we consider that the majority of new ventures fail within their first years of operation (Timmons, 1990), putting the person back to stage zero (possibly even with debt). So if we encourage young people to drop out of college to try and become one of those rockstar entrepreneurs but ultimately fail, what should they then do? On average, they would end up in a below-average profession, given that tertiary education still results in higher average income (cf. table 232 in US Census Bureau, 2012).

Nonetheless, there is a valid assumption made that underlies the bold statement of "drop out of college if you want to become a successful entrepreneur," which is that you need to learn the skills and capabilities on the job and do not expect to learn them in school. As long as one is aware of this fact, I believe there is no harm in entering tertiary education and still trying to become a successful entrepreneur. In the end, the stories written about these billionaire college dropouts only tell part of the story, mainly obscuring the true story of when, how and why they dropped out and most certainly offer a skewed view on entrepreneurship given that journalists hardly ever write about the majority of entrepreneurs who either fail or end up earning less than they would in regular employment.

4.4   Glimpsing into Entrepreneurship

As a result of young people's growing interest in exploring entrepreneurship as a viable career path, we can observe the emergence of a variety of job portals that focus on free positions in startups (either as internships or full-time employment as well as co-founder positions). The costs of posting positions in regular job portals are typically too high for startups, which is why the broad public traditionally does not see open positions inside startups. Hence, through the introduction of such portals many more people are exposed to career opportunities in up and coming new ventures. The following case study provides a short insight into such a job portal and the impact it has on youth employment.

– Rajeeb Dey, Founder and CEO –

"We need to take an open-source approach to tackling youth unemployment. We simply cannot maintain the status quo; an entire generation is depending on us to act now."

Rajeeb Dey

Enternships has developed a new "positive" learning-based approach to recruitment where all candidates can benefit from the process of applying for a job irrespective of if they are hired. Through the process of acquiring new skills and insights from employers they convert those who would otherwise be rejected into advocates.

Enternships was created after the founder—President of Oxford Entrepreneurs at that time—was constantly being approached by startups and SMEs who wished to advertise jobs to the members of Oxford Entrepreneurs. On reflection he felt that whilst aspiring bankers, lawyers and accountants did internships what was there for an aspiring entrepreneur to do? Other than setting up your own business he felt that the best way to learn about entrepreneurship was to work within a startup or small business. However, these companies had no visibility on campus. Startups don't have the time, resources, and brand awareness to directly come on campus and engage talent and so he launched Enternships as a solution to bridge these worlds.

Upon starting as a basic listing site for Oxford students and then launching as a standalone service in 2009 Enternships has helped over 6,000 startups and fast growing businesses find talented interns and graduates.

Enternships also develops innovative talent programs for clients such as Telefonica, Santander Bank and Havas. For example, we launched "Wayra Enternships" with Telefonica's global accelerator program (Wayra) to provide a platform to connect all European startups that Wayra invest in to talent. In doing so it became the world's first accelerator to provide a dedicated talent solution and Enternships has advertised over 150 opportunities through the platform, reaching candidates from over 450 different universities in Europe. They also hosted a startup careers fair within the Wayra London Academy and which was launched by His Royal Highness The Duke of York.

CASE STUDY: OPERATION HOPE

– John Hope Bryant, Founder Operation Hope –

"The HOPE Business In A Box Academy intervention reconnects the power of aspiration with the power of education in our children's lives, helping them to start a business through linking financial literacy, financial dignity and entrepreneurship training and support together."

John HOPE Bryant

What does Operation HOPE do to tackle youth unemployment?

The mission of Operation HOPE is a financial literacy and entrepreneurship program. It represents silver rights empowerment, making free enterprise work for everyone and working on the ground as the non-profit private banker for the working poor, the underserved and struggling middle class. Operation HOPE provides financial literacy empowerment for youth, financial capability for communities, and ultimately, financial dignity for society. One fairly new initiative created by Hope in 2013 to address the issue of job creation and youth entrepreneurship is HOPE Business In A Box Academies (HBIABA) which channels and transforms youth's natural aspiration and state of hope into practical and life changing action steps such as:

1. Youth complete the Gallup-HOPE Index (GHI) each fall semester to measure their attitudes and feelings about hope, dignity, entrepreneurship, financial literacy and wellbeing in order to gain insight into how they envision their economic future.
2. Youth are led through the financial dignity program, Banking on Our Future (BOOF), which gives them access to the knowledge and tools they need to take control of their financial futures.
3. Youth complete the four-hour HBIABA primer course on entrepreneurship where they learn the process of turning a personal interest, dream and skill into a viable business idea and the art of

pitching that idea. The course, taught by local professionals and business owners, helps kids develop skills in public speaking, critical thinking, and project management among others.

4. Next, those youth interested in turning their idea into a fully operational business have 120 seconds to pitch their idea to a panel of judges and their peers.

5. Winners of the school-wide pitch competition will be paired with a business role model who works with them over a ten-week period to further develop their business plan and budget. Youth are presented with a tablet to develop their plan and help operate their business.

6. The new youth entrepreneurs then present their business plan and their budget to HOPE and have access to a HBIABA business start-up grant of up to USD 500.

7. At the end of the ten-week session, the new young entrepreneurs receive their HBIABA business start-up grant and launch their new business ventures with the assistance of their business role models.

8. They then have the opportunity to post their idea on a crowd-funding site.

The youth who complete the HBIABA initiative will be introduced to key business and financial concepts, which will provide them with the tools required to successfully compete in the global economy.

The key performance indicators (KPIs)

HOPE has been dedicated to elevating the dignity, hope and economic self-sufficiency of people in low-wealth and underserved communities for the past 22 years. HOPE has served more than two million individuals, directed more than $USD 1.5 billion in private capital to America's low-wealth communities, maintains a growing army of over 20,000 HOPE Corps volunteers and currently serves more than 300 US cities, South Africa, Saudi Arabia, Morocco, and the United Arab Emirates.

The Banking on Our Future program focuses on keeping the most at risk youth from repeating the cycles of poverty and despair that has trapped so many in their families and communities by teaching them basic financial literacy, or what HOPE calls "the global language of money." Banking on Our Future has educated and inspired 755,000 youth in the US and 40,000 youth in South Africa.

HBIABA is in its first phase of existence and has inspired 1,661 students in 11 Academies. There are currently 43 HBIABA commitments in progress. Ultimately, this program provides our youth with vital life-skills such as critical thinking, problem solving and communication so they are prepared to turn their dreams into reality

Learnings and recommendations

Our future depends more than ever on the success of our youth. Yet, in the US alone, more than 1.2 million students drop out of high school each year, restricting themselves to a near certain lifetime of economic hardship and jeopardizing the country's competitiveness in the global economy. For youth to have the opportunity to achieve financial success, they must first be empowered to navigate today's economic complexities.

By gaining insight into how youth envision their economic future, we can inform interventions and education to eliminate the gaps that marginalize some students from full and meaningful participation in the labor market. The Gallup-HOPE Index is a first-of-its-kind survey that sets a baseline around economic energy, telling a story about how we are failing to recognize and maximize entrepreneurial talent and aspiration in our youth. But the data also tell a story of hope, shining a light on the path that educators, policymakers, and community leaders must navigate to build and sustain thriving communities. This path we must navigate is lined with positive role models for youth. According to Malcolm Gladwell's *Tipping Point*, five percent of role models will stabilize any community.

HOPE's advice to other organizations or people looking to get involved in this mission is simple. Help increase the proportion of business role models in our communities and this will change everything. Kids want a good job or a shot at economic opportunity. We can spur a generation of entrepreneurs, small business owners and engaged workers school by school across the globe.

This will do more than lessen inequalities in income, this will spur and grow very real new wealth creation, new ownership and a new era of jobs for all.

4.5 Entrepreneurship Initiatives for Marginalized Groups

4.5.1 The Entrepreneurs' Ship: Promoting Youth Entrepreneurship in Developing Countries

The Entrepreneurs' Ship is a non-profit project fostering entrepreneurship as a viable career option in areas where high levels of youth unemployment or difficult employment situations leave little room for young individuals with high ambitions.

The project's primary goal is to ensure a healthy labor market for tomorrow's youth by establishing functional and healthy entrepreneurship ecosystems around the world. The Entrepreneurs' Ship helps governments (national and regional) as well as universities in developing entrepreneurship promotion strategies and establishes programs to turn these strategies into reality. Based on a unique understanding of the different factors and actors of entrepreneurship ecosystems, programs are being tailored to the local conditions.

4.5.2 Ecosofft and SAAMARTH: Helping Unemployed and Uneducated Young Women Become Independent

– Content for this section is provided by Stanley Samuel, Founder and CEO of Ecosofft and Managing Trustee of SAAMARTH (India) –

> Unemployment is not only a by-product of capitalism, socialism or failure of capital markets, it is borne out of poverty, policy and failed programs.
> *Stanley Samuel, Founder and CEO of Ecosoff*

Ecosofft's (Eco Solutions for Tomorrow – Today) philosophy is that everyone deserves a fair and equal opportunity. In most cases, people are not aware of their rights and benefits from government programs. In other cases, the programs fail to reach the desired impact for various reasons. We are taking skills and value-based training to the grass roots level and integrating them with programs related to water, sanitation and livelihood improvement. We aim to develop and support one million micro-entrepreneurs by 2050 or before.

We serve as a catalyst to solutions related to poverty in selected regions in India. We take an integrative approach by involving the community, companies, public policy, and educational institutions. In this context, we launch and operate different community-based projects that help people gain necessary skills and qualifications and as such allow them to manage their lives in a self-sustaining manner. In particular, we focus on young women and girls.

About ten years ago, we commenced a vocational training program with unemployed and uneducated young women, by teaching them sewing, cutting, designing, needlework and related skills. These are six-month intensive programs (structured programs combining theory, classroom work, and hands-on practical work).

To date we have trained over 400 women and young girls. The participants of our programs have significantly improved their quality of life and economic situation as they make up to INR 200 per day, which allows them to support their families and gain recognition within the family—an important fact as they are now regarded as less of a "burden to the family." Some are even able to re-enter education. Next steps will be to offer micro-credits to our program participants to ensure that they can afford their machinery and tools to become even more independent.

4.5.3   *The Big Issue*: Off the Streets with Micro-Entrepreneurship

The Big Issue is a magazine sold by homeless and long-term unemployed people. It was launched in 1991, during a period of economic recession, in the United Kingdom by John Bird and Gordon Roddick. The concept was very simple. The newspaper, compiled by professionals, was sold to homeless people, who then can sell it on the streets at a profit. They are working, not begging. They are getting off the streets through micro-entrepreneurship. In the beginning they receive a few copies on credit; just enough to get them going. With the first profit they can then buy more newspapers and from there they start making profits. Since its inception, *The Big Issue* has helped thousands of vulnerable people take control of their own lives. At any given time, roughly 2,000 individuals work with *The Big Issue*, earning a legitimate income. Roughly 100,000 copies are sold every week. In 2013 alone *The Big Issue* put more than GBP 5 million in the pockets of their vendors, releasing them from a dependence on handouts and providing an alternative to begging. In 1994, the International Network of Street Papers (INSP) was launched to help other organizations worldwide launch similar initiatives. Through this initiative, street papers in more than 120 countries have received inspiration, leading a global self-help revolution.

4.5.4   Generation Enterprise: Launching Startups in Slums

Generation Enterprises works with at-risk youth (unemployed, NEETs, under-employed) in underdeveloped and impoverished urban areas (e.g., slums) to launch community businesses with the goal of creating decent employment for them and their peers.

Since 2009, the team has been operating small incubators in Lagos, Nigeria, having trained 150 young people as Fellows. More recently, a pilot project in New Delhi was launched.

4.5.5   Prison Entrepreneurship Program (PEP) and Project Leonhard: From Prison to Startup

Prisoners are oftentimes dismissed with the statement: "Once a blaggard, always a blaggard." What is being disregarded, however, is that many prisoners want to lead a different life and re-integrate with society. One of the biggest problems for re-integration in society is that prisoners oftentimes lack the knowledge, confidence and external support to transition back into the outside world and earn money in a legal and honest manner. Once released from prison, they oftentimes need to wait a long time for regular employment, which may result in them becoming recidivists, bringing them straight back into prison.

Project Leonhard, having been inspired by the Prison Entrepreneurship Program (PEP) in Texas, tries to provide a solution to this never-ending spiral in that it educates and trains prisoners to become self-employed. Prisoners from all 36 prisons in the German state of Bavaria can indicate their interest in participating in the program, from which a core group is selected. They then enter a three-stage program. Stage 1 takes place while still in prison, teaching them the basics of entrepreneurship, transmitting entrepreneurial skills and helping them prepare a business plan. Stages 2 and 3 take place once they have been released from prison, focusing on re-integration into the world of work with weekly business training and mentoring sessions as well as formal support for starting the business.

PEP has, to date, helped 700 prisoners re-integrate into society with a relapse rate of less than 10% (normally it is 50–70% in Texas). Project Leonhard is too new for solid statistics, but so far it looks like a promising approach for the individuals as well as society.

4.6   Building Entrepreneurship Ecosystems as a Solution

An entrepreneurship ecosystem is a dynamic and interactive community within a geographic region, composed of varied and inter-dependent actors (e.g. entrepreneurs, institutions, and organizations) and factors (e.g. markets, regulatory framework, support setting, and entrepreneurial culture), which evolves over time and whose actors and factors coexist and interact to promote new venture creation. (Vogel, 2013b)

4.6.1   Arabreneur

– Content for this section is provided by Dr. Abdul Malik Al-Jaber, Founder of Arabreneur –

Arabreneur is an accelerator and investment fund aimed at contributing to the development and growth of a socially conscious economy and civil society in the Middle East and North Africa (MENA) region. Arabreneur consists of different pillars that collectively constitute an entrepreneurship ecosystem. The ultimate goal is to encourage young people to start their own companies and investors to support regional economies. It supports young people that have a business idea through access to facilities, networking opportunities, events, competitions, funding, and mentors. The program encourages young people to create companies based on their ideas through the organization of ideathons, and startup weekends.

Arabreneur closely collaborates with universities with the goal of creating an environment of entrepreneurial behavior and skills development. National and international mentors and investors help in the process of bringing the ideas to the market. After early acceleration, the most potential candidates will pitch their ideas to the Arabreneur Venture Fund and other angel investors. Through this multi-stakeholder approach, Arabreneur contributes to building a stronger entrepreneurship ecosystem in the MENA region.

Over the past two years, Arabreneur and its mother company MENA Apps, has supported startup weekends and bootcamps. In these events, we have trained and mentored over 200 startups. Arabreneur is recognized as a major player in the entrepreneurship ecosystem in the MENA region and is part of many initiatives such as the Oasis Venture Fund, Kuwait SME Fund, Startup Bootcamp, Vital Voices, and the Cherrie Blair Foundation. All these partnerships focus on building a stronger entrepreneurship ecosystem in the MENA region. Through these partnerships Arabreneur was involved in the mentorship of over 250 startups that have collectively created over 600 jobs.

Additionally, Arabreneur and MENA Apps invested in 15 early-stage companies, which as a result created an additional 150 jobs. The organization is rapidly expanding operations throughout the MENA region.

Arabreneur was initially privately funded. This was a critical starting point to build and prove a new model for entrepreneurship development in the MENA region. The fact that Arabreneur was creating facts on the ground rather than promoting its plans to investors and sponsors provided the organization the credibility through its initial successes. Success stories are very important to mobilize entrepreneurs in emerging markets where finding a job is the first thing people think of when it comes to economic development.

Through the initial success stories many entrepreneurs started to develop ideas and participated in our events. For example, when Arabreneur launched in Ramallah, nobody could identify early growth startups that were ready for investments of USD150,000. Within four months, Arabreneur received 60 company applications for such investment. This was mainly due to the lean approach that Arabreneur took to identify, select, and invest in companies. Arabreneur made the commitment to invest in four companies per quarter, and is still on track on this commitment.

The other major recommendation is to build a big network of partners to support the ecosystem. We have entered partnerships with most local universities to support their students in creating new startups. Moreover, we partnered with various NGOs and incubators to increase our visibility and outreach. The underlying benefit of these partnerships is that they create a win-win situation for both parties (e.g., partnering with incubators gives Arabreneur access to early-stage ventures while the incubator can report successful investments and networking for their graduated startups).

The last recommendation is to build a global network of partnerships that allow startups to access international resources. The presence of international partnerships accelerates growth and reduces the risk of investments for all parties.

4.6.2   Elgazala Technopark

– Content for this section is provided by Farida Kamel, Program Manager at Flat6Labs Cairo –

In recent years, MENA governments have started to take active steps in creating national entrepreneurial ecosystems to spur and promote job creation. Tunisia's Elgazala Technopark, the first technology hub to open in the Maghreb region, was launched in 1999 in line with the country's ambitious plan to bring together in one place business incubators, research centers, local and multinational firms, and government entities, to create an entrepreneurial ecosystem where cross-synergies can materialize between these different players in the hope of creating thousands of local job opportunities. A decade after its inception, Elgazala Technopark had successfully created over 2,000 job opportunities, with 70% of the park's employees' holders of a masters-level degree in engineering or an equivalent degree. The success of Elgazala Technopark prompted the Tunisian government to open two new technology parks in the country as well as similar hubs targeting other sectors such as textiles and renewable energy amongst many others. Similar industry-centric hubs of innovation are shaping the region's entrepreneurial ecosystem contributing to job creation. A pinch of salt is to be added. While the proliferation of innovation-centered hubs in the region is encouraged, the sustainable success of the latter is dependent on governments becoming visionary catalysts, not merely putting in place the infrastructure needed to host these innovation hubs, but more importantly creating a climate favorable to entrepreneurship and knowledge-sharing. Otherwise, these hubs will be nothing more than real estate ventures, a burden to the government and a curse to the country's youths.

4.7 Conclusion

To tackle youth unemployment we need to establish both short-term and long-term solutions. Short-term to help today's youth and long-term to prevent tomorrow's youth from ending up in the same problematic situation as today's youth.

As part of the portfolio of suggested long-term solutions to the youth labor market crisis, youth entrepreneurship has gained importance over the past years. Why? Because entrepreneurs are among the main drivers of innovation, economic development, and job creation.

By fostering youth entrepreneurship we turn tomorrow's job seekers into job creators. However, it must clearly be mentioned that youth entrepreneurship should not be regarded as *the* solution to youth unemployment but rather as one critical element in a portfolio of active labor market strategies (Schoof, 2006).

We teach our children one of the most critical 21st century skills and with it a whole set of other relevant skills that are relevant in the 21st century world of work, such as negotiation skills, financial literacy, presentation skills, problem-solving, among many more. It helps our kids reflect early on what they want to do with their life, and if they figure out that it is not entrepreneurship then at least they advanced by narrowing down the choice set through exclusion principle. It further helps our kids contextualize what they learn in school and it helps them accept and cope with failure. Lastly, because young people are more likely to hire fellow youths (Meager et al., 2003), there are positive secondary effects on the youth labor market.

However, we need to be aware that youth entrepreneurship requires different support structures than does adult entrepreneurship due to the differences in reasons to launch a business, prior human-, and financial capital endowments, opportunity types that are exploited and availability of alternative career options. As a consequence, any support programs need to factor in these specific characteristics and needs and ensure that supplementary skills are being developed through training and mentorship.

Ultimately, the promotion of entrepreneurship is a difficult and multi-faceted issue and it requires a coordinated and collaborative approach—an ecosystem approach (see details on creating an ecosystem (or multi-stakeholder) solution in Chapter 9). It requires the involvement of all the stakeholders, ranging from parents to educators, policymakers and companies.

5

Addressing the Gap between the Education System and the Labor Market

Chapter written in collaboration with Michelle Blanchet, The Social Innovation Institute for Educators

> The illiterate of the 21st century will not be those who cannot read and write, but those who cannot learn, unlearn, and relearn.
>
> *Alvin Toffler, 1970*

Today's young men and women are the future. While it may sound clichéd, it is important to make this realization. Our young people need to tackle the greatest challenges of the 21st century. They will determine the future of work and they will be responsible for guiding society forward. Considering the challenges that lie ahead, young people are now expected to have an entirely different skill set than any previous generation. They must be able to adapt and shape a rapidly changing world, and generate opportunities that never before existed. To invest in our future, we must give young people the sort of education that will enable them to find their place in a 21st century society. We are currently confronted with the paradoxical situation that despite the high rates of youth unemployment, employers in developed economies are complaining that they cannot find the skills that they need (Mourshed et al., 2014). As outlined earlier, this serves as evidence for the growing skills mismatch that we are experiencing. Educators can also step up and play their role in combating youth unemployment. Historically, educational institutions focused predominantly on teaching some core subjects, while ignoring their responsibility to facilitate their students' transition into the world of work upon graduation.

One of the best ways education providers can prepare students to succeed in the 21st century is by providing them with the tools and skills they will need to compete in the job market. Work is important. It allows individuals to be productive while simultaneously advancing society. By finding employment, individuals can deliver needed goods and services to the public thus providing a social benefit. At the same time, individuals earn a living, ensuring they will have a decent quality of life. Considering the importance of work for the future of individuals and society, it would only make sense to ensure that we are enabling our young people to find employment so that they can both contribute to society and improve their own quality of life.

Yet, for many schools and universities, preparing youths to find employment is still not a main priority. Due to this lack of focus, many youths are not adequately equipped to tackle 21st century problems and to find their place in a 21st century job market. If young people are the future, it has become time for us to materialize necessary transformations in our education system that will allow more young people to find work and create the sort of future we need.

many youths are not adequately equipped to tackle 21st century problems

By contextualizing these facts with the current youth unemployment crisis, we must ask ourselves what role education providers need to play to ensure that students are better prepared for the 21st century world of work?

Schools and universities need to be responsible for not only building skills but also for increasing student engagement and promoting lifelong learning; all of which are essential in our current job market. They need to instill certain value sets that enable students to tackle 21st century problems and give them the tools they need to aptly perform jobs or create their own jobs. Education providers need to be at the forefront of the solution to youth unemployment and establish support structures and collaborative frameworks that will enable them to help their students as they transition from school to work. Moreover, education providers need to ensure that the education they are providing enables all students to have opportunities and access to employment.

This chapter highlights some steps that schools and universities can take to better align the education systems with the labor market. While this task seems overwhelming, there are many feasible bottom-up initiatives that education providers can create to engender an educational paradigm that emphasizes the future and the world of work, without having to wait for the next educational reform to pass. More specifically, the first part of this chapter will focus on 21st century teaching, introducing 21st century skills followed by a discussion of the day-to-day practices that can help transform the classroom into a dynamic space apt for teaching 21st century skills, values, and content. The chapter will go on to explore the importance of entrepreneurship and innovation in stimulating a new mindset amongst our youths. If students are to create the jobs of tomorrow, we need to provide outlets that help them train their minds and exercise their ideas. In this way, they will have the confidence, skills, and tools required to successfully innovate. This leads to a discussion of the role of education providers in establishing collaborative frameworks that engender education for employment (E2E) ecosystems and better enable students to transition from school to work. In the final part of this chapter we take a holistic look at our education systems and outline additional opportunities to generate more outlets for our youths to attain success.

5.1   21st-Century Teaching

When we think about a 21st century education system we must envisage a system that addresses the mismatch between what is being taught in our schools and the skills, knowledge, and experiences demanded by the current labor market. We must ask ourselves what the curriculum of tomorrow might look like, what skills are most important for our students, and which methodologies and resources will best transmit these new themes and skills to our young people; and ultimately how schools and universities can best prepare students for the workplace. All education providers should take the following four areas into account to tackle many of the issues related to youth unemployment:

1. Fix skills mismatch: By realigning the curriculum, education providers have the possibility to fill the gap between the skills students receive and those skills that are demanded by the labor market, which is currently a central issue contributing to youth unemployment (Tirapani, 2012). By creating a skills framework and focusing on skills within daily instruction, educators ensure students will have job mobility and be better equipped to stimulate future economic growth. (OECD, 2013).

2. Boost engagement: There are a significant number of youths who fall into the NEET category (IOE, 2009). By keeping students engaged they

not only learn more but they are also more likely to continue with their education.

3. Promote life-long learning: If students view learning as a lifelong endeavor, they will be more likely to build skills throughout their career thus helping them to have more job mobility and be more productive (OECD, 2013).

4. Career readiness: Education providers need to get their students strategically thinking about their future and their goals in life. By equipping them with a 21st century skill set and providing them with the relevant experience they will need for the workplace, students will be better prepared to enter the job market.

If education providers were to keep these four points in mind, they could drastically improve the work readiness of their students. Fortunately, awareness of the youth unemployment issue is increasingly causing schools and universities to make strides to improve the effectiveness of pedagogy and support systems. So which are the relevant 21st century skills and how can we ensure that students acquire them prior to entering the world of work?

5.1.1 21st Century Skills and Curriculum

There need to be major changes to both how we teach and, in particular, what we teach. One of the first issues to be addressed as we discuss education is the content and skills being emphasized within our curricula. Today, employers are arguing that students need to demonstrate that they have acquired applied knowledge within their field, which would better prove they could aptly perform in the workplace. On top of this, employers are also emphasizing the need for skills, which can often be fostered in any classroom regardless of subject content. This signifies that labor market requirements are demanding a shift in classroom instruction. While historically teaching was centered on core knowledge-creating subjects such as languages, math, natural sciences, arts, music, history or geography, there are a variety of new skill-centered approaches that need to be considered.

Yet, despite the increasing skills mismatch (Mourshed et al., 2014) the majority of the world's education systems continue to operate on a strikingly outdated model, thus inhibiting students from exposure to more relevant global themes and skills.

In addition, focus is often placed on students' knowledge of content thereby overshadowing the importance of skill-building in the classroom. At this point in time, schools and universities can no longer continue to ignore the importance of 21st century skills and must transition from a content-based classroom to a skills-based classroom. Figure 5.1 illustrates some of the 21st century skills.

To materialize the shift from exclusively content-based to a balanced content-and-skill-based curricula, education providers should make it their goal to establish a guiding skills framework that allows teachers and professors to see the types of skills and applied content they should be transmitting to their students. All educational institutions should work towards adopting or creating a suitable skills framework that aligns with the labor market, which is flexible enough for educators to adapt to their subject or grade level. Moreover, this framework should act as a living document that schools and universities can modify to fit their communities or to accommodate changes in the market.

The creation and implementation of a skills framework is a challenging task that requires a paradigm shift in how we teach and learn, and entails the

FIG 5.1   21st-century skills

support of a variety of actors. Through collaboration (which we will discuss in 5.3), we can design and implement skills frameworks that can realistically be materialized in the classroom (Committee of the Regions of the European Union, 2012). By encouraging dialogue between policymakers, educators, and employment experts we can overcome obstacles preventing skills from being emphasized in the classroom. Together, we can find the most appropriate means to generate awareness about the skills mismatch, discover the best means to assess students for skills, and support educators so they can better transition from the traditional classroom to an applied classroom. We must be aware, however, that if we add skills to the list of top priorities for teachers, we need to ensure they are also assessed based on that and not just on the traditional "what knowledge have you acquired" type of assessment. We might need to reassess our grading system and teacher training programs to ensure they're compatible with these new changes.

L E A R N   M O R E

A variety of initiatives have been created over the past decade or two, aiming at redesigning the curriculum to be relevant to the world in the 21st century. First and foremost, we would like to highlight the "P21 initiative for 21st century education," but also other initiatives such as the Apple Classroom of Tomorrow (Apple, 2014).

Recommended readings: Trilling & Fadel. *21st Century Skills: Learning for Life in Our Times* (2009). Wiley.

Now that we know what needs to be done with regards to integrating skills into the curriculum, the question arises how these can be taught. What are some of the methodologies that can be employed by educational institutions and teachers to teach students 21st century skills? These will be discussed next.

5.1.2   21st Century Teaching Methodologies

[U]nless we want to just forget about educating Digital Natives until they grow up and do it themselves, we better confront this issue. And in so doing we need to reconsider both our methodology and our content. (Prensky, 2001: 3)

A modernized curriculum that emphasizes skills is a vital component in improving E2E outcomes. However, equally important, is how we transmit those skills to our students. In many schools and universities, the classroom often takes on a traditional dynamic that is organized by subject and exhibits a vertical power structure between teacher and student. This dynamic is often ineffective for giving students opportunities to gain skills and experiences that complement their learning; skills and experiences that are demanded by the labor market. To transform the classroom into a center that engages students, and provides them with the skills they will need for the future, we need to utilize new teaching strategies and models that are better suited towards the 21st century.

With access to technology and greater awareness of the needs of the 21st century, many innovative teaching strategies, techniques, and programs are being utilized that generate dynamic new classrooms. The following list highlights a few popular trends exhibited within the teaching profession that allow for a healthier balance between content, applied knowledge, and skill building.

- *The flipped classroom* is now becoming a popular tool for teachers to utilize classroom time to devote towards skills and hands-on practice. Educators assign content from text or online sources and give lectures via video requiring students to cover the content at home. Once in school, educators can devote more time to hands-on interaction, debates, simulations, experiments, and other forms of applied practice. This makes the classroom much more conducive to learning skills.
- *Project-based learning, challenge-based learning, and problem-based learning* are similar teaching strategies that induce critical thinking, team building, and problem solving. Each model aims to spark creativity and innovation by asking students to solve real-world problems often leveraging the use of technology. While each methodology may have subtle differences they all enable students to learn new content while simultaneously gaining skills. Teachers act as mentors and facilitators in each of these learning models, thus changing the dynamic between teacher and student.
- *Gamification* can be used in the classroom by applying game-design elements to learning modules. Many educators believe gamifying the classroom not only increases student engagement, it also helps build skills.
- *Learning by doing* encourages educators to apply knowledge by giving students the opportunity to use content to perform tasks. Educators might create their own initiatives or might work with external organizations that offer hands-on programs to students.

In addition to these new teaching strategies, pedagogical values are also changing, allowing greater emphasis to be placed on student engagement, socio-emotional learning, sustainability, creativity, and ethical responsibility

(High Level Group on the Modernisation of Higher Education, 2013). This new climate aims to instill a 21st century value system in our students that complements the skills they will need to have to address 21st century challenges as well as to succeed in the labor market.

Many of the 21st century skills as well as 21st century teaching methodologies are linked to and rely on technology. Consequently, we will briefly discuss the role of technology in the shift towards a 21st century classroom.

5.1.3 The Use of Technology to Teach 21st Century Skills

> I think online learning is going to be transformative. Traditional education is never going to be the same again. (Anant Agarwal)

Technology has become a vital part of the 21st century and constitutes a pillar on which our society and economy functions. In the classroom, it has become an invaluable tool whose many facets are changing the face of education. Technology enables students to have access to content, apply knowledge, and build skills. Likewise, it offers students who do not necessarily have access to a school (for various reasons, including cost or geographic constraints) the opportunity to get an education at low cost (or no cost, cf. Khan Academy).

Technology enables students to have access to content, apply knowledge, and build skills

Despite the revolutionary changes we are experiencing as a result of online learning, technology has much more to offer to the education system. In fact, its importance has become so apparent it has no longer become a question of whether we should use technology, but rather how we should use technology.

If we think about the world of work it quickly becomes apparent that without technology our everyday life, and with it our economies, would collapse. The vast majority of Millennials and Digital Natives cannot imagine how their parents and grandparents built and operated international businesses without having access to email or Skype. Where did they store all the information if not on a shared drive or in the cloud? How did they build organizational knowledge across departments if certain knowledge is stored on some paper that is physically kept in some folder in someone's office? All these changes have had such a massive impact on the world of work, that the adequate use of these tools is inevitable. Being able to quickly browse through the web and filter the relevant content from a million different pages and summarize it in a comprehensive manner for the C-level executives is a necessary skill. All these things are essential in the 21st century workplace. Consequently, our education system has the obligation to prepare the students for this world of work.

Since the introduction of technology in the education system, a core question that remains is to what extent technology can replace classroom learning. Studies have shown that blended instruction is more effective than either traditional education or online education (IBIS Capital Report, 2013), thus proving the need for all educational institutions to leverage the use of technology in classroom instruction. However technology can never be a 100% substitute for real-life learning. Nonetheless, it has become an inevitable tool for the 21st century classroom. Given the possibilities that new technologies provide and their multifaceted use there are a multitude of options educators have to teach students how to utilize technology to its fullest potential.

At the content level, technology initiatives are helping to facilitate needed changes that make learning more dynamic and effective. As of 2012, Apple announced that it had over 20,000 educational apps built into the iPad (Techcrunch, 2012), designed to improve the quality of instruction and learning in a variety of ways. For example, video and presentation software allows teachers to make online tutorials and flip the classroom, which frees up time that can be dedicated to skill building. New applications and online modules help make learning more engaging by providing interactive tools for students to learn and apply classroom material. For students who need extra support with their studies, programs like Khan Academy and the Learnia offer free online tutoring assistance enabling students to perform better in subject areas they find difficult.

In addition to assisting with classroom instruction, technology is providing students with opportunities to learn about technological skills and use advanced technology as part of their regular educational programs. Learning about certain aspects of technology is a skill in itself, and students are able to use technology to build skills in a hands-on way; skills that are inevitable in today's labor market, giving young people a competitive advantage as compared to their older colleagues (see reverse mentoring in Chapter 6). For example, new programs offer students the ability to learn about web design or how to code. Devices like 3D printers are promoting the use of visual thinking, critical thinking and hands-on problem solving skills as students learn to develop new products. It is critical that educators tap into this potential to ensure that students are both engaged and building skills.

Technology has also provided a new means for educators, students, and other institutions to generate awareness, collaborate, and connect. It has now become easier than ever before to learn about new initiatives and bring them into the classroom. As seen with programs like Skype in the Classroom or TED-Ed, collaboration between external institutions and educators can take learning to new dimensions. Online platforms like Edutopia or InformEd, promote lesson sharing and enable teachers to learn about the latest trends in education. Through such outlets, best practices are shared and instruction is continuously modernized.

The benefits of technology are vast, and many recognize the potential technology has in shaping the lives of our students and their futures. However, many students still do not have the ability to use technology in an apt and appropriate manner. While digital natives might be good at using technology it does not signify they know about or use technology in a way that would enhance their employability and provide them with new opportunities. Many students still need guidance in utilizing advanced programs, learning how to look up useful information, researching, and applying technology in a variety of contexts. Schools and universities must play their role in preparing youth for life in the digital age.

LEARN MORE

The following examples illustrate how technology is revolutionizing the classroom in the 21st century education system:

- *Nearpod*: An interactive system that engages students to take part in lessons.
- *Socrative*: Enables teachers to create games and educational exercises through smartphones, iPads, or laptops.
- *ShowMe*: An online tool to help teachers create video tutorials and flip the classroom.
- *World of Warcraft in School*: Teachers are using popular video games to gamify curriculums and engage more students.
- *Khan Academy*: A series of online video tutorials for a variety of subjects and topics

Online programs to gain skills, content, and certifications

- *Skillshare*: A platform that enables experts to teach real-world skills in an informal setting.
- *Coursera*: Free, high quality online courses from leading institutions.

Programs that give technological skills

- *CodeNow*: Provides programming training to high school students.

- *Monkeywrench CAD*: Gamified tutorial to teach industrial engineering students how to use novel CAD software.

Program to help educators utilize technology

- *Apple distinguished educator*: Supports innovative teachers and helps them to develop new ways to teach and learn.
- *Google for Education*: Provides training programs to educators enabling them to better incorporate Google tools in the classroom.

Technology initiatives in education offer fast, cheap, and efficient ways to reach a wide audience. They enable people to have more autonomy and choice in their learning, and offer seemingly endless possibilities to innovate. As of now, there are numerous online programs and applications that aim to improve education by providing quality programs and modules to the general public. In producing these products and services, more people are able to gain access the tools and resources they need increase their employability.

The following list provides a few examples of the many ways e-learning is helping youths to build skills and obtain credentials:

- MOOCs and open universities: By providing free, high quality online courses more students now have access to knowledge that once only came with full enrollment at university.
- Strategically placed learning stations: As seen with organizations like Hole in the Wall and The Center for Digital Inclusion (CDI), access to technology is providing a viable outlet for marginalized youths to obtain skills and receive quality educational opportunities.
- Encouraging technological skills: Individuals can now utilize programs to learn to code, design websites, or gain other applied skills. These skills can then generate other opportunities for individuals.
- Promoting community-based learning initiatives: Organizations such as Acumen Fund and Skillshare use an online platform to connect community members and deliver content. Through this model individuals can work together in an informal setting to learn real-world skills.

5.1.4   Hands-on Skill Training

In the 1960s, Edgar Dale developed a concept he called the "cone of experience" which stated that students remembered 90% of what they learned when they actually did something themselves. About half a decade later, educational institutions are finally doing more to tap into this idea by creating outlets in which students can gain 21st century skills and experiences in a less traditional context. This new movement, of *Learning by Doing,* gives students real-life skills and experiences that increase engagement, encourage autonomy, and enable students to gain a better profile for the workplace.

Learning by Doing is currently being achieved through a variety of outlets. Within schools and universities, technology and new teaching methodologies are acting as mediums through which students can learn in a hands-on and applied manner (as discussed in the previous two sections). In addition, education providers are now attempting to offer more interdisciplinary programs that implement hands-on application. If we want to best prepare youth for the labor market, it has to become commonplace for academic programs to incorporate some sort of project-based assessment or fieldwork to complement students' academic instruction thus making students more marketable as they enter the workforce.

External organizations and companies can also do more to help education providers deliver applied learning experiences to students. There need to be more vocational opportunities for students to take on during their studies to gain valuable work experience prior to graduation. Education providers must do more to connect and partner with companies and organizations that provide students with hands-on work experience. In generating such opportunities, students get exposure to prospective careers while simultaneously applying their instruction in a real-world setting.

Another interesting advancement in the Learning by Doing movement is the new rise in education ventures. In the past decade, many new initiatives have been sprouting up that aim to boost skills and instill values not currently emphasized in traditional curricula. For example, programs on leadership, empathy, sustainability, and social impact have had tremendous success in attracting youths and building 21st century mindsets. Not only do many of these programs foster greater diversity in learning (by offering more choice), they also invoke real-world application. Furthermore, these types of programs boost student engagement (since students often self-select to participate), and give students tools that will enable them to become lifelong learners (OECD, 2013). It has been said that experience is the new degree. So hopefully many educational institutions will adopt such programs to enable students to gain experiences that will enhance their employability.

Makerspaces

- *Project H Design*: A public school curriculum that incorporates design and construction into its program. It promotes community development through the materialization of real projects.
- *Fab Labs*: In-school or mobile workspaces that allow for digital fabrication.
- *D.schools*: Designed to ignite creativity, the d.school applies the concept of design thinking as a problem-solving technique.
- *Maker Education Initiative*: Encouraging educators to create innovate learning spaces that turn students into "makers."

Vocational opportunities and company programs

- *Enstitute*: An apprenticeship program that enables students to work in companies and gain necessary skills.
- *Leadcap*: A program in which young people get to closely interact with corporate leaders, through initiatives such as "CEO shadowing."
- *Experience Institute:* A 12-month program designed to give young people a hands-on experience by pairing them with innovative companies from tech, business, design, and social innovation.

Applied programs

- *Quest University*: A university specifically designed to adapt to a 21st century world by offering hands-on programs and assessments.
- *Emzingo*: Works with leading business schools to provide a hands-on curriculums so students can practice their business and leadership skills in the field.
- *Think Impact*: Institute offering eight-week sessions in the field to learn about social innovation, entrepreneurship, etc.

Education ventures providing hands-on experience

- *Euforia*: Offers external programs that encourage students to work on social/environmental problems with leading organizations.

- *Coderise*: Empowers high-school students with demonstrated potential by giving them the tools and inspiration to dive into tech innovation and tap into their entrepreneurial spirit.
- *Makerbot Academy*: Aims at putting a 3D printer in every school in the United States to ensure that students gain hands-on experience at making things themselves.

5.2　From Job Seekers to Job Creators

By addressing the skills mismatch and ensuring students have the sort of applied knowledge and experience needed for the 21st century world, education providers can help alleviate the youth unemployment issue. However, there is another issue that requires education providers to take their efforts a step further. A key problem of today's youth unemployment issue is that there are not enough jobs to cater to the large amount of high school and college graduates who enter the labor market each year (Mourshed et al., 2014). This requires schools and universities to generate new outlets so that young people can create their own employment opportunities.

Throughout the world there is a severe lack of quality employment opportunities for young people. The economic crisis has aggravated the situation causing major strain on young job seekers (ILO, 2013). To overcome these challenges, we must enable our young people to be more forward thinking and innovative than any previous generation. This requires us to generate a different sort of student profile than was emphasized in prior decades. Today's youths are now expected to be creative, flexible, and entrepreneurial; qualities that will help them overcome the challenges of tomorrow and spark economic growth (Audretsch, 2002; Acs, 2006; Carree & Thurik, 2010; High Level Group on the Modernisation of Higher Education, 2013).

As outlined in Chapter 4, entrepreneurship is also becoming an increasingly desired career path for young people. By encouraging entrepreneurship and innovation, and ensuring students receive support for new ideas and initiatives, education providers can help youths to design the jobs of tomorrow. For the success of our young people as well as our own economic growth, this area needs to be developed within our schools and universities.

5.2.1   Entrepreneurship Education

How can we encourage students to become job creators and turn their intentions into action? If today's youths are to create the jobs of tomorrow, education providers must equip them with the tools, skills, and mindsets needed to innovate. Starting from an early age, students can be exposed to activities that promote entrepreneurial thinking thus giving them the confidence and know-how to understand how markets work. By exposing young people to the principles of business and encouraging financial literacy, students grow up better equipped to enter the workforce and start their own initiatives.

Many education providers are now working on new programs to support students with entrepreneurial ideas (Committee of the Regions of the European Union, 2012). Studies have shown there is a correlation between individuals who have taken courses in entrepreneurship and have started their own businesses (European Commission, 2012b; Rosen, 2013). While it kind of makes sense to say that attending an entrepreneurship course or training is likely to be beneficial for the young person, we need to be careful with normative statements about the specific effect of entrepreneurship on young people's employability, given that most entrepreneurship courses are still elective classes resulting in a selection bias of who actually decides to participate in these programs. Moreover, when taking into account the graduates' skills which are most valued by employers, we have to take a somewhat critical perspective on these findings. Nonetheless, it is certainly beneficial to train our children the art of entrepreneurship and have them explore it early on in a fun and risk-free manner.

As a result of a growing awareness of the importance of entrepreneurship we have also witnessed a rise in entrepreneurship courses (Katz, 2008), online applications (that encourage entrepreneurship and financial literacy), innovation labs, and in-house business fairs that enable education providers to foster an entrepreneurial mindset amongst their students.

In addition, many external organizations are also working to bring entrepreneurship into the classroom in a practical and applied manner. By partnering with schools, these organizations bring start-up weekends, business mentor programs as well as youth crowdfunding platforms to young people. Through these initiatives, more students are encouraged to learn the principles of business and pursue start-ups. In doing so, a new paradigm has been sparked that enables young people to take charge of their own transition from school to work.

CASE STUDY: OPEN UNIVERSITY OF WEST AFRICA (OUWA)

– John Roberts, Co-Founder and President of OUWA –

"The model of the Open University of West Africa is to educate, incubate, and invest. By providing access to high quality affordable higher education, support services in ideation, business plan formation, and investment, we believe that a generation of entrepreneurial West Africans focused on significant contributions to economic development can emerge."

John Roberts

What does OUWA do to tackle youth unemployment?

OUWA leverages affordable online educational resources, including MOOCs, to create accessible pathways to higher education for West Africans who were otherwise denied access to traditional institutions. We specifically support young talented individuals to become better business leaders by placing high quality tools into their hands.

OUWA runs multiple programs, each with their own format. The most popular course is a Certificate in Entrepreneurship, which we believe is training the next generation of entrepreneurs. We operate this course from a co-working space (Hub Accra) that has some similarities to an internet café. In this space young people get access to hardware and the Internet to access online learning resources. Where the model goes deeper than a tradition internet café, is in the dynamic community, and numerous workshops that also operate within the space. OUWA accelerates young peoples' online learning experiences by leveraging trained facilitators to enhance weekly peer-to-peer learning meet-ups. We also offer a satellite model, the first instance of this involves OUWA bringing laptops and USB internet sticks to primary schools. OUWA offers teachers access to a yearlong professional enrichment course designed by the Commonwealth Education Trust via Coursera. This helps them understand the value of modern teaching methodologies and therefore empowers them to teach their students in a more effective manner.

The key performance indicators (KPIs)

OUWA started operating its first physical campus in Accra (Ghana) in April 2012. From this space we operated an unaccredited

Certificate in Entrepreneurship program with 150 young participants, following an online training module, "Technology Entrepreneurship," taught by Professor Chuck Eesley via Stanford Venture Lab. OUWA added to the curriculum offline co-founder ideation sessions, mentoring, a business plan competition and seed funding. Through such programs (blending online and offline training) OUWA tackles several challenges that are associated with online education/MOOCs, particularly in lesser-developed countries. These challenges include lack of offline support, a lack of internet access and a lack of accreditation. OUWA has been very successful at addressing the first two issues, and at the time of print, OUWA has just entered into a collaboration with University of the People to solve the final point.

Since the creation of OUWA, various companies have been started out of our educate, incubate, and invest model. With four noteworthy companies to mention: SliceBiz (Kickstarter of Africa), Hub Accra (co-working hub), Agripro (empowers farmers to grow their income) and Made in Africa (helps African artists enter new markets via online sales).

Learnings and recommendations

There are two key learnings from our experience:

1. *It is often easier to ask for forgiveness afterwards rather than permission first.* For the first number of months that we were operating, we were not a registered company and certainly not an accredited school. We operated below the radar until we had enough money to make the proper legal arrangements. We did this because we were operating on the timeline of our upstream MOOC partners, and they were launching their courses irrespective of our ability to offer facilities to our students. To avoid bureaucratic hoops preventing us from meeting the needs of our students, we started off in this below-the-radar manner, despite the riskiness involved. It should be noted that this is a dangerous game, and careful consideration must be given to any such strategy before adopting this *modus operandi*.
2. *Empower those around you and get local expertise onboard.* OUWA has come so far because we are made up of an

amazing team of dedicated West Africans, combined with industry experts from around the world. If we hadn't empowered our local West African students to become staff members, let them advise our decision-making progress through their local understanding of context, we certainly wouldn't be as successful as we have been.

L E A R N   M O R E

- Junior Achievement: Enables students to create actual mini-enterprises that compete at the regional, national, and international levels. They also develop company programs for young people to gain experience in the business world.
- Student start-up competitions: Programs that enable young entrepreneurs to receive support and funding for their enterprises.
- MoneyThink: Trains college volunteers to deliver financial education to local schools.
- Manpower Group and Microsoft's "Build your Own Business" curriculum: This program focuses on the Middle East and Africa and aims at supporting youth employability and entrepreneurship.
- The Fitzroy Academy: In a four-week program in which industry rookies are trained to become industry experts.

5.2.2   Innovation in the Classroom

How do we invoke a new mindset that engenders a culture of innovation? Many educational institutions could do more to encourage student creativity and imagination. In fact, educational providers should strive to create a culture of innovation throughout their curricula and programs. By developing an environment in which students can pursue and strengthen their ideas, we form a generation of independent, critical thinkers who are able to solve problems on their own accord. As discussed in the previous section, we need to see whether this is, in the long run, a desirable thing for the labor market as a whole given that employers are not particularly keen on hiring entrepreneurial and creative graduates. What we can be sure of though is that if the incumbent employers

cannot provide sufficient numbers of jobs then an entrepreneurial next generation can become the key providers of solutions for their own problems. Schools
and universities that prioritize creativity and freethinking are able to get their
students to think beyond what exists. In having the opportunity to question
the world, they become better equipped to tackle 21st century problems and
are better prepared for the future of work.

As outlined above, many of the 21st century skills (Figure 5.1) require a more
dynamic classroom. Skills like social intelligence, design mindset, novel and
adaptive thinking, and sense making are skills that cannot be taught through
traditional instruction, but rather through experience and practice. It is therefore imperative that education providers do more to encourage a culture that
promotes creativity and innovation within their framework. This will not only
boost skill building, it will engage students and allow them to easily adapt to
changes in the workforce.

Education providers should therefore strive to generate outlets that encourage
student innovation. While innovative teaching methodologies and Learning
by Doing initiatives are contributing to this new climate there are many other
initiatives that could be promoted within schools and universities and which
would help establish a culture of innovation. For example, the "maker" movement and the design thinking movement have led teachers and students to
create in-house innovation labs, makerspaces, courses on innovation, and innovation clubs, which are changing the ways in which students learn. In addition,
in-house libraries and computer labs have been transformed into interactive
spaces that promote new media literacy. While these dynamic spaces and
programs have yet to become a standard part of school infrastructure they
are major building blocks in supporting innovation. These activities, allow
education providers to foster creative, entrepreneurial mindsets, among their
students while also helping them to develop some of the crucial skills needed
to innovate, for example discipline, project management skills, resourcefulness,
and social intelligence.

In addition to in-house initiatives, there are many external programs that are
trying to bring new skills and values into educational institutions. By utilizing
such programs, students can pursue creative outlets that suit their interests or
find mentors who could help them to materialize independent learning projects. A great example of one such program is The Future Project. This organization matches schools with "dream directors"—coaches who are specifically
trained to help students work on innovative long-term projects of their choice.
This program has proven worthwhile in boosting student engagement and

giving students the ability to take risks, thus boosting their confidence and entrepreneurial ability. In working with this type of organization, schools can encourage creativity and innovation without disrupting their traditional programs. In undertaking such activities and promoting a creative, entrepreneurial mindset, students gain 21st century skills as well as valuable work experience. By allowing students to use their natural curiosity, we keep them engaged while encouraging them to become independent learners.

There are of course many obstacles, which inhibit education providers from developing a culture of innovation in the classroom. For one, students and teachers are often overloaded with content-based learning that prevents them from focusing on skills and innovative projects. The curriculum is often presented in a very contrived manner, which can prevent educators from adapting their teaching methodologies or stifle student creativity. In addition, rigid assessment guidelines might stop students from exploring their ideas. Many grading schemes do not allow for trial and error, thus discouraging a healthy dose of failure. In allowing for innovation, and developing a new mindset that promotes creativity and entrepreneurship, we can offer some flexibility for educators and students.

CASE STUDY: SOCIAL INNOVATION INSTITUTE FOR EDUCATORS (SIIE)

– Michelle Blanchet, Founder of SIIE –

At SIIE, we feel that one of the best ways to alleviate the mismatch between school and the workplace is to better equip our teachers with the relevant skill set and values they will need to pass along to students. However, many professional development workshops and teacher training programs fail to provide teachers with this relevant skill set thus preventing them from emphasizing 21st century skills in the classroom. SIIE aims at alleviating this gap by revolutionizing professional development programs. We do not offer prescribed solutions on how to fix education, but rather provide a space in which educators can learn about new trends in business and society, apply what they feel is relevant to their students, and get support in implementing any needed changes to their instruction, classroom, or schools.

At SIIE, we believe that if teachers are made more aware of the education to employment process, they will do more to ensure their students have the skills and experiences they need to attain success. We are confident in the power of teachers and believe they are an invaluable resource in reducing youth unemployment and transforming schools to meet the demands of the 21st century.

- Ashoka U Changemaker campus: Promotes social innovation in higher education by creating a network of individuals who work to solve real world problems in creative ways.
- Piggybackr: Supports student innovation as well as financial literacy by offering a crowdfunding platform just for teenagers.
- The Future Project: Enables schools to hire dream directors whose aim is to get students engaged.
- Labster: Virtual lab used to teach life sciences.

5.3   Creating Education for Employment Ecosystems

We need to recognize and prioritize the importance of transitioning our youths from school to work so that we can design more efficient and effective education to employment (E2E) ecosystems. Education providers can make many internal strides to improve education to employment outcomes for young people, but this is only a part of what needs to be accomplished to alleviate youth unemployment. Education providers need the support of many external actors to overcome E2E challenges, which is why young people, educational institutions, companies, and governments need to work together to address this issue. Due to the impact each of these bodies can have on alleviating youth unemployment, we need more collaboration among our political, economic, and educational institutions so that we can construct outlets that enable all young people to gain skills and find opportunities in the market.

5.3.1   Collaboration

How do we work together to actualize E2E efforts? At all levels, not just university, we need to ensure that employment experts, policymakers, and education providers are working together to ensure that students can find job opportunities. Important discussions need to take place among these actors to invoke education policy that supports needed structural changes and educational paradigm shifts. No single institution can be held solely responsible for boosting youth employment, as many new initiatives require buy-in from a variety of actors. The success of E2E efforts—just like the majority of other initiatives discussed in this book—depends on the level of coherence between these bodies (Figure 5.2).

Figure 5.2 demonstrates the interdependence that often comes into play in actualizing educational initiatives. Be it at the national, regional, or local level, there must be dialogue, collaboration, and implementation of activities among a variety of stakeholders to ensure that E2E initiatives are successful. A perfect example of this would be the implementation of a skills framework. As many reports suggest, employers are now demanding that new recruits have a different set of skills than are currently promoted in most schools (CACEE, 2014). To actually address this issue, employers have to communicate this need to education providers (a report itself is often insufficient). Even better would be if they actually get involved in the education part itself (e.g., participating in courses and training or through the provision of internships or industry-related bachelor- and masters-degree theses). If there is no communication, then education providers will not be able to implement an industry-related skills framework (Mourshed et al., 2014). Government bodies may need to approve the skills framework before education providers can utilize it and they may also need to ensure that education providers have the resources and funds needed

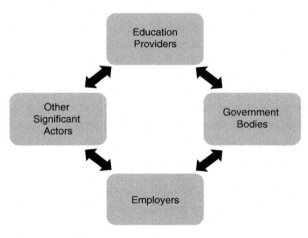

FIG 5.2   E2E ecosystem players

to incorporate this new skills framework into their daily operations (High Level Group on the Modernisation of Higher Education, 2013).

However, as soon as there is governmental approval involved, processes become more complex and time-consuming. So we need to focus on how we can build and operate such E2E ecosystems in a rather lean and effective approach without the unnecessary overheads. One of the first steps that can be taken to promote this sort of collaboration would be for education providers, employers, and government bodies to employ someone directly responsible for overseeing E2E efforts. McKinsey's recent report on education for employment labeled this individual/unit a "system integrator" (Mourshed et al., 2014), someone who implements and maintains partnerships with external organizations, someone to streamline communication and coordination among the partners and ultimately someone to monitor the effectiveness of the initiatives taken to tackle youth unemployment. The latter is one of the most essential functions of such a unit, because the constant monitoring and evaluating of initiatives will allow them to help achieve good E2E outcomes and to offer suggestions for other initiatives and programs. Moreover by creating such system integrators, educational institutions could be better informed about the latest E2E initiatives and programs being offered by governments and companies and vice-versa. This would ensure that there is awareness about the actions different bodies are taking to boost E2E outcomes as well as to facilitate the effectiveness of youth employment programs.

At the local level, there is even more that can be done to promote collaboration among the different stakeholders. Data has shown that local level collaboration is the best way to overcome community issues (High Level Group on the Modernisation of Higher Education, 2013) and having such opportunities for citizens to engage in issues is an ideal way to overcome E2E obstacles. All stakeholders, including youths, should therefore take advantage of their proximity and decision-making power to induce feasible changes that best suit the needs of youths. By working together, local actors can tailor-make solutions appropriate to the needs of their young people, employers, and education providers. One suitable setting for interaction could be the school board meetings.

Finally, many external organizations have made it their mission to bridge the gap between various actors and foster the multi-stakeholder dialogue to tackle youth unemployment. Some organizations have started to host events such as education start-up weekends, datathons, and schoolyard scrimmages, which attempt to bring these local actors together under one roof so that they can tackle challenges within the school system. Such collaborative efforts help in clearly identifying problems, proposing solutions and implementing successful strategies.

- Cedefop (European Centre for the Development of Vocational Training): Cedefop's mission is to support the development of European VET policies and contribute to their implementation.
- Hackathons and schoolyard scrimmages: Organized events that bring together community members, educators, and other professionals to tackle education design challenges.
- 4.0 schools: An education incubator that supports education ventures, individuals, and schools to work on challenges in education.

5.3.2   Career Services

To tackle youth unemployment and promote collaboration, education providers need to make it a priority to help their students find work. A career services department can act as the internal liaison between educational institutions and external actors. Many college graduates have difficulty finding jobs upon graduation and do not have access to adequate support services (FutureWork Forum, 2010; Mourshed et al., 2014). This difficulty is even greater for those who do not have a secondary education degree. It is therefore imperative that both schools and universities have built-in support structures to help students find employment. This signifies developing an efficient career services department in each school and university, which can help students find opportunities, offer career guidance, and enable students to gain connections.

Establishing and maintaining a career services department is still a complicated and costly operation for many education providers. The following four items appear to be major obstacles in instituting an efficient and effective career services department for youths:

1. *Lack of funds and resources:* Some educational bodies lack the funds and resources needed to create and/or maintain this department within their schools.
2. *Lack of responsibility for career guidance:* Some schools and universities do not see it as their responsibility to provide a career services department for their students. This is especially true at the secondary level, where counseling is often geared towards prospective university students, and not those who need career guidance.
3. *Ineffective management of the centers:* Many schools and universities have created career service centers, but oftentimes do not running them professionally,

in part because these centers are not being operated as profit centers but instead as subsidized units.

4. *Lack of relevance*: Many career service professionals have an industry focus and lack skills to offer students the full exposure to the diverse career opportunities they have ranging from corporate to academic, non-governmental organization (NGO)/Non-profit organization (NPO) and entrepreneurship.

As outlined above, educators (particularly in Europe) have until recently largely ignored their responsibility to help their students transition into the world of work. However, since the onset of the financial and employment crisis this mindset has been gradually changing. Nonetheless, the vast majority of universities outside the US still do not have fully functional career guidance or alumni services. This was, in fact, our motivation, back in 2008, to launch Jobzippers (later HR Matching) as a service provider to bridge the gap between universities and employers. In 2010, the FutureWork Forum conducted an international research project to assess student's desires and perceptions towards work (FutureWork Forum, 2010). One of the key findings was that more than 75% of students either did not have a functional career service at their university but really would like to have one or have one but do not find it useful. Students feel like they are left alone in the planning of their own future career and would wish for stronger guidance by their educational institutions; this holds particularly true for times like these.

From an employer's perspective it is not economical (particularly in times of an economic downturn) to invest heavily in graduate recruiting if educational institutions make it particularly challenging to reach out to their students. In turn, they will reach out to professionals rather than go through the hassle of connecting with hundreds of universities in order to recruit a few graduates who they then need to train on the job for one or two years. Consequently, educational institutions need to open up towards employers and embrace a multi-stakeholder perspective to tackle youth unemployment.

THINK PIECE: THE ROLE OF UNIVERSITY CAREER GUIDANCE

– Rajeeb Dey, Founder and CEO of Enternships –

Looking at the UK the youth unemployment situation is a complex one. On the one hand we are facing youth unemployment levels close to 1 million, yet an increasing number of employers are complaining of an inability to fill job vacancies. The mismatch of skills and lack of preparedness for the world of work points to a failure in our education system and the need to radically rethink the way we prepare youth for work and the role employers need to play. We have institutions in place that guide young people through their formative years—hold their hands through examinations, through certificates, through the cornerstones that make up how they learn. But once out in the real world, there is no support.

There is no backbone to rest on, no more tailored advice, or pointers to what to do next, instead there is just the chaos of grappling for increasingly scant graduate schemes, the worried scramble for reputable internships, the endless sending out of CVs to harassed hiring managers, who don't have the time or the inclination to train up a young person waiting for their real lives to start.

This isn't just unfair—it is a total and utter waste of potential. As of 2011, obligatory careers advice was removed from the national curriculum. What could be more important to a young person than what they are going to do with the rest of their lives? How can these young people know in what direction to push, when the options were never really explained to them to begin with? More than half of all graduates don't feel like higher education has prepared them for the world of work. More than half of all employers agree. However if you want to describe the current system of student and graduate employment—or lack thereof—one thing is clear: what we're doing isn't working. It's time for a big, big change.

This leads us to ask ourselves what an ideal career service department would look like. Not only is the job market overwhelming for students, but also employers are having difficulties finding talents. The role of any career services department could therefore include the following (see Figure 5.3):

- Prioritize work readiness: Many education providers need to pay greater attention to what will happen to youths as they leave education for work. By making work readiness a priority, education providers can ensure students are strategically thinking about their futures (Mourshed et al., 2014)—early on and not just shortly before graduation.
- Awareness: In many countries, students need to make important career decisions as early as fifteen years old (Mourshed et al., 2014). However, many students are unaware of the programs and services available to them. In the EU, lack of awareness of EU programs is a huge barrier preventing youth employment initiatives from getting results (Tirapani, 2012).
- Career counseling: The mentality of today's youth has changed. Today's young people are less money-oriented than previous generations, and are

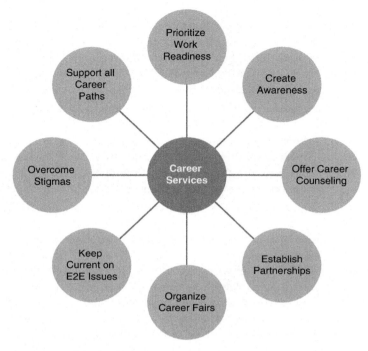

FIG 5.3   **Responsibilities of career services**

more likely to seek meaningful employment that interests them (this is especially true for the highly educated) (Tirapani, 2012). Given these trends, many youths will probably need guidance to strategically think about their career moves and to learn about what options are available to them. A career services department could inform students as to the types of post-secondary courses available to them, which would best help their futures. Moreover, this department could teach students about interviewing techniques, which résumé formats to utilize, and provide guidance on job-hunting techniques.

- Staying up-to-date in recruiting techniques: A career services department should act as the liaison between employers and education providers. It should therefore be their responsibility to stay current on market trends, most valued skills, and new recruiting methodologies. This department should then have to disseminate this information to staff and students and be evaluated based on a more holistic performance measure.
- Holistic support: Students, when graduating, have a variety of career opportunities ranging from a corporate career to academia, a career in an

NGO/NPO to entrepreneurship. Career service centers, however, often focus only on the corporate track and ignore the other paths. This needs to change given that each individual will be taking a different path.

• Creating partnerships: Staff from career services should be in charge of establishing and maintaining partnerships with external organizations that offer training programs, internships, and vocational opportunities for students. They should reach out to potential employers as well as keep track of government E2E programs. By ensuring this task is fulfilled, education providers will know about opportunities available to their students and will be better equipped to disseminate this information.

• Career fairs: Career fairs are wonderful opportunities for students to learn about employers, for employers to attract talent, and for students to network. Education providers should host career fairs to both create awareness and help students find employment opportunities. However, besides the classical career fair they can also offer career talks and dedicated workshops.

• Overcoming stigmas: Unfortunately, in some societies, there is currently a stigma against vocational training, thus making university the most attractive option for social mobility/job mobility. Career services can attempt to normalize vocational education and make it more appealing to youths.

A dynamic career services department could do a lot to bridge the gap in the E2E process. Not only would this department be responsible for collaborating with external bodies, it could offer much-needed support to youths. Moreover, by implementing this sort of department in each school or university, education providers can stay more up-to-date on E2E issues while simultaneously providing students with the opportunity to receive personalized support as they look for work.

CASE STUDY: JOBZIPPERS

"Building a European network of university-integrated job portals to bridge the geographic boundaries of the skill gap and replace location-based recruiting with skill-based recruiting."

Peter Vogel

The recent economic crisis has led to a disproportionate increase in youth unemployment around the world. In Europe, youth unemployment rates increased by 60% over the past four years, leaving every fourth employable young person without a job. If no suitable active labor market policies (ALMPs) are identified, the result will be economic waste, an undermined social stability and a marginalization of the local workforce, a valuable natural resource for any country. In times of exorbitant youth unemployment rates it is essential to create incentives for employers to engage in youth recruitment.

Jobzippers was launched in 2008 when the youth labor market crisis was just on the verge of formation, aiming at revolutionizing the way youth recruiting works. This is done by establishing a pan-European network of campus career communities, thus helping employers recruit the best talents, and support schools and universities in setting up professional career portals and helping students shape their individual career path. More specifically, schools are offered free-of-charge job boards that are customized to their corporate identity (CI) and integrated to their websites with as little effort as 5 minutes time to create a piece of code and integrate it into the website. This is a highly scalable solution and tackles one of the most fundamental issues of youth unemployment – the gap between the education system and the world of work.

On the other end, Jobzippers helps companies spread their job opportunities across many universities and schools through a fully automated technical integration. Moreover, there is a clear monetary advantage for employers, given that HR employees do not need to spend any time manually posting jobs across multiple universities but instead can focus on the candidates. Jobzippers offers a scalable solution to graduate recruiting that makes it both cost-effective and time-saving for employers. As a consequence, this solution increases the employers' willingness to engage in youth-specific recruiting activities, and in particular to replace "location-based recruiting" with "skills-based recruiting." We have the standing commitment from many large companies that have understood that it is their mandate to invest into youth recruiting.

CASE STUDY: CAREER INTEGRATED LEARNING PROJECT

– Dr. Robert Shea, Vice-President Marine Institute –

What does this project do to tackle youth unemployment?

The Career Integrated Learning project was developed to help students make the transition between education and work. One of the issues associated with the "skills mismatch" is that employers seek competencies or skills developed through experience, and students define themselves by their degree name, not by the skills, abilities and talents that they possess—often as a result of completing a degree program. The Career Integrated Learning Project addresses this issue by helping students to identify and articulate the broader skills and attributes acquired through completion of a degree—making a clear connection for employers to see the potential in a prospective employee.

The concept of identifying career competencies or graduating student competencies (GSC) is not new, especially for students who participate in experiential learning activities. What is innovative about this project is translating the process to classroom-based courses, especially in Arts and Science faculties. The fact that the project began at a grassroots level, working with interested faculty and put responsibility for career development in the hands of students, is also innovative.

Working individually with faculty at Memorial University of Newfoundland, project staff and course instructors collaborate to identify GSC associated with course evaluation activities. Each activity required by a professor involves the practice of skills that are transferable to life after university. For example, in a folklore course, when students complete a group assignment they are developing teamwork skills, communication skills, responsibility and ethics as well as learning about their own work preferences. The key is to challenge students to reflect on those skills and to consider the competencies they may have or are developing in other courses and other aspects of their lives.

The Career Integrated Learning Project has also expanded to include employers and other universities across the country. To truly address the issue of a skills mismatch employers and all post-secondary institutions must be engaged in the conversation. This project encourages students, professors, career center staff and employers to think more broadly about the skills that are developed during the completion of a post-secondary degree.

The key performance indicators (KPIs)

The project was piloted in 2012 with a small group of students in one course and then expanded during the 2013/2014 school year to include arts and science faculties. Participants included undergraduate and graduate students who ranged in age from 18 to 65. Of those involved in the project, 437 responded to a survey and 72% of those respondents said that becoming aware of the graduating student competencies that they were practicing in the classroom was helpful to them. Many students gave examples of how they could now articulate these competencies to improve a resumé or apply for graduate school, or simply recognize opportunities in their current studies. Here are a few quotes:

- "I had never thought about competencies before this class. Before this class, all I thought about was completing courses and marks."
- "Though I am not graduating this year, it has opened my eyes to things to think about and things to pay attention to in class that will develop my skills for employment."
- "Until this course, I had not considered what GSC I was developing as a student. I knew I was learning how to do different things in my courses but did not recognize that some of these competencies set me apart from other individuals who will be applying for similar jobs."

Learnings and recommendations

To launch a similar project it is important to get buy-in from your organization and colleagues. Start with people who are like-minded—solution champions—but also focus on how you might align your project with organizational goals. For example, we adopted the language of our university's teaching and learning framework. The use of this common language provided the framework that enabled us to connect with colleagues and achieve common goals.

Invite input from students, and faculty—and be willing to try different approaches as you go along. Working directly with students and instructors in the classroom allowed us to see first-hand the results of our efforts. We adjusted or changed content and direction when we received feedback and this helped the project grow and progress.

- URGuarantee: A wrap-around career support program of the University of Regina (Canada) that guarantees their graduates a free year of tuition if they don't find a job in a field related to their education within six months (Bell & Benes, 2012).

5.4 Alternative Methods for Dealing with Academization

If education providers are to best tackle youth unemployment, there is one more area of concern that must be addressed: academization. In most countries, employers decide upon talent by selecting those who have performed the best in university and have earned relevant degrees. This behavior has spawned a system of credentialization, in which students must receive a degree or certification within a field to perform a certain task. Due to the need for formal credentials, students are often obligated to attend university before finding quality employment. Unfortunately, this trend towards academization has somewhat undermined our need to fulfill labor market requirements, forcing education providers to focus on university enrollment as the main stepping-stone in the E2E process.

In many countries, the system of academization proves itself to be far too limiting for many students since using quantitative assessments and university degrees to determine employability leaves too many students without options. Considering that those who have college degrees are more likely to find employment than those who do no, we especially need to create systems and initiatives that ensure all students get the skills and experience they need to become employable. This signifies designing programs and systems of credentialing that engage students and prevent them from falling into the NEET category, as well as guaranteeing students are ready for work when they leave secondary education.

5.4.1 Developing a New Mindset for Success

While it is widely known that the trend in academization has added further strain to the youth unemployment problem, university still remains one of the most popular outlets for students to enhance their employability. The cultural and social value placed on university degrees has in many societies become even more significant than the actual value of the degrees themselves. Historically, tertiary education was regarded as a privilege and the pathway to a better life. This view persists until today, causing significant pressure on the education system and the world of work (with the exception of countries like Germany, Austria or Switzerland which have established strong dual education systems; see next chapter). Figure 5.4 visualizes the tertiary education gross enrollment ratio (GER) for different regions of the world. Across all regions we can observe an increase in tertiary education GER the past years. What is interesting (not visible in the figure) is that Germany (61% in 2012), Austria (72% in 2012) and Switzerland (55% in 2012) have lower tertiary education GERs as compared to the Western European average (78% in 2012), an indication that more tertiary education is not necessarily always a good thing but that there needs to be a balance between tertiary and vocational education. Consequently, it does not appear viable for universities to remain the main outlet for attaining quality employment and success.

By encouraging all youths to enter tertiary education, the following issues may arise:

- Value of a secondary education diploma decreases: For many careers, a high school diploma is no longer sufficient for entry-level positions. Many

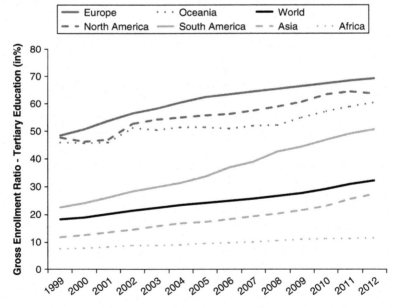

FIG 5.4   Rise in tertiary education gross enrollment ratio (GER) in selected regions

Source: UNESCO Institute for Statistics

students feel forced to attend university to attain decent employment, as job choices are more limited for those who only hold a secondary school diploma.

- Drift into theory: If universities continue to fail to provide experience and skills while more young people enter universities, an even greater number of young people will have an academic and industry-unrelated training, thus aggravating the situation that students will have a problem attaining employment. A university degree is not enough to attain employment as employers want to see students who have experience: university in itself can be inefficient in filling market gaps (Clancy, 2013).
- Secondary education providers emphasize university counseling over career guidance: Many schools strive to push their students into university programs (Selingo, 2012). This leads to a lack of career guidance and support for the many young people who might seek an alternative path.
- Costs of university are high: Cost is still one of the main barriers to entry for many university students (Mourshed et al., 2014). Regardless of the price of tuition, many young people still struggle to pay the cost of living during their time of study. The expenses that are incurred can hinder many students from affording this opportunity. Moreover, if costs are too high, students might not deem the investment in university as worthwhile (Selingo, 2012). This trend might intensify as more young people move into universities due to increased organizational costs.
- Students turn away from vocational opportunities due to stigma: A study conducted by McKinsey & Co. found that of the students learning about vocational opportunities, only half actually enrolled in vocational courses due to social pressures against it. The push for a university degree has caused many students to overlook other outlets to find a career (Mourshed et al., 2014).

By changing our mindset towards education and work, and providing alternative outlets towards attaining employment, we can improve E2E outcomes. Of course, this requires a huge paradigm shift in how we view university. Parental pressure, unnecessary demands of employers, and a lack of awareness about these flaws prevent us from seeking alternatives to address this issue. We need to make university a choice, not a necessity, and vocational opportunities more socially acceptable in order to get more students into the workplace. In the following section we will discuss dual education systems.

5.4.2 Dual Education Systems

The overuse of academization can have significant consequences on our young people as well as on our economies. When comparing national education systems we can see major differences with regards to the presence of vocational training (Figure 5.5). Some countries have developed dual educational models that are more robust in their offerings thereby facilitating the E2E process. These models provide educational streams that enable students either to pursue a vocational track or an academic track that will guide them into suitable employment upon graduation.

Predominantly found in the German-speaking part of the world, dual-education systems demand that students choose career trajectories upon completion of compulsory education. While some students do choose a more academic route, thus continuing to a higher-level secondary school followed by university, many students select a vocational route. The latter mixes theory and practice by requiring students to split their time between classroom instruction and apprenticeships. Due to the large amount of vocational opportunities, young people have a wide range of choice in selecting their career paths (Swiss Education, 2014).

The dual system model provides a viable alternative to current trends we see in academization. Moreover, considering the economic well-being and low levels of youth unemployment rates exhibited by these countries, it would make sense to consider this E2E process in other contexts. Several countries are now

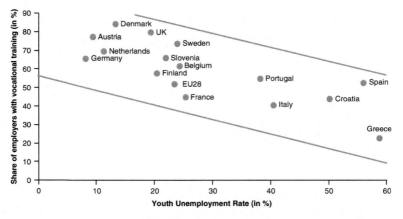

FIG 5.5   **Cross-country comparison of vocational training**

Data Source: Eurostat

trying to implement such dual education systems with a strengthened apprenticeship model, following the examples of Germany, Austria and Switzerland. As we will see in the following case about the Swiss banking sector, this system has evolved over many decades, which makes a 1:1 replication elsewhere tricky, at least in the short-run.

CASE STUDY: APPRENTICESHIP SYSTEM IN THE SWISS BANKING SECTOR

– Sandra Elmer, Credit Suisse –

What does Credit Suisse do to tackle youth unemployment?

There is a long-standing tradition in Switzerland of apprenticeships and the dual system of professional training—a successful example of a public-private partnership (PPP). Depending on the profession, apprentices learn their trade three to four days a week at private companies over the course of two to four years. The remaining days are spent at a public educational institution, where they acquire theoretical skills and broaden their practical skills and knowledge of general subjects. Each year of the apprenticeship, they spend a set number of days taking specific industry courses to enhance their professional expertise.

Over 60% of young people begin their professional careers in an apprenticeship after completing compulsory education. An extensive and diverse range of apprenticeships in over 250 professions—from SMEs to major corporations and public administration—gives these young people an opportunity to further their education and begin their professional careers. This model can be adapted to the changing needs of the economy and the varying challenges of job profiles, which helps to keep youth unemployment low in Switzerland.

In a normal economic environment, these young people have no problem finding permanent positions as trained specialists after completing their apprenticeships. In addition, various programs by non-profit organizations provide individual assistance to these young people for their integration into the workforce.

Not only are the graduates of these training systems highly sought-after on the labor market, but with additional tertiary education, they can advance as far as the executive levels of a major bank—as demonstrated by the example of Hans-Ulrich Meister, CEO of Private Banking at Credit Suisse.

This traditional training approach has achieved greater significance recently, despite increasing competition from university training programs in Switzerland. The economic crisis at the end of the previous decade struck young people particularly hard. In September 2009, roughly 30,000 young people in Switzerland aged between 15 and 24 were unemployed. Within a short period of time, the youth unemployment rate doubled from 2.3% to 5.4%.

The risks associated with a long-term high youth unemployment rate have spurred Credit Suisse into action, as the bank considers itself an integral part of Swiss society. In response to the crisis, Credit Suisse launched the "Together We Can Tackle Youth Unemployment" initiative. For the period from 2010 to 2015, the bank is investing up to CHF30 million in training and individual support offered in Switzerland by six non-profit partner organizations, with the aim of improving employment prospects for young people.

The key performance indicators (KPIs)

Between 2010 and 2013, more than 4,200 young people successfully completed one of the programs provided by the initiative. Of these, over 2,500 participants received a permanent employment contract, more than 850 obtained temporary employment and over 800 more signed a training contract. Since 2012, the youth unemployment rate has also dropped back down to 3.2%. At the same time the bank set a goal of raising its own apprentice count from 600 to 750 by 2013. This goal was reached thanks to a series of measures.

Moreover, the bank aims to recruit at least 80% of all apprentices to a permanent position once they have completed their apprenticeships. Many of these apprentices subsequently undertake part-time further education at a vocational school or a university of applied sciences. Some opt for full-time study and return to their employer afterwards. Apprenticeship training thus paves the way for specialists of the future, not only for the bank, but also for the industry as a whole.

Different sectors in Switzerland offer apprenticeship programs. In 2013, 7,223 young people completed business apprenticeships in a total of 21 sectors. With 1,255 successful apprenticeships, the banking industry is the third-largest training sector in this profession. Institutions ranging from the smallest banks to the major banks offer these three-year business apprenticeships in the banking sector.

The trainees complete six half-year placements within the bank during which they get to know different areas and can develop their practical skills on the basis of specific educational targets. They also acquire banking expertise at the Center for Young Professionals (CYP). Swiss banks established the CYP as a center of competence, with the goal of centralizing specialist bank training and expertise and as a means of pooling resources. It was used to form the basis for an innovative environment focused on excellent teaching supported by technology. Finally, these young people learn about general and business-related subjects at vocational business schools. The optimal interaction of these three centers of learning is central to successful completion of the trainees' education, but presents challenges both to them and to the representatives of the individual training centers. Close cooperation among the three locations supports the transfer of knowledge between theory and practical application, as well as just-in-time learning of the necessary business skills.

Investment in apprentices not only makes a great deal of sense from a business perspective, but also has a social element. With these apprenticeships, employers can secure long-term access to candidates. They also offer a unique opportunity to familiarize young recruits with a corporate culture right from the beginning of their careers. Young professionals can pass on their knowledge and gain their first leadership experience in the role of mentors to apprentices. The bank also derives substantial benefits from the young generation, which brings fresh ideas and a certain carefree mindset to the company. The apprentices are not only the employees of the future, but also the clients of the future. Most notably, apprentices can be employed productively in their final year of training, which makes them valuable and sought-after workers. This experience gives them self-confidence. At the end of their training, the apprentices know the company well, have established a large network of contacts and have held their own in a new environment time and again. Consequently, they possess strong social and methodological skills, laying strong foundations for their further personal and professional development.

Learnings and recommendations

Switzerland has a long tradition of apprenticeships and such an established system cannot be replicated overnight. However, opportunities certainly exist in other countries.

This system of professional education is based on close cooperation among the different stakeholders. What keeps this system running is the readiness of companies to train apprentices and organize themselves into sectors so as to ensure professional training and development. At the same time, there needs to be a conviction in society—among parents and young people as well as the economy at large—that youth development through apprenticeships provides good opportunities for a lifelong career that allows for recognition in society with the option to switch between different types of education and good prospects for advancement. An additional important factor contributing to success is the constant adaptation of the system to developments in society and the economy.

It is possible to transfer the system to other countries and cultures, but this will require an appropriate change of attitude in their economies and societies and a trade-off in the contribution of the government between support and legislative regulation to the point of placing requirements on companies. What is needed above all is time, since the companies that train apprentices have to adapt and develop training staff. Companies that are familiar with the system from their parent companies (based in Switzerland, Germany, and Austria) can use their branches to lend a helping hand as pioneers in countries that wish to establish the dual system. Moreover, it should be possible to offer the training model as a joint endeavor right from the start. This raises the value of the training, and it is only then that the graduate trainees can move freely on the labor market. The companies must provide entry-level positions with tasks that can be managed by graduates and must support them in their development. A long-term perspective that does not expect an immediate benefit is essential, as is patience in a fast-paced world.

5.4.3   Creating Opportunities for All

How do we ensure that all students have access to educational and employment opportunities? No matter the system of education provided in a country, education is still the main source for youths to build skills and have access to future employment. It is therefore imperative that we do more to ensure our education providers can provide a quality education for all. Youths who fail to attain academic success are likely to suffer from disengagement, lack of economic opportunity, and a poorer standard of living than youths who attain academic success. Moreover, ignoring this population of students adds further strain on the economy as we fail to unlock their potential possibly causing them to seek employment through informal means. To overcome this issue, we need to ensure that all young people are integrated into some sort of education system.

There are still many marginalized groups that are completely isolated from the rest of society. Youths from remote parts of the world, impoverished communities, and street children might never have an opportunity to attain an education. To reach these groups, we need to design innovative learning spaces or support educational initiatives that are proving they can provide a quality education to disadvantaged youths.

> **LEARN MORE**
>
> Khadijah Niazi of Lahore, Pakistan, is an inspirational example of how online education is revolutionizing learning. She was only ten years old when she first took the Artificial Intelligence online course on Udacity. She managed to finish the course and, the following year, Khadijah completed Udacity's Physics course with highest distinction, being the youngest ever girl to complete it. Just two years later, Khadijah sat next to Udacity founder Sebastian Thrun, Bill Gates of Microsoft, Larry Summers of Harvard, Thomas L. Friedman of The New York Times, and other panelists at the Victor Pinchuk Foundation's 6th Philanthropic Roundtable, which took place at Davos in conjunction with the 2013 World Economic Forum, discussing the future of education.

While these models exist, they need further support to scale up and have a greater impact. For example, some organizations are working on programs that empower street children through entrepreneurial training. Others are designing new types of schools that help students obtain relevant skills thus increasing their employability. By providing education through new means, these bodies are ensuring that more students have access to some sort of quality education. We need to generate awareness about these successful educational models, so that we can enable them to grow and increase their impact. Moreover, if such knowledge is shared, these educational models could be replicated and adapted to fit similar contexts.

Social enterprises are also proving to be another effective means in addressing gaps in our education system. Underfunded schools and disadvantaged youths are now finding some relief through enterprises that effectively channel needed funding and resources to their recipients. Other enterprises are working hard to fight discrimination and violence so that schools can provide a safe and productive environment for their students. To engage students and encourage them to stay in school, some social enterprises are using sports, like football, to motivate students to take their education seriously. Although these enterprises are addressing a wide range of issues, they are enabling more students to succeed academically and have a fighting chance when it comes to seeking employment. It is therefore important that we create awareness of successful social enterprises tackling education so that they too can be scaled and achieve greater impact.

L E A R N   M O R E

Initiatives providing educational opportunities to the marginalized

- *Hole in the Wall*: An organization that puts learning stations in underprivileged communities so that students can explore their natural curiosity.
- *Mobile Schools*: An organization that develops and delivers an entrepreneurial education to street children.
- *DevEd*: An organization designing a school that aims to provide students with the relevant skills they'll need to succeed in their community.
- *Coderise*: Teaches young people from developing nations to develop web applications.
- *Social Ventures Australia*: Creating better education and employment outcomes for disadvantaged Australians.

Initiatives providing funding and resources

- *Aiducation*: An organization that provides high-performing students from developing countries with academic scholarships.
- *DonorsChoose*: An online charity that enables teachers to receive funds for needed supplies and school projects.

5.5 Conclusion

As society works together to address youth unemployment, we will continue to see new initiatives being developed that attempt to revamp educational institutions and improve E2E processes. While these will hopefully help society to move forward, there are still a few underlying factors that might undermine our ability to transform the role of school and university. Until these factors are addressed, it will be difficult to transform education so that it better suits 21st century needs.

We need to generate more data on youth unemployment and how schools and universities can better align themselves to the marketplace. We need to encourage organizations that are helping education providers (e.g., PanoramaEd or Kickboard) to produce more data. In having some sort of means to analyze and assess problems, we can then monitor and evaluate the success of initiatives and programs meant to facilitate the E2E process.

Any change in the education system requires supporting our teachers. Empowering educators and giving them a voice in the decision-making process promotes engagement and allows educators to implement initiatives that best serve their student body. By investing in modernized teacher training, providing educators with the resources and support needed to revamp classrooms, enabling more communication and collaboration between administrators, business professionals, and educational organizations, we can engender needed changes in our educational institutions. Establishing a skills framework can only be accomplished if teachers are aware and prepared to implement these new skills. Creating applied learning experiences or partnering with external organizations takes time and resources, often not provided to educators in their workday. By supporting teachers and encouraging them to make the transformations we seek, E2E initiatives are more likely to succeed.

All university students should receive a quality education, which largely depends on the quality of their professors. Professors should therefore be encouraged to focus on pedagogy in addition to their research and be made aware of the E2E process. This can, however, only be achieved if academics are not solely evaluated by their publication track record.

Schools and universities might need to adopt different assessment tools that better cater to new classroom dynamics. Oftentimes, grades, scores, and grade point averages (GPAs) are still the main means for assessing student performance. These metrics can make it difficult to evaluate skills and applied knowledge, as many 21st century skills are difficult to quantify. By using a combination of assessments, for example portfolios that include test scores, projects, and teacher evaluations, we could provide a more well-rounded view of students to potential universities and employers. Moreover, these new assessment tools might make it easier for educators to focus on skill-building and hands-on learning.

Education providers are not the only institution responsible for providing education and training. Employers must also adapt to the workforce and play their part in providing adequate training to our youths. In fact, employers who invest in training and partnerships are more likely to be satisfied with their new recruits than those employers who do not (Mourshed et al., 2014). By sharing the responsibility to train young people, employers can reduce costs for education providers while simultaneously providing students with the specialized skills they seek in the workplace (OECD, 2013).

Finally, we need to prioritize career readiness as an essential function of our schools and universities. Too often fads in education cause us to focus our energies on initiatives that miss the big picture of the relationship between school and work. Work will occupy a large portion of students' adulthoods as well as shape our society. It will provide our youths with purpose and enable them to obtain a higher quality of life. Career readiness is therefore essential to the wellbeing of our youths as they become adults. We must ensure that our school and universities are playing their parts in adequately equipping our students for the future.

chapter 6

Employers' Contribution to Tackling Youth Unemployment

> While policymakers have a role to play in pushing forward reforms to strengthen the economy and foster job creation, the private sector is Europe's largest employer and its contribution is essential to help solving the issue.
>
> *Laurent Freixe, Nestlé*

For many global organizations the recession is history and all effort is focused on growth and new investments. Yet as the economy recovers, the C-levels of these organizations are left to realize the workforce has changed and therefore their recruitment and retention strategies require systematic rethinking. In addition the youth unemployment crisis leaves a large proportion of the future workforce without a job, scarring them for life. Therefore, employers must not close their eyes to what is happening to their prospective future employees.

In fact, employers have an important role to play in tackling youth unemployment. They not only provide jobs that allow young people to enter the world of work; they are also important sources of training and knowledge creation for young people that leave the education system without the adequate skills and capabilities (as discussed in Chapter 5). While it generally sounds relatively straightforward, it is everything but simple given that the youth unemployment crisis is accompanied by major generational changes.

As outlined in Chapter 2, the 21st century workforce (the Millennials and the Digital Natives) has entered the labor market bringing with it fundamentally different characteristics, traits, attitudes towards work and expectations from work. Employers are slowly trying to adapt to this change, but it is challenging given that they now need to figure out how to manage a workforce of four (sometimes even five) generations, help them collaborate and find incentive structures that satisfy the expectations of the Baby Boomers, the Generation X-ers, Generation Y-ers, and the Digital Natives (GES, 2013).

We are faced with the somewhat awkward situation of many highly educated young people not finding jobs and a majority of employers complaining about not finding enough qualified people. There is an uneven distribution of skills around the world (see Chapter 3, and Deloitte, 2014) and an ever-increasing mismatch between employers' expectations and future employees' expectations. Employers are asking for many upfront credentials from young people, including excellent grades, prior work experience, multiple languages, a global, entrepreneurial, team-focused, hard-working, open, friendly and goal-oriented mindset, among many other things that make it close to impossible for the majority of tomorrow's employees to enter the workforce with the confidence of being ready for the job. At the same time, employers are left with a non-committing, fast-paced, less loyal generation that wants a career filled with mentoring, growth, flexibility, rewards, global opportunities and immediate promotions. So employers are obviously scared of getting them onboard and training them on the job to acquire the necessary skills only to then see them leave again two years later.

Employers, small and large, hire individuals if they feel that doing so is in their interest. Oftentimes companies report to investors which unfortunately are mainly driven by the profitability of the company and less by the employers' contribution to tackling youth unemployment (exceptions prove the rule!). So it is essential to understand how employers can benefit from recruiting young people. What do they gain compared to hiring more experienced workers? How can that be achieved without neglecting the older generations?

We're left with a clash between tomorrow's employees—including tomorrow's leaders who will be running these organizations—and the world of work as it stands today. As part of multi-stakeholder solutions to youth unemployment, employers play a central. They must assume their responsibilities in preparing youth for the world of work by closely collaborating with the education system, providing internship and mentoring opportunities, giving lectures and talks in schools, attending career fairs and other career-related events, and opening up their doors for young people. They need to ensure that young people are aware of the available opportunities. Employers also need to ensure that they build adequate vocational training opportunities to counteract increasing academization and help build relevant skills and capabilities on the job. They will need to build a workforce management system that allows them to effectively work with four or five generations of employees. Moreover, they need to ensure that there are sufficient youth-compatible jobs available in their companies, taking into account the Digital Natives' characteristics and expectations from work. Linked to that, they will need to ensure that tomorrow's leaders find a stimulating and satisfying work environment in order to ensure continuity when the older managing employees retire. This needs to be done by building a 21st century workplace. In the following I will discuss these points in greater detail, starting off with two fundamental points: (1) Is there a business case for hiring young people; and (2) how can employers better interact with the education system.

6.1   Is There a Business Case for Hiring Young People?

There have been various studies that tried to answer that question, bringing forth mixed results. While the CIPD (2012) and Hasluck (2012) found a clear business case for employers to hire young people—going beyond altruistic motives, others (Cominetti et al., 2013) did not find a clear business case, with employers highlighting both positive and negative aspects of hiring young people.

Given that companies like business cases in order to change their course of direction, I would like to start off by highlighting a few key benefits that employers will get out of hiring young people, followed by some of the downside effects.

6.1.1   Some of the Benefits of Hiring Young People

First and foremost, employers will have to hire young people anyway at some point in time—given that they want their organization to outlive their older employees. From a business perspective that argument alone should make a suitable business case for hiring young people. In fact, it feels like many employers are just postponing a move that they know is inevitable but may not be particularly comfortable. It means change, it means adaptation, it means turmoil and it maybe also means (at least in the short-run) financial disadvantages until employers have fully understood how best to utilize young people with their new skills and abilities. Nonetheless, it is just a matter of time that they will have to do it anyway. So why not start right away? In the end, it is the early bird that catches the worm.

Second, employers can benefit from hiring young people in that they can still shape them to perfectly fit their organization. As some of the interviewees of the study of Cominetti et al. (2013) indicated: "I like starting with a blank canvas" or "We train them the way we want them to be." Employers can imprint their organizational culture on young people—a process that is much more complex for older employees. Young people are much easier to train and willing to learn. Linked to this argument, the employer can form an entire workforce that is well aligned with the overall organization's goal and specific needs.

Third, employers can greatly benefit from young people's digital literacy. As Prensky (2001) described, the Digital Natives have grown up in a virtual world and have an intuitive understanding of technology whereby the Digital Immigrants (those who grew up before the internet, computers, and smartphones) had to transition into this new world. They typically bring along many new technologies that can be adopted by the employer and at the same time they are faster at getting used to the in-house IT systems. So depending on the industry, this ability can be of tremendous value to employers. This, among other qualities of young people, will help bring the organization to the 21st century.

Fourth, young people bring with them a lot of enthusiasm, energy, a global mindset, motivation, and willingness to learn and to make a difference in the world. If employers clearly state their vision and goals, young people can align themselves and feel like they are a part of something bigger.

Fifth, young people are much more flexible than their older counterparts. While this can also be seen as a disadvantage, it can be helpful when it comes to hours they are able to work, international work opportunities that need to be filled, etc. Young people are also changing their jobs more often, which can allow some employers to flexibly move them around across functional units (e.g., as part of a trainee program) and as such train them even better and in a horizontal manner.

Sixth, linked to their digital literacy, the fact that they just left education with the newest stock of knowledge, and their general willingness to make a difference in the organization, employers can greatly benefit from hiring young people by involving them in reverse mentoring programs—programs where they purposefully train their older work colleagues (see Chapter 6 for an example).

Seventh, young people are generally less costly than older workers, saving the employer a lot of money. As Cominetti et al. (2013) show, the minimum wage level depends on the employee's age. Employers who offer minimum wage jobs can therefore greatly benefit from hiring young people. But also in industries that do not work with minimum wage jobs, young people are still typically less costly.

Last but not least, many employers hire young people as part of their Corporate Social Responsibility (CSR)—particularly now during times of high youth unemployment. If they are regionally embedded employers, they can contribute to the region's development by preventing a brain drain, as such ensuring that they will be seen positively by policymakers, educators, and other stakeholders from the region. From a business case perspective it makes a lot of sense to engage in recruiting youth as it will shine a bright light on the organization with various positive effects for the organization.

6.1.2   Some Downside Effects of Hiring Young People

The biggest argument against hiring young people is their lack of work experience (general and specific) as well as their lack of adequate skills. More generally speaking, many companies complain that young people are not employable upon graduation from school or university but first need intensive on-the-job training in order to add value to the organization.

Second, many employers see an issue in the young people's attitude towards the company. This holds particularly true with regards to their reduced loyalty. While historically employees would join an organization to find a job for life (as we still see oftentimes in Japan), employees today change their jobs every few years. This high turnover rate puts a lot of financial pressure on an organization (higher recruiting costs, higher on-the-job training costs) and it bears some risk for the organization because in today's digital world highly sensitive information can leak outside the organization as employees leave.

Third, young people oftentimes have false expectations from work and of their value to the organization and the level of job they "deserve." They do not want to see a classical hierarchical system anymore but instead work with older employees as if they were peers, no matter if they have been with the organization 20 times longer or not. This false expectation from work also shows in their salary expectations, which are oftentimes not aligned with the actual job.

6.1.3   Conclusion

So is there an overall business case for employers to hire young people? After this short discussion I would clearly say yes. While there are obvious downside effects of hiring young people as compared to older employees, there are many more positive effects. Ultimately, employers cannot go around hiring Millennials and Digital Natives given that at some point there will be no Baby Boomers and Generation X-ers left to be hired. Consequently, it is advisable to start early on and train them on the job.

6.2   Employers Integrate with the Education System

It is important that young people gain first hand insights into the world of work early on during their education to ensure that they go back to the classroom with a better understanding of what work is and why it is important to acquire certain types of knowledge and skills. Without this early exposure to the real world it is difficult for young people to develop an intrinsic motivation for learning and, in particular, the ability to filter the relevant from the irrelevant. Moreover, such exposure allows students to go through a reflective process about their own interests and capabilities.

The latter is of utmost importance when it comes to an individual's career development. The sooner a person understands what he or she wants to do with life, the better the preparation will be prior to transitioning to the world of work. This improved understanding of where one wants to be in the near future has to take place on different levels. First, the young person must understand the broad direction/field/industry he or she is interested in, be that science, engineering, humanities, healthcare or some other field. Second, the individual needs to reflect on whether he or she wants to enter a corporate career, academia, an NGO/NPO or become an entrepreneur. Lastly, the person needs to understand his or her core abilities when positioned within a team. This will allow him or her to clearly find the right position within the labor market. Belbin (1981) has developed a set of nine team roles that individuals can take on, ranging from action-oriented roles (shapers, implementers, and completer-finishers) to people-oriented roles (coordinators, team workers, and resource investigators) and thought-oriented roles (planners, monitor-evaluators, and specialists).

Employers can play a critical role in helping young people go through this reflection process and better identify their dream career. Employers can grant access to their employees—from line workers to the top management—so that young people can observe the everyday work routines of those employees, the activities they have to undertake, and their roles and responsibilities (see case Leadcap in Chapter 8). Young people can then use this information to understand whether or not they can see themselves in that position. Understanding what they like and what they do not like is equally important during this reflection process.

One of the simplest things that employers can do to help students is to actually go into schools and talk about their company, their industry, and their everyday job. This helps young people gain a better understanding for what the world of work looks like and what their interests and competencies are. Employers can volunteer as classroom visitors, give talks, and run classes similar to those developed by Junior Achievement (JA), designed to educate students about work readiness, entrepreneurship, and financial literacy. Employers can provide speakers, lecturers, and mentors, and offer activities such as participation in career fairs as well as career-shadowing programs.

CASE STUDIES: WORLDS OF WORK (WOW) AND WORK INSPIRATION

– Andrew Brough, Foundation for Young Australians –

"Employers can have a massive impact on the lives of young people by offering inspiring work exposure programs."

Andrew Brough

Foundation for Young Australians

The Foundation for Young Australians (FYA) is a national independent non-profit organization dedicated to all young people in Australia. In the careers learning space, its role is to equip young people with the tools and connections for the changing world of work.

Young people need a specific set of skills to be able to navigate the world of work. To facilitate work exposure and the development of networks we need to connect young people with the world of work as early and as often as possible. Currently, career learning starts too late, and there are too few, inadequate and fragmented work exposure opportunities.

FYA takes a multi-stakeholder approach by working closely with businesses, not-for-profits, and education partners to provide career learning for young people across Australia. Through our programs Worlds of Work (WOW) and Work Inspiration, FYA and their partners provide meaningful work exposure for thousands of young people every year.

Worlds of Work

Worlds of Work (WOW) is a national FYA initiative that supports young people to make successful transitions to work and life beyond school. The program enhances young people's understanding of the changing world of work, builds their capabilities and confidence to participate in the workplace, and cultivates skills for lifelong career development.

Each year thousands of young people across Australia visit hundreds of workplaces, made possible by the support of hundreds of WOW partners who open up their boardroom doors. For many of the young people it is the first time they look behind the scenes of a real workplace environment, allowing them to meet employees and ask them questions about their work and life. The WOW partners understand how critical it is for young people to be exposed to workplaces, which is why they participate in their career discussions in order to support them in their considerations for their career journey.

Work Inspiration

Work Inspiration is an Australia-wide, employer-led campaign to change the face of work experience in Australia through meaningful work exposure opportunities and career discussions between employees and young people. The National Australian Bank (NAB) is a founding partner of Work Inspiration, with FYA and the Smith Family. Since its launch in August 2013, Australian businesses have pledged over 2,500 Work Inspiration placements to young people across Australia.

FYA, NAB and the Smith Family are assisting organizations across Australia to adopt a Work Inspiration by providing program materials that capture the collective learning of other Work Inspiration organizations and support organizations to develop and offer Work Inspiration in their workplace to young people in their local area. Work Inspiration is one example of the ways in which businesses can positively influence how young Australians participate in work experience in our country.

Learnings and recommendations

FYA prides itself on being partner powered. In order to solve massive challenges such as the current youth unemployment crisis it creates multi-stakeholder solutions. It is through collaboration with partners that FYA can amplify its impact. With the right partners and opportunities related to work exposure and career opportunities our young people will be able to uncover their full potential.

Building on our collective experience, FYA is working in partnership with the Beacon Foundation and Social Ventures Australia to develop a new model of careers learning called "Beyond the Classroom" designed to be implemented at scale across Australian secondary schools. Beyond the Classroom links industry with teachers so students experience and understand the practical application of what they are learning. This will help young people think about what they want their future to look like and how that can be achieved by the choices they make as they progress through school. FYA is relentlessly optimistic about young people, their capabilities and their desire to earn and learn.

LEARN MORE

- **Manpower training-to-employment program**: Such programs focus on job-specific training of individuals with skills and capabilities that are customized to available jobs. They help employers to by-pass the skill shortage issue and help jobseekers get access to jobs they otherwise would not have been able to apply for due to a lack of skills. It is an effective and efficient way reskilling disadvantaged workers to move to where the demand is greatest.
- **ccINspire**: ccInspire is an online career exploration tool that pairs employers with middle- and high-school students. It allows students to gain early insights into different career

opportunities and employers to begin interacting with students while those students are still in the classroom, building relationships that can last for a lifetime.

- **LYNX (aboriginal career program)**: In various countries, including Canada, the aboriginal communities are experiencing disproportionate youth unemployment rates. Surprisingly, these communities appear to be entirely ignored in the ongoing debate about youth unemployment which focuses on those nations and groups in which hitherto we were not used to seeing high youth unemployment rates. Canada is running a public-private partnership (PPP) between employers and post-secondary educational institutions to help aboriginal students and graduates seek meaningful employment and to help employers find qualified aboriginal post-secondary students and graduates.

6.3   Vocational Training and Apprenticeships

In most countries, a university degree is considered a better and more valuable preparation for the world of work. Yet, it does not make a lot of sense that all individuals go for an academic university training. In fact, dual education systems with a strong on-the-job training system—such as those in Germany, Austria and Switzerland—have been shown to successfully bring young people to work. Consequently, dual education systems are considered a central approach to tackle youth unemployment and employers need to take a leading role in the promotion of vocational training and apprenticeships as an attractive career opportunity.

6.3.1   Lobbying for Hands-on Professions

Employers need to get active early on in the education system to improve the overall image of apprenticeships in particular and vocational training generally. Employers can send speakers into schools to showcase the benefits of vocational and technical work and the career opportunities students can have by joining such professions. As illustrated in Chapter 5 based on the Swiss banking industry, individuals can have great careers and even reach the C-levels of multinational companies having started off with an apprenticeship.

By advocating vocational education employers can make a strong contribution in tackling youth unemployment, help address the skills mismatch and simultaneously reduce their own skills shortage while helping young people consider a wider range of potential career opportunities. To export the apprenticeship model to other countries, employers with established and well-functioning apprenticeship programs in countries such as Germany, Austria or Switzerland could expand their programs to other countries. This will likely lead to greater success than companies who do not yet have such programs, launching them in countries where there is no strong dual education system.

6.3.2   Apprenticeships and Traineeships

> There is a big stigma hanging over young people at the moment regarding their readiness ... it does not take an awful lot to get them ready.
>
> *Mike Thompson, Barclays; House of Lords, 2014*

One of the best things employers can do is to increase the amount of young people they take on right out of school to enter their apprenticeship and traineeship programs. Knowing that the education system does not sufficiently equip students with the necessary skills and competencies for the world of work, employers need to get involved proactively. As outlined above in Chapter 6, there are a number of advantages to hiring young people early on, such as the ability to align them with the organization's structure, vision, and goals. In his article entitled "Over 20 Percent Youth Joblessness and Still No Apprenticeships," economist Robert Lerman argues that the only solution to youth unemployment is to systematically implement apprenticeship programs, which will help raise the skills and capabilities of young job entrants (Solman, 2013). This requires a strong commitment from the employer but, as we will see in the subsequent example, it is expected to pay off in the mid- to long- term.

CASE STUDY: "NESTLÉ NEEDS YOUTH"

– Laurent Freixe, Executive VP Europe –

How does your organization tackle youth unemployment?

At Nestlé, we have a long tradition of recruiting young people directly from schools or universities. We invest in them, build their capabilities and develop their professional career plan. We do so whilst embracing diversity of cultures, traditions and opinions. In the current economic context we felt like we can do even more to help address youth unemployment, which is why we decided to launch the 3-year program Nestlé needs YOUth in 2014. There are some key areas in which this programs seeks to address the youth unemployment crisis:

- Direct recruitment: We plan to hire 10,000 youths (under the age of 30) by 2016.
- Apprenticeships and traineeships: We plan to strengthen our apprenticeship and traineeship programs to reach 10,000 youths over a 3-year period.
- School-to-work transition: Deploy readiness for work activities mobilizing our employees and managers to help young people prepare for their entry into professional life.
- Engage our suppliers: We motivate our suppliers to also participate in the initiative. All partners of the "Alliance for YOUth" have agreed to sign the pledge of the European Alliance for Apprenticeship, a project promoting apprenticeship schemes across Europe.

Our overall target is to hire 20,000 young people across all our European businesses and offices. This goal has been communicated to the EU Commission and the media, in full transparency.

The key performance indicators (KPIs)

To track the success of our program and to ensure that we fulfill our promises, we put in place a monthly reporting system based on the input of data from 22 markets in Europe (including our Headquarters). The report is divided into two sections:

1. Direct recruitment (broken down on the level of business units as well as countries):
   - Number of regular employees below 30 years old (hired in the reporting month)
   - Number of temporary employees below 30 years old (hired in the reporting month)
   - Number of apprentices (total & aged 15–24)
   - Number of trainees (total & aged 15–24)

- Number of apprentices and trainees hired in factories and distribution centers.

2. Readiness for work (related to the number of undertaken activities and the number of employees & retirees who have participated):
   - Number of CV clinics—Universities
   - CV clinics—Schools/Colleges
   - Unemployment offices
   - Job Fairs
   - Company Information Lectures
   - Open days

We ask each market to inform us in advance about the planned readiness for work activities for the following month. This allows us to coordinate activities across different markets and leverage it on social media. In addition, we plan to ask the markets to report the number of temporary employees/apprentices/trainees that have received a permanent contract (i.e. the conversion rate from temporary to permanent employment).

As a reference: The first four months of the program have resulted in 4,135 new hires; 1429 regular youth employees and 1181 youth temporary employee were hired. In addition, 1525 trainees and apprentices have been given a job opportunity. From those, 650 were hired in factories and distribution centers (often located in rural areas). Regarding the readiness for work initiatives, 660 events (CV clinics in schools and universities, job fairs, unemployment offices etc.) have been organized across Europe with more 1,900 Nestlé employees participating.

Learnings and recommendations

Why did we get such a good traction around the initiative in such a short period of time?

- Coherence: We are well aware of the importance of the private sector in solving youth unemployment. In a period of crisis growth remains at the core of our strategy. Overall, we achieved good alignment of our approach with the Commission EU2020 agenda targeting smart, sustainable and inclusive growth.

Moreover, our initiative is well aligned with our "Creating Shared Value" approach.

- Legitimacy of Nestlé in youth employment: We have always recruited young people from schools and universities to develop them in their career within the company.
- Excellent execution: Our initiative is driven centrally by a small team at the head office, but then deployed locally in all countries across Europe simultaneously.
- Engagement with policymakers: From the beginning we have interacted with the relevant stakeholders, at the Brussels level and national and local levels. We have been very transparent on our objectives and frequently report our progress, an approach that is very much appreciated by the EU Commission.
- Our people are mobilized: By taking such a strong stand on an issue such as youth unemployment, our people across Europe are very proud, which positively reinforces their commitment to Nestlé's values and engagement.

LEARN MORE

These are a few more company-driven apprenticeship and training initiatives that have been launched in response to the youth unemployment crisis.

- Barclays apprenticeship program: In an attempt to contribute to tackling youth unemployment, Barclays has created an additional 1,000 apprenticeships and launched a new program to support 10,000 young people into work (Barclays, 2013).
- Souq.com: Souq.com, the leading e-commerce platform in the region and often dubbed the "Amazon of the Middle East," in collaboration with the Education for Employment center in Egypt, have put in place in 2013 a dedicated e-commerce training program, providing training opportunities for 120 Egyptians in the field on online business and e-commerce trading.
- Diageo: Diageo tackles youth unemployment with a GBP 5 million program to train unemployed young people in Scotland (Herald Scotland, 2014).

6.3.3 Helping Adolescents with Difficulties to Enter and Complete Vocational Training: Foundation "Die Chance"

– Content for this section is provided by Dr. Markus Rauh, Founder and Member of the Foundation Board of the Swiss Foundation "Die Chance." –

Dr. Markus Rauh created the Swiss-based foundation "Die Chance" (English: The Chance) in 1999. The foundation's aim is to support young adolescents (aged 16–22) with social problems, learning difficulties, insufficient educational achievements or migrant backgrounds to find appropriate vocational training, to successfully complete the training and to find employment afterwards.

The foundation focuses on the most difficult cases, which means that they need to specifically seek out those individuals who require special support to take their first steps into the world of work. The success of the foundation lies in its holistic approach to tackle a systemic problem. It does so not only by mentoring and training young people but also by closely collaborating with vocational schools, employers, government agencies, and other relevant stakeholders. This multi-stakeholder approach is important given that the young people oftentimes have below-average grades and therefore might not be able to find suitable apprenticeships on their own. The foundation needs to do a lot of lobbying with employers to ensure that sufficient numbers of these more basic apprenticeships are available.

While the organization has a clear rule of helping everyone who seeks their help, there are still some core requirements that applicants need to fulfill. Potential candidates need to be between 16 and 22 years of age; they need to show sufficient motivation to successfully enter and complete an apprenticeship; they need to be motivated to collaborate with the foundation's team and express a willingness to learn. They also need to prove that they have been in contact with the regional vocational counseling service. Lastly, the young applicants must not have completed higher secondary education.

The foundation depends on fundraising as the philosophy is that it should only exist as long as private donors are willing to support the cause. In addition, the foundation collaborates with the public sector for promotional purposes and for financial support. Yet, to date the success of the foundation is evident. From 2000 to 2013, the foundation has looked after 1,312 adolescents with a total of 201 supporting companies (Die Chance, 2013). The foundation's goal is that at least 80% of the participating young people successfully complete their apprenticeships. To date, a total of 91.5% have completed their apprenticeships, which is a huge success for the foundation, given that with completed vocational education the young people will be less likely to become unemployed.

To replicate such a program elsewhere it is essential that young people with a difficult background or problems receive integrated long-term support, starting with help to find a suitable apprenticeship, ongoing mentoring throughout the apprenticeship and ultimately also support in finding employment afterwards (if the employer with whom they did their apprenticeship is not taking them on as permanent employees). The interconnection with various stakeholders ranging from employers to policymakers and the vocational schools is critical.

6.4   Designing a 21st-Century Workplace

If employers build a work place that is suited (and ready for) the next generation, many of the "negative" characteristics (as outlined in Chapter 6) can be turned into opportunities for building effective multi-generation workforces. It is important that employers understand how to make tomorrow's leaders (i.e., the talents among the Digital Natives) happy, given that they will imprint their way of thinking and doing into the organizational structure and serve as role models for all other future employees from that generation. To build a 21st century workplace, organizations need to address a few key issues.

In my talent management seminars, I focus on the following action-items to build a workplace of the future (Vogel, 2013a).

IMPORTANT ELEMENTS OF A 21ST CENTURY WORKPLACE FOR TOMORROW'S LEADERS

- **Meaning and vision**: Young people want to see how their own contributions fit into a bigger puzzle and how they can have an impact on the organization's success. It is therefore important that the organization not only has a clear written vision and mission statement but actually lives these values at the core of their organizational identity.
- **Culture and community**: Employers must create a culture and community with which young people can clearly identify, or else they will quickly leave the company. The workplace of the future will become increasingly interconnected and as

such it is important that, on a small scale, employers create a community-driven work environment (Johnson Controls, 2009).

- **A system of passion and purpose**: Over the past decades we have witnessed the emergence of a system of knowledge-based workers. While these types of workers have been around before, the proportion of knowledge workers has rapidly increased. Consequently, talent retention is of critical importance to organizations in order to avoid tacit knowledge from leaving. Among the most critical factors of talent retention is employee engagement. The 21st century worker is looking for meaningful work—work that supports a greater purpose for society.

- **Instant rewards**: Young people are used to instant responses (i.e., sending out a Whatsapp as compared to sending a snail mail across the Atlantic). This fast-paced way of thinking and collaborating strongly affects the workplace, forcing employers to adapt their reward system. Instead of giving promotions every three to five years, they should maybe consider installing smaller but quicker reward structures.

- **Customized recruiting and rewarding**: While traditionally individuals are recruited to fit one specific position it might be worth looking at the person's profile and customizing a position around that profile. While this certainly cannot be done in every organization and not in every type of position, there are still many jobs that could be filled based on this principle. Likewise, the reward structure could be customized to the individual. While some are financially driven, others are driven by challenges, and again others are driven by visibility and appreciation. Understanding these differences will help retain the talents.

- **Social media:** Be open about social media. Don't ban Facebook, Twitter, and other channels at the workplace, because young people will use it anyhow. If not at the desktop computer, then on their smartphones. While it is important to make sure that they do not spend the entire day chatting, it is critical to embrace young employees as central brand ambassadors. You would be surprised how much individuals talk about their employers on social media channels. Use that to your advantage!

- **Flexibility and guidance**: Employers should be more flexible while still offering guidance for their young employees. Young people enjoy flexibility in the way they work but at the same time also enjoy guidance from more experienced individuals. Combining these two is key to having happy Digital Natives in the workplace. Mentoring and reverse mentoring programs can help build cross-generational support structures that allow all team members to feel important—the older generations can teach the younger ones the rules of the game in the company and the younger ones can help the older ones acquire new technological or language skills.

- **Virtual and physical teams**: Linked to the argument of flexibility, it is important to build a modern workplace that combines both virtual and on-site work. This approach is being adopted by more and more employers and will be the guiding principle for the 21st century workplace.

- **Intrapreneurship**: Young people are increasingly interested in entrepreneurship. Yet, many will never actually get to start their own company. This is a major opportunity for employers given that they can attract these individuals by building intrapreneurial ecosystems—work environments that allow young people to try out their entrepreneurial thoughts and ideas in the interest of the organization (Vogel & Fischler-Strasak, 2014).

6.4.1   Driving Forces of the Changing Workplace

Let's analyze the driving forces behind the changing workplace. These are very similar to the trends that drive the overall labor market (see Chapter 3). In the following I would like to outline some of these driving forces.

First, we are experiencing an overall population growth, an ageing workforce resulting in multi-generational workforces of up to five generations, urbanization, and changing family patterns (two-income households and fewer children).

Second, the changing generational characteristics (Chapter 2) require adapted work environments given their different lifestyles and working patterns.

Third, we are steering towards a major pension crisis, which is a result of changing demographics, forcing older employees to work longer, and creating multi-generational workforces.

Fourth, employment itself is changing with the rise of more flexible as well as temporary work contracts, the youth unemployment crisis, and increased competition for talent.

Fifth, the technological revolution has fundamentally changed the way we live and work. International travel has been partly replaced by video-conferencing, and permanent connectivity and availability is demanding much from the workforce. Plus the increasing amount of knowledge and information creates major strains on individuals. Work without virtual assistance is difficult in the 21st century.

the technological revolution has fundamentally changed the way we live and work

Sixth, we are witnessing societal changes. Intensified working patterns lead to phenomena such as the quarter-life crisis. As a consequence, people are seeking a better balance between work and life, which is becoming increasingly difficult as a result of the blended nature of both. People are replacing real-life contacts with virtual contacts. The power of one genius mind is being replaced by the power of the collective mind.

Seventh, we are becoming more environmentally conscious and the youth population seeks to preserve whatever is possible from our planet.

Eighth, global collaboration (near-shoring and off-shoring of jobs), increasing global competition and a sustainability agenda all drive changes in the way we work and the way companies do business.

In response to all these factors, our office spaces are fundamentally changing as is the management system that keeps everything together, ranging from facility management to talent management.

6.4.2 Rethinking Recruitment for the Digital Natives

As discussed earlier (Chapter 1) young people have smaller and weaker social networks as compared to their older counterparts. This puts them at a disadvantage when looking and applying for jobs. This is particularly true if employers fill many of their positions informally without ever announcing the jobs publicly. This practice can form a real barrier to youth recruiting and companies need to do much more to make their recruiting youth friendly (Cominetti et al., 2013). These "hidden jobs" need to be eliminated if we want to fight youth unemployment. This can be done in various ways, including the open and pro- active promotion of available positions through online and offline channels and through an integrative recruiting approach in which employers collaborate with educators.

young people have smaller and weaker social networks

First, employers need to embrace modern technology and the readily available online recruiting channels to showcase their open positions to youth. When we launched Jobzippers back in 2008 as a graduate recruiting portal to bridge the gap between the labor market and the education system, we oftentimes heard employers saying that they did not want to pay to post jobs for young people and that the internet should be free anyhow. They recruit young people only through their trainee programs, attending some career fairs or by posting the jobs on their own website. So there was a clear barrier for them to actively engage in online recruiting for young people. If employers want to contribute to tackling youth unemployment they will need to change their attitude in this regard given that young people spend an enormous amount of time on the Internet and on social media sites.

Second, due to the rapidly changing world of work with new jobs and indus- tries emerging (and old ones disappearing) (see Chapter 3), it is important that employers are forward looking in their recruiting strategy, seeking to hire based not only on their current needs but also based on their potential future needs—in terms of knowledge and skills.

Third, the individualism of applicants is becoming an increasing trend in recruiting. Consequently, companies are trying to customize job profiles to tal- ents instead of trying to fit a candidate into a specific position. This, however, is not possible in every type of position.

Fourth, predictive metrics and the use of big data are becoming inevitable in 21st century recruiting. Going beyond historic metrics, managers can now look at real-time and predictive metrics to better understand their current and future recruiting needs.

Fifth, mobile-, social media-, and video-based recruiting have been and continue to be powerful sources for recruiting talents. Direct and instant applications from mobile devices are becoming increasingly mainstream.

Sixth, many talents no longer update their resumés but instead maintain LinkedIn profiles with reasonably up-to-date information. Employers need to adapt to this trend and remain flexible enough to accept applications with a link to a LinkedIn profile as compared to a formal resumé in the classical format. Many talents simply do not have the time to maintain both and therefore companies will lose out if they remain "old-fashioned." Likewise, the question remains open as to whether big companies with professional talent management systems will be able to recruit the best individuals if they force applicants to put all their information into the talent management systems they operate instead of simply accepting a LinkedIn profile link.

THINK PIECE: INTEGRATIVE RECRUITING

– Rajeeb Dey, Founder and CEO of Enternships –

With the recent boom in online learning via Massive Open Online Courses (MOOCs) and the endless learning possibilities that the web can offer, power is starting to shift. We no longer have to rely on our educational institutions to provide us with learning tools. If anything, the more exciting possibilities are starting to exist outside university walls.

There is now the opportunity for employers to take greater ownership in preparing the talent it is looking to hire. Companies have at their disposal learning materials but guard these behind corporate intranets; they have insights into the skills they require but often keep this knowledge to themselves. What would happen if we adopted a more open-source approach to learning, development and hiring? Instead of guarding training materials why not make them openly available to candidates to interact with even before they have joined your company? In doing so their interaction with your brand becomes interaction based around learning rather than merely a transaction of applying for a job whereby one person wins (and is hired) and everyone else, many of whom may be existing or future customers, are left feeling like a reject (and ultimately negative about your employer brand).

6.4.3   Reverse Mentoring: A Bridge between the Generations

While mentoring has a long tradition within organizations—older employees training young job entrants—there is a reverse trend of young people training older employees with respect to novel technologies among other things.[1] This is called reverse mentoring and an increasing amount of employers are starting to embrace this approach to handle the complexity of multi-generational workforces.

The aim of reverse mentoring is to foster an exchange of ideas between the young generation in a company (between 20 and 30 years of age) and employees of the experienced generation (over 50 years), to provide extra space for innovative ideas, to learn from each other, and to expand personal networks. It is a logical counterpart to the regular mentoring programs, given that the younger generation can help the older generation acquire new skills. In today's time it is of great value to create an inter-generational work environment alongside a strategy and mechanism to attract and retain young talent by offering them appreciation, perspectives, and new experiences.

Credit Suisse, for example, has recently launched a reverse mentoring program, which lasts for six months. Following a pilot program in 2013, it was successfully deployed throughout the organization in summer 2014. During the six-month period, mentees and mentors will meet four to six times for 60 to 90 minutes. The program starts with a joint kick-off event and it involves two workshops. Traditional mentoring topics, and the advantages of mixed-age teams will be discussed and tested during the workshops.

This pilot program has been well received by the participants. The young mentors on the one hand enjoy the fact that they can add immediate and tangible value for more senior employees, a concept that has not been so evident in the more traditional hierarchical workplace. The older mentees, on the other hand, value that they are able to rediscover the organization from the point of view of a new entrant, an insight that helps them reflect on their own career. Both parties experience recognition and appreciation for their concerns and perspectives. A bridge of respect and trust is built between the generations. Generation Y is eager to learn, expects feedback on their performance, their behavior, their personality. The mentoring program contributes to this need for feedback in particular. Older employees incorporate the new findings in their management behavior, creating a ripple effect.

To successfully implement a reverse mentoring program, a company needs to have a critical size and a multi-generational workforce. Moreover, it is of great value if the organization already successfully operates a traditional mentoring program, given that this indicates a "mentoring culture" which is supported by the top management. In addition it is helpful if professional mentoring tools and specific skills related to mentoring are available within the organization. Last but not least, the organization needs to have a clear awareness of inter-generational tensions and knowledge and experience gaps across generations, given that these can serve as the source of growth and innovation for the entire workforce and ultimately the organization.

6.4.4 From Cubicles to Coworking Spaces—Learning from Startup Communities

– Content for this section is provided by Daniel Ramamoorthy, Founder of Treehouse –

> The reason Treehouse and other coworking spaces work is because it's lead, managed, and composed of this generation once frustrated now empowered.
>
> *Daniel Ramamoorthy, Founder of Treehouse*

The coworking movement started hardly five years ago but there are already over 3,000 such spaces around the world. The unprecedented growth is proof that there is a clear shift in the expectations of work and work environment. Coworking spaces are the antidote to offices, so properly balancing physical needs (e.g., larger open floor spaces, minimal walls, meeting rooms, event space, welcome desk) with social needs (e.g., fireside chats, networking meetings, classes, retreats, and expeditions) is essential. Coworking is an organic bottom-up approach to a global economic downturn and a solution from those most affected.

No longer the solution and home to just this generation, coworking is in fact recalibrating workspaces across industries and around the world. Given that the majority of members of coworking spaces are in their 20s and 30s (i.e., the Millennials and the Digital Natives), it's clear that the very generation that is/ was jobless is now redefining what work is and how work happens. Some of the fundamental characteristic traits of the next generation are well reflected in these new working environments, which is why it may be worthwhile for larger organizations to read through this section and see how such structures may be implemented within their own organizations.

- It's the era of collaboration. There was a time when invention was done behind closed doors and experiments were conducted in sterile hidden laboratories. Now these innovators harness the power of modern technology to develop cross-continental teams to tackle global problems and to develop solutions and applications. Where people once valued privacy, this generation now sees real power in linking with partners and sharing information. Hence, it is not necessarily only the large incumbent firms that drive economic development and innovation, but smaller firms or even individuals—individuals who are well connected throughout the world, capable of pulling together all the necessary resources and capabilities to outperform the behemoths of established industries.

• It's the era of removing barriers. Engineers working with app developers working with education specialists working with fashion designers working with artists. This is the modern workplace. Suits with free spirits. Night owls working across borders to those with a local heart and purpose. No more are disciplines meticulously separated and narrowly defined. In fact, it is the grey areas and potential synergies in overlapping areas that seem to hold the most potential.

• It's the era of sharing while learning. Tenured professors compete with practitioners who lecture and hold workshops about the lessons they've learned while conducting business. Teaching is no longer just for the experts and the success stories. Our favorite four-letter F word is Fail and entire conferences are organized to provide a platform to share and learn from our greatest mistakes (see for example Failcon). Learning comes from peers as much as from authorities on the subject.

• It's the era of scaling. When it comes to funding, where once only Venture Capitalists monopolized the investment market, now new online platforms turn family members and friends into co-investors and funders. When it comes to networking, everyone's influence has exponentially improved with social media and ever-growing professional and social circles. When it comes to accessing resources, everything, and everyone is hardly a couple degrees of separation away.

Treehouse, like other coworking spaces around the world, is home to the generation that embodies these values. It's a natural melting pot of dreamers and doers from various disciplines who collaborate, share, and scale. And like other coworking spaces, it's an epicenter of the global shapers of this generation; a carefully curated community which ensures that everyone is collaborating with people who have the networks and resources to propel each other forward. Office space equips the community with the resources required to build companies but at a price that is actually affordable. Event space celebrates the many victories and provides a platform for learning from the many mistakes. Design rooms see the creation of many experiments and products. Meeting rooms explore new cross-pollination of ideas and skills. And the café is the epicenter of serendipitous new partnerships.

The recent unemployment crisis rendered many aspiring global shapers, future leaders and highly skilled young workers jobless. And while for some there might have been frustration or resentment, others were empowered to use those same parameters to usher in a whole new world order; one ruled by innovators who explore the synergies between previously distinct disciplines. Skilled workers turned freelancers who offer their services to the masses, and entrepreneurs who bravely pave a path through uncharted territory.

So the question remains how incumbent firms, those that currently cannot provide sufficient employment opportunities for these young talents, can learn from these organic bottom-up communities of shakers and doers to build a workplace of the future—one where tomorrow's leaders feel like they can thrive. Coworking spaces are transforming the work environment and the offices of the largest new age social media companies are proof of how it's even being implemented within larger organizations. If done well, such coworking spaces will naturally become a hotbed of entrepreneurial (or intrapreneurial) activity. See Chapter 6 for more insights on building an intra-organizational architecture for entrepreneurship and innovation.

6.5   Building a Global Skill Supply Chain

Given the complexities and continuous disruptions in the global economy, one of the main issues for employers worldwide is to build their global workforce skills, as well as finding them, accessing them, developing them, and bringing the work to them. Companies that develop a deep understanding of their capability gaps can build a global skill supply chain to address critical needs. This supply chain can be filled by tapping into new skills pools in new locations, creating innovative new ways of working that provide access to a broader range of talent, and developing skills throughout the workforce—from the youngest recruits to the most experienced employees. (Deloitte, 2014)

We find ourselves in a paradoxical situation with high unemployment rates, indicating a surplus of labor, and simultaneously companies reporting great difficulties to recruit and retain employees with the right skills. These difficulties are most prevalent in newer business areas, such as computing, big data management, life sciences, and energy technologies among many others (Deloitte, 2014). Over the past decades, largely triggered through technological advancements, companies automated many transaction-based jobs or shifted these jobs to low-wage countries, while positions that require extensive human interactions remained largely untouched (Johnson et al.,

2005; Lund et al., 2012). Changes in global competition, increasing skills shortages and changing demographics force employers to make the most out of their highly paid talents. Likewise, employers in advanced economies are left with the challenge of an increasing lack of college-educated talents (McKinsey, 2012).

Given these challenges, employers are starting to implement supply chain approaches to develop the capabilities of their workforce. It requires continuous mapping of their demands and adjustments of recruiting and retention strategies, instead of a one-time adjustment. Employers not only need to understand their current skill and capability gaps but also their future skill requirements. Likewise, they need to understand where the skilled workers are located, how they can access them (e.g., via global mobility programs) and how they can redesign work to access these skills in different places.

As highlighted in Chapter 3, talents and the necessary skills are available, but oftentimes not in the desired geographic location. This leaves employers with the challenge of either moving people around the globe to embed them into their workforce in another country (with another culture), or to find more creative ways of engaging these individuals without having to go through this strenuous effort. In times of Skype, Dropbox, Salesforce, and 37signals, among many other virtual means of communication and collaboration, this seems to be a much more feasible approach than 20 or 30 years ago.

RECOMMENDATIONS FOR BUILDING A GLOBAL SKILLS SUPPLY CHAIN

Linked to the concept of tradable tasks (presented in Chapter 8), the following actions may be taken by employers to facilitate such an approach:

- Breaking down jobs to allow the skilled workforce focus on what they're best at and outsource those tasks that can be done by someone else. Such an approach may be particularly interesting in the context of youth unemployment given that highly skilled Millennials and Digital Natives from countries of lower labor demand (such as Spain or Greece) can be employed in places of great labor demand (such as Germany) without them having to leave the country (i.e., avoiding a brain drain), thus contributing to their own country's economic development and stability. Combining an office-based workforce with a remote and flexible workforce allows employers to make excellent use of globally distributed talents.

- Employers can build virtual workforces, by embracing cloud computing and ubiquitous technologies, that are no longer confined to one specific location but instead can work from anywhere in the world. This approach of bringing work to the skills (and not vice-versa), can not only help employers fill their skill gaps but also help tackle youth unemployment. This is particularly relevant for Millennials and Digital Natives (see Chapter 2), given that they strive for more flexible lifestyles and that they are well suited to work remotely (virtually), having grown up in a largely virtual world. As Bonny Simi, VP of Talent at JetBlue says: "It does not matter to me if they work better from six at night until three in the morning or if they can do their work in six hours instead of eight" (McKinsey, 2012). It is the result that matters!
- Employers can extend the global supply chain by building relationships with "talent factories" in emerging economies, such as universities or specific institutes. Likewise, companies may consider getting access to talents through the acquisition of specialized firms.

To understand how to build a virtual workplace, I recommend reading *Virtual Teams: People Working Across Boundaries with Technology* (Lipnach & Stamps, 2000).

6.6 More Business-led Initiatives

One book is not sufficient to showcase all the great examples of business-led initiatives that exist around the world. Nonetheless, I would like to showcase some more that I came across while preparing this book.

6.6.1 WORKing for YOUth

WORKing for YOUth is a UK-based initiative that has been created by leading businesses that have coalesced to collaboratively tackle youth unemployment

by creating additional job opportunities and offering mentoring support for young people across the country. The goal is to create 200,000 additional jobs for young people by 2015, by investing over GBP 1 billion.

6.6.2   Generation Success

Generation Success is an Australian initiative that brings together some of the country's biggest employers to collaboratively tackle the issue of youth unemployment. It provides practical tips and advice to support employers, young people, educators and parents with the goal of ensuring that there is a pipeline of young talents in the future.

6.6.3   Education for Employment Foundation

The Education for Employment (EFE) Foundation offers tailored training programs for unemployed youth in the Middle East and Northern Africa, building a bridge between local employers and unemployed youth. EFE closely collaborates with local employers to secure job commitments ahead of training and then, once a commitment is secured, train the unemployed young people for these positions, giving them the necessary skills and tools to succeed in the job. EFE works with university graduates who cannot find employment. EFE runs interactive courses that prepare students for the jobs, including accounting, banking, construction, sales, textiles, teaching, and entrepreneurship.

6.6.4   Manpower Placement Program for the French Government

Focusing on "hard to serve" candidates, including disconnected youth, Manpower collaborates with the French government to build the candidates' necessary skills and sufficient confidence to present themselves for employment. This program is structured in a step-by-step fashion starting off with a first temporary work engagement that helps young people gain confidence and build a portfolio of work experience. However, this is not the end of the program. Instead, it ensures that the young person will subsequently transition to career-oriented work. The program helps 5,000 people per year of which 65% are successfully placed in long-term employment (Manpower, 2012).

6.6.5   Job Sharing

The Swiss association "PTO" advocates the job-sharing concept whereby two or more employees (for example a junior job entrant and an older person shortly before retirement) can share one full-time position. Such an approach has multiple advantages. First of all, it allows both young workers and older workers to be in the workforce simultaneously without one or the other having to be unemployed. Second, concepts of mentoring and reverse mentoring could be applied in that the two individuals sharing the same job can learn directly from one another. Third, it offers a lot of security for the employer because even if one of the two were to quit the job, the position would not remain vacant and tacit knowledge would not be lost. Such a task-force approach would ensure continuity for the organization at the same cost. Many young people are actually looking for part-time positions, but oftentimes have major difficulties in finding something adequate.

6.7 Conclusion

Employers play a central role in tackling youth unemployment. If they do not create jobs for young people then there is not much that educators or policy-makers can do to tackle youth unemployment besides trying to inspire young people to become entrepreneurs—an avenue that is fruitful but certainly not for everyone.

It is important that more employers look beyond their balance sheets and take a socially responsible attitude by implementing the different low-hanging fruit solutions that I have been outlining above. But even if employers primarily focus on the business aspects, I argue that there is a business case behind hiring young people. In the mid- to long-run it will pay off to hire more young people as opposed to ignoring those profiles because of a skills mismatch. Employers need to integrate more with the education system, to help educators make education more relevant for the workplace and to promote their open positions early on during education. Employers should also become more active in fostering vocational- and on-the-job training through apprenticeships and traineeships. In many countries around the world, these types of careers are not considered "sexy" enough for most young people. Consequently, there's a lot of lobbying work to be done by the employers who rely on apprentices. Employers can also contribute to tackling youth unemployment by redesigning their workplace for the 21st century, to make it more appealing to the next generation of leaders who, in turn, will drive organizational change and attract more young people into the organization. Moreover, employers should build skills supply chains to prevent another skills mismatch occurring again. Understanding their skills requirements ahead of time will allow them to prepare for the future. In conclusion, employers are one of the key drivers of job creation for young people and I urge all companies to take a more socially responsible position and create employment opportunities for young people.

chapter 7

Designing Active Labor Market Policies to Tackle Youth Unemployment

> Improving youth labor market outcomes requires an in-depth understanding of employment and labor market issues that are country specific. Analysis of youth labor markets, with particular emphasis on the issues that characterize youth transitions to decent work, is crucial for determining country-specific needs and for shaping policies and programmatic interventions. A global movement framed by the ILO's Call for Action is required to break the vicious circle that keeps so many millions of youth out of education and stuck in non-productive employment and poverty.
>
> *ILO, 2013*

What if one percent of the bailout money that policymakers paid to bail out those who caused the recent financial crisis had been invested in youth employment initiatives? Would we still be seeing these exorbitant youth unemployment rates around the world? That is a question I had asked myself a few years back while writing an essay for the St. Gallen Symposium (Vogel, 2010). In 2013, at the verge of a generational meltdown, European policymakers finally started to make a move in this direction with large-scale programs such as the Youth Guarantee. But the question is whether such a reactive move could have been anticipated in order to avoid the situation we are in right now if policymakers had given youth a greater priority and not just those who have the biggest lobbying power? I guess that the question "could we have avoided it?" is asked after all major catastrophes. And the answer is yes and no. Of course it is only afterwards that one understands that something of such magnitude can happen and it is only after an in-depth assessment of the catastrophe's drivers that we are wise enough to understand the indicators that need to be observed to avoid something similar from happening in the future.

We certainly cannot change the past, and in the case of youth unemployment it is useless to look for one particular stakeholder to blame, because it is such a complex multi-stakeholder issue that it would be naive to point the finger at only one group. Nonetheless, we are in big trouble and need to fix it quickly to avoid a Generation Jobless while simultaneously building a sustainable system to avoid a repetition in the future. But where should we start? Preferably with those who have both the means and the power to pave the road towards a better future: policymakers. The aim must be to create a framework based on which all the other relevant stakeholders can build effective and efficient solutions.

There are many things that policymakers can do (and actually have already started doing) to tackle youth unemployment and build a more robust system for future generations. First, policymakers can push forward dedicated Active Labor Market Policies (ALMPs) that focus on helping young people in the education system transition efficiently into the labor market, young unemployed to move into employment, and young NEETs to find employment, education, or training opportunities. Second, policymakers can act as a coordinating unit by bringing together all the relevant stakeholders—educators, policymakers, employers, entrepreneurs, international organizations and of course youth—to facilitate the development of multi-stakeholder solutions to the problem. Third, in line with the previous argument, they can embrace public-private partnerships (PPPs) as central cornerstones to solving youth unemployment. Fourth, they can catalyze these solutions through facilitation, not through regulation. Fifth, to avoid repeating the situation we are facing today, they can implement effective youth-specific labor market monitoring schemes that function as early warning systems. Having gained an improved understanding of the different causes and drivers of the crisis (e.g., the skills mismatch) we can now implement such monitoring schemes.

This chapter discusses a variety of ALMPs that have been implemented (or have been suggested for implementation) in different regions and countries around the world. The goal of this chapter is to provide an international overview, an improved understanding and heightened awareness of existing youth-specific ALMPs, facilitating the exchange of best-practice solutions and ultimately helping policymakers improve existing programs as well as implement novel programs. All the programs have the potential to contribute to solving the youth unemployment crisis and to stimulate secondary effects such

as the relief of the welfare system, increased societal well-being, economic growth and of course the avoidance of a Generation Jobless.

The chapter starts off with a brief insight from the ILO; it goes on to highlight some programs within the portfolio of EU measures to tackle youth unemployment; it then discusses a dedicated ALMP that helps unemployed individuals transition to self-employment—the topic on which I have written my PhD thesis. This chapter also analyzes PPPs as an essential part of the solution to youth unemployment and concludes by showcasing a variety of national youth ALMPs ranging from Peru to Germany, the UK, South Africa and the Arab world.

7.1   ILO Initiatives

The ILO has outlined five policy areas that can be adopted by national and regional policymakers to tackle youth unemployment: (1) policies related to employment and economic policies to increase aggregate demand as well as access to finance; (2) policies that address the skills mismatch between the education system and the labor market and to smoothen the transition from school to work; (3) labor market policies to foster employment for disadvantaged youth; (4) labor market policies that foster entrepreneurship and self-employment among young people; and (5) labor rights that ensure equal treatment of youth across countries (ILO, 2013). The ILO has implemented a variety of youth employment projects. Here are two examples:

- **Work4Youth (W4Y):** W4Y is a five-year public-private partnership program between the ILO and the Mastercard Foundation, aimed at promoting decent job opportunities for young people around the world.
- **The ILO Youth Employment Programme (YEP):** Different regional ILO offices have launched projects and initiatives to tackle youth unemployment. The diverse projects are listed on the ILO website, structured into Africa, Americas, Arab States, Asia and the Pacific, Central Asia, and Europe.

7.2   Portfolio of EU Policy Measures

In Chapter 1 I discussed the particularly tough situation for Europe's youth, with above-average youth unemployment rates in places such as Greece, Portugal, and Spain among others. As a consequence of this grim situation, the EU has implemented a variety of policy measures that aim at tackling youth unemployment. In the following I would like to introduce a few of these EU policy schemes.

7.2.1　EU Funding Programs

7.2.1.1　European Social Fund (ESF)

The European Social Fund was created in 1957 and it aims at creating employment opportunities. Among its central goals is to improve the employment situation for young people, NEETs, and the socially excluded. Programs run for a period of seven years and are allocated a part of the overall EU budget. The ESF distributes funds to the Member States to operate the programs that have been collectively decided on. Its activities are structured in four main pillars:

1. **Strengthening employment and mobility:** By opening pathways to work for those with outdated skills or without education, creating career chances for NEETs, boosting small businesses by helping them train their workers, and helping individuals develop missing skills.
2. **Improving education and training**: By helping young people complete their education and as such reduce school dropouts, improving vocational and tertiary education opportunities, and building a culture of training and life-long learning.
3. **Creating equal opportunities for all**: By helping marginalized and minority communities gain skills and get access to jobs that might otherwise be unavailable to them and by helping them enter the world of work with similar qualifications as their counterparts.
4. **Improving public services**: By reducing regulatory and administrative burdens and promoting standards of transparency, integrity, and accountability, by increasing the organizations' effectiveness and by forming a platform for collaboration amongst the organizations.

7.2.1.2　European Regional Development Fund (ERDF)

The European Regional Development fund was established in 1973 and aims at creating economic cohesion and reducing imbalance between different regions across Europe. Its primary focus areas are to support small- and medium-sized enterprises (SMEs) and to foster innovation. Through these initiatives, the fund might also contribute to tackle youth unemployment in that these SMEs are drivers of job creation.

7.2.1.3　Youth Employment Initiative (YEI)

In early 2013, the European Council agreed to launch the Youth Employment Initiative, which, over the period of 2014–2020, will focus on creating opportunities for NEETs in regions with a youth unemployment rate that exceeds 25%. In particular, the funds are made available to EU countries to fund measures related to the Youth Guarantee scheme (see below).

7.2.2   EU Legislative and Non-legislative Proposals

The European Union is among the regions in the world with the highest youth unemployment rate. It therefore does not come as a surprise that employment policies, although they are typically a national competency within the Member States of the EU, are now on top of the agenda for EU policymaking. The heads of states collaboratively have agreed on a variety of specific measures to tackle youth unemployment—particularly focusing on those Member States with the highest youth unemployment rates such as Greece, Portugal, and Spain. I will briefly present these.

7.2.2.1   *Youth Guarantee*

The Youth Guarantee is a new policy-driven approach to combat youth unemployment in Europe. It is based on best practice examples from Austria (launched in 2008 under the label "Ausbildungsgarantie") and Finland (launched in 2013 under the label "Nuorisotakuu"), where similar programs were put in place several years ago. The Youth Guarantee ensures that all young people under the age of 25—independent of whether or not they are registered with an employment service—get a good-quality, concrete offer of employment, continued education, apprenticeship, or training, within four months after leaving formal education or becoming unemployed (European Commission, 2014a). The total estimated cost of implementing a Youth Guarantee scheme across the EU countries is EUR 21.4 billion per year (ILO, 2012b). However, when comparing this figure with the estimated EUR 153 billion per year that NEETs cost the EU, this is a much more reasonable and promising figure (Eurofound, 2012).

As the Commissioner for Employment, Social Affairs and Inclusion, László Andor, commented at a meeting in July 2014: "Many Member States are actively implementing measures to make the Youth Guarantee a reality with the support of the 6 billion euros available from the Youth Employment Initiative and of the European Social Fund, worth over 10 billion euros every year. The YEI funding has a crucial role to play since it shall directly support young people by providing a first job experience, a traineeship, an apprenticeship or training courses" (European Commission, 2014h).

7.2.2.2   Youth on the Move

Youth on the Move is one of the Europe 2020 flagship programs. It aims at unleashing all young people's potential. While it focuses on all youth, it also puts particular emphasis on the NEETs and how they can be led back into education, training or employment (Eurofound, 2012). Its particular target is mobility within Europe in that it incentivizes governments to implement apprenticeships that are available across Europe and by operating EURES, an online portal that aims at matching young people and job vacancies across the EU (European Commission, 2014b).

7.2.2.3   Erasmus+

Erasmus+ aims at boosting the skills and employability of young people as well as modernizing of the education system. Over the period of seven years (2014–2020), a total of EUR 14.7 billion will be spent on new programs related to education, training and youth (European Commission, 2014c).

7.2.2.4   Action Teams

In 2012, Greece, Ireland, Italy, Latvia, Lithuania, Portugal, Slovakia, and Spain—the eight countries with the highest youth unemployment rates—implemented action teams with the aim of mobilizing funds that was still available within the 2007–2013 European Social Fund and European Regional Development Fund (European Commission, 2014d).

7.2.2.5   Quality Framework for Traineeship

The European Council adopted a framework that enables trainees to acquire high-quality work experience under safe and fair conditions. It states that traineeships need to be based on written agreements, provide more valuable learning content for young people; must be of reasonable duration, and allow for cross-border mobility. By offering EU-wide traineeship opportunities, the Council hopes to smoothen the school-to-work transition (European Commission, 2014e).

7.2.2.6   European Alliance for Apprenticeships

The European Alliance for Apprenticeships aims at bringing together public authorities, businesses, social partners, vocational education and training providers, youth representatives, and other key actors to promote apprenticeship schemes and initiatives across Europe. The key activities are: (1) to reform of apprenticeship systems; (2) to promote the benefits of apprenticeships; and (3) to smartly use resources (European Commission, 2014f).

7.2.2.7   EU Skills Panorama

The EU Skills Panorama aims at improving the ability of the different stakeholders to understand and anticipate skills requirements from the employer's perspective and to adopt education and training systems early enough, resulting in a better match between the skill supply and demand—in particular a "real-time match" without long time lags between the expression of skill demands and the provision of these skills from a supply side. This program's goal is to build a lively and interesting platform that connects various stakeholders and collectively—in a crowdsourced and big data approach—ensures the best match (European Commission, 2014g).

7.3   From Unemployment to Self-employment

As discussed in Chapter 4, entrepreneurship is considered to be among the main drivers of innovation, economic and societal prosperity, and job creation (Audretsch, 2002; Acs, 2006; Carree & Thurik, 2010). It therefore does not come as a surprise that entrepreneurship is a central strategy to combat global youth unemployment and to re-ignite the labor market. In response to the growing awareness of its importance, policymakers around the world have implemented various policies to foster entrepreneurship and self-employment (Fayolle et al., 2006; Card et al., 2010).

One ALMP on which many governments have placed great hope is the attempt to tackle unemployment by directly helping unemployed individuals transition to self-employment. Despite some early studies that have investigated this type of new venture creation (Pfeiffer & Reize, 2000; Blanchflower & Street, 2004), there has been relatively little research on these programs. Scientists have not investigated this specific form of entrepreneurship and the public have not seemed to care too much about it, given that no one really thought that it made sense to help unemployed start their own companies.

However, formerly unemployed founders are highly motivated to become self-employed and their companies have high survival rates (e.g., Brüderl et al., 1992). Despite making up a relatively small portion of national ALMP expenditures (1–6% of ALMP spending, OECD, 2000) firms established by the formerly unemployed make up a large proportion of all new firms in an economy (30% in Sweden,

Statistics Sweden, 1998) and more than 25% in France (Désiage et al., 2010)). It is surprising that until recently, not more scientists and policymakers have shown interest in this particular strategy considering the severity of the labor market crisis and the potential impact it can have on fighting unemployment.

During my PhD at the Chair for Entrepreneurship of the École Polytechnique Fédérale de Lausanne (EPFL) under the supervision of Prof. Dr. Marc Gruber and co-supervision of Prof. John Dencker, PhD, we worked with several European ministries of employment to study the effectiveness and efficiency of these programs. This was a follow-up study on some of my co-supervisor's earlier work (Dencker et al., 2009a, b; Dencker & Gruber, 2014). We found remarkable results with regards to survival rates, jobs that are being created and the overall well-being of the individuals, indicating that these programs function very well.

In a pan-European study of 12 of these national policies we analyzed and compared specific characteristics of these policy schemes (Haas & Vogel, 2015). Table 7.1 displays the different ALMPs.

TABLE 7.1   Overview of public policies that help unemployed transition to self-employment

Title/Agency/Launch date	Description
Austria **Title**: Gründerprogramm **Agency**: Arbeitsmarktservice **Launched**: 1998	**Support**: The support consists of financial aid of up to 6 months (exceptional extensions) through continued unemployment payments or emergency state payments (Arbeitslosen- und Notstandshilfegeld), training (accounting, marketing, etc.) and financial support (Gründungsbeihilfe) during the first 2 months after a firm's creation. **Eligibility & procedure**: Unemployed persons with intentions of starting a company based on an idea that matches their previous professional experience can apply for the program. Once these prerequisites are fulfilled, external advisors assess the business plan for its eligibility for funding.
Belgium **Title**: Prêt Lancement **Agency**: Office National de l'Emploi (ONEM) **Launched**: 1992	**Support:** Unemployment insurance can be extended for another 6 months to enable the administrative tasks necessary for setting up the company prior to generating sales. Eligible persons can also receive favorable starter loans. Professional support from a coaching and mentoring program is furthermore offered for a maximum duration of 18 months. In addition, there are special support programs for younger as well as older persons, including special funding and coaching support.

(continued)

TABLE 7.1 Continued

Title/Agency/Launch date	Description
	Eligibility & procedure: Unemployed, jobseekers (more than 3 months registration with the regional employment office), and beneficiaries of waiting allowances. Assessment criteria include the project's chances of success, the person's business competence and the outlook for repayment capacity. Repayment of the loan takes place in monthly increments starting from the 2nd (optionally 3rd or 4th) year.
Czech Republic **Title**: Překlenovací příspěvek **Agency**: Ministerstvo práce a sociálních věcí České republiky **Launched**: 1989, expanded in 2004	**Support:** The program constitutes a bridging contribution for three months that amounts to the average monthly wage. **Eligibility & procedure:** Registered unemployed who have had previous employment of at least 12 months in the last 3 years.
France **Title**: ACCRE/NACRE **Agency**: Pôle Emploi **Launched**: 1977	**Support:** ACCRE ("Aide au chômeur créant ou reprenant une entreprise"/"Assistance to those starting a business out of unemployment" in English) offers exonerations from some social security contributions (for 3 years maximum), and monetary support paid in two tranches of 50% each of their remaining credit in unemployment insurance. In some cases, applicants can also get a loan bonus if a bank approved their application. NACRE: coaching/training program for 3 years after company creation. **Eligibility & procedure:** Registered unemployment including the right for monetary support (exceptions: young people under 30, people with disabilities or those whose employer has declared bankruptcy). The applicant has to (1) create a new company or take over a company, (2) apply no later than 45 days after business registration, and (3) cover more than 50% of the start-up capital.
Germany **Title**: Gründungszuschuss **Agency**: Bundesministerium für Arbeit und Soziales **Launched**: 2006 (previously "bridging allowance" and "Me Inc" since 1986).	**Support:** Founding subsidies offer financial support (6 months continuation of last unemployment benefits + EUR 300, with a possibility of a 9-month extension if the business performs well), the allocation of industrial real-estate space and founding-related coaching (in cooperation with the KfW Bank). The "Einstiegsgeld" (start-up grant) is a monetary support mechanism for those people who are not eligible for unemployment benefits but who still want to start a business. **Eligibility & procedure:** Subsidies are granted to those entitled to unemployment payments (ALG II), having at least 150 days of unemployment benefits remaining. Sufficient knowledge and the viability of the idea need to be proven.

(continued)

TABLE 7.1   Continued

Title/Agency/Launch date	Description
Greece **Title**: Πρόγραμμα Νέων Ελεύθερων Επαγγελματιών (New Freelancers) **Agency**: Greek Manpower Employment Organisation (OAED) **Launched**: Early version: 1980s (larger program: 2008)	**Support:** It consists of counseling and funding of varying duration and amounts (EUR 18,000–24,000 in multiple installments throughout the funding period, depending on age and pre-conditions). In addition, the government offers specific programs for young people and unemployed women. If the firm survives for more than 12 months, a monetary bonus can be requested. **Eligibility & procedure:** Granted to registered unemployed (Greek or EU citizens) who have attended OAED entrepreneurship courses, have at least 30 days of unemployment support remaining, and have registered with the tax office.
Netherlands **Title**: Besluit Bijstandsverlening Zelfstandigen (BBZ) **Agency**: Dutch Public Employment Service (UWV) **Launched**: 1996	**Support:** Income support (maximum of 18 months), loans (maximum of 26 weeks with 70% of prior income), tax-incentive programs for private investors ("Aunt Agatha Scheme"), micro-financing (loans of less than EUR35,000 and coaching). **Eligibility & procedure:** People receiving unemployment benefits (WW) whose business plans are approved by the "Werkbedrijf" ("work-coach") of the Dutch Public Employment Service (UWV).
Poland **Title**: Ustawa o Promocji Zatrudnienia i Instytucjach Rynku Pracy **Agency**: Ministerstwo Pracy i Polityki Społecznej **Launched**: 2004	**Support:** One of the mechanisms is to support self-employment, but also re-employment, with grants provided consisting of a loan of up to 20 times the national average wage from the Labor Fund. Immediate repayment is required if the business is not started. According to our sources, the loans are rather uncommon. **Eligibility & procedure:** Unemployed are eligible if (1) they did not reject a valid job offer during the previous 12 months of unemployment, and (2) they did not receive any public funds for starting a new business during the previous 5 years. Strict criteria are applied, limiting the program to a small number of applicants. The business has to be started at latest 2 months after signing the contract.
Spain **Title**: Prestaciones por desempleo Capitalización (Unemployment Capitalization benefit) **Agency**: Servicio Público de Empleo **Launched**: 1985	**Support:** One-time payment of parts or the full amount of the remaining unemployment allocations as well as a coaching component. The Institute of Employment (Instituto Publico de Empleo) promotes different courses for unemployed people, allowing them to develop specific skills that may help in setting up a business. **Eligibility & procedure:** Registered unemployed (with more than 3 months of unemployment benefits remaining) who have not received unemployment capitalization during the previous 4 years and start business not later than 1 month after receiving the money. A detailed viability check is made prior to the funding.

(continued)

TABLE 7.1   Continued

Title/Agency/Launch date	Description
Sweden **Title**: Start-up Grants Program **Agency**: Arbetsförmedlingen (Swedish Public Employment Service) **Launched**: 1985	**Support:** "Startup Grants" are equivalent to the remaining unemployment allocations and are paid for a maximum period of 6 months; less generous grants are also available to those without unemployment insurance. There is also a micro-financing program in place (Almi mikrolån) and special programs for young people under the age of 26. **Eligibility & procedure:** Registered unemployed or those at risk of becoming unemployed. The Public Employment Service decides whether to grant financial assistance based on external consultants who rate the potential of the business and the candidate's abilities. Registration is required prior to producing the first revenues. Candidates must not have received a prior bank loan.
Switzerland **Title**: Taggelder **Agency**: Swiss federal secretary of economy (SECO) **Launched**: 1996	**Support:** Unemployed individuals can receive maximum of 90 days of their unemployment benefits (Taggelder) and work on their business ideas without having to actively look for jobs. At the end of this period, they decide to proceed or not. Tax reductions exist for investors. Special support programs exist for disadvantaged regions (e.g. Valais, Jura, etc.). Other forms of support include an online information portal, further monetary bonds as well as a coaching program. **Eligibility & procedure:** An individual is eligible for the support program if they became unemployed without actual fault, are 20 years of age or older and have a project proposal for the business endeavor. The business must be related to their prior professional experience and no revenues may be produced during the period of support.
United Kingdom **Title**: New Enterprise Allowance (NEA) **Agency**: Department of Work & Pension **Launched**: 2012 (earlier programs since 1983)	**Support:** The New Enterprise Allowance (NEA) consists of a weekly allowance worth GBP 1,274 over 26 weeks, paid at GBP 65 a week for the first 13 weeks and GBP 33 a week for a further 13 weeks and a facility to access a loan of up to GBP 1,000 to help with start-up costs. **Eligibility & procedure:** Jobseeker's Allowance (JSA) claimants aged 18 and over who want to start their own business can get extra help though the New Enterprise Allowance (NEA). After submission of a business plan, experts will evaluate the eligibility.

Source: Adopted from Haas & Vogel (2015)

We were surprised to find that only Belgium and Greece offer dedicated programs for unemployed youth to start their own companies. This is surprising because many young unemployed have never worked before and therefore would need a specific and different support program than their older counterparts. In fact, the only other dedicated program to help unemployed young people to start their own ventures that I could find is a UK-based program offered by The Prince's Trust (see below). This is the problem with many entrepreneurship promotion programs; that they do not account for the specific characteristics and needs of young would-be entrepreneurs and treat them as part of the general adult population (Lewis & Massey, 2003; Schoof, 2006).

CASE STUDY: BELGIUM, THE YOUNG SELF-EMPLOYED SCHEME

– Michèle Baukens, General Advisor, ONEM –

As a result of the disproportionately high youth unemployment rate, the National Employment Office (Office National de l'Emploi, ONEM) started implementing new policy schemes and modified existing ones to better cater for the needs of young unemployed people and help them integrate (or re-integrate) into the labor market. One of the wider policy measures that ONEM has implemented since the 1970s is the integration benefit scheme; a scheme consisting of a variety of different programs. Young people can benefit from this scheme and receive unemployment benefits despite never having paid into unemployment insurance to either seek employment or to start their own company. To qualify for integration benefits, an unemployed person should at least have completed some type of studies, be under the age of 30, and have gone through an integration period (changed from 9 to 12 months in 2012) when he or she has been seeking regular employment.

Within this integration benefit scheme, ONEM has launched a dedicated self-employment promotion program, called Young Self-Employed Scheme. While similar programs helping unemployed transition to self-employment exist in the majority of European countries (Haas & Vogel, 2014), Belgium is among a few countries that offer tailored programs for young unemployed individuals. This is crucial given that young unemployed individuals have systemically different profiles and needs and therefore cannot and should not be channeled through the same programs as their older counterparts who have already gained professional experience.

The Young Self-Employed Scheme encourages people under the age of 30 to become self-employed and start their own business. It grants a preferential rate loan and provides assistance for young people in the early stages of their start-up, including coaching and training.

The Participation Fund (a public credit institution) is the institution that helps young people to carry out their business project under advantageous conditions. The young person submits a preliminary project description based on which the fund decides on whether or not he/she will be invited to join the program and prepare a more detailed business plan. In 2013, the fund recorded 410 claims on the Young Self-Employed Scheme.

After outlining a business plan, the young person receives assistance and advice during a maximum of six months from one of the structures recognized by the Participation Fund. The support is free and tailor-made to the young person's needs.

During the preparation of his/her project the young person receives a monthly reimbursement of EUR 375 for his/her expenses as well as an allowance for starting up the business. The latter is called the New Enterprise Allowance and is paid by ONEM, in addition to the funding provided by the Participation Fund.

At the end of the support phase, a start-up loan of maximum EUR 30,000 can be claimed from the Participation Fund. However, not all business plans result in a loan from the Participation Fund. During the first 18 months of the loan, the supporting structure continues to guide and advise the founder. As a fallback solution, the young people can re-enter unemployment insurance (without any further admittance conditions) if the business fails within the first 15 years. Thereafter, the regular admittance rules apply.

To cope with the problem of young people's integration, which is a structural as well as cyclical problem and which represents an essential challenge in most of the countries, a lot of federal and regional measures (of which some have been briefly described above) exist in Belgium.

A miracle cure does not exist, but putting together the measures implemented on different levels can limit the effects of the problem. These measures include integration benefits, early guidance given by the public employment office, more intensive follow-up of the active job-seeking behavior, recruitment aid, benefits for a resumed schooling program or in the case of vocational training, the possibility of training programs in a working environment, financial advantages to start up a business, among other measures.

Besides programs that are provided by the ministries of employment, there are also a few (but really just a few) programs that pursue a similar goal but are not directly offered by the ministry of employment. One of these programs is The Prince's Trust Enterprise Programme in the UK, which, since 1983, has been helping young unemployed individuals start their own companies. The following case provides some insights into this particular case—a case that from my point of view is a great success and should serve as a role model for other countries.

CASE STUDY: UK, THE PRINCE'S TRUST

– The Prince's Trust Enterprise Programme –

"Youth charity The Prince's Trust helps unemployed young people gain the skills and confidence they need to find a job."

How does your organization tackle youth unemployment?

The Prince's Trust helps disadvantaged young people to get their lives on track. It supports 13 to 30 year-olds who are unemployed and those struggling at school and at risk of exclusion. Many of the young people helped by The Prince's Trust are in or leaving care, facing issues such as homelessness or mental health problems, or they have been in trouble with the law. The Trust's programs give vulnerable young people the practical and financial support needed to stabilize their lives, helping develop self-esteem and skills for work.

One of the courses provided by The Prince's Trust is The Prince's Trust Enterprise Programme, which helps unemployed 18 to 30 year-olds interested in self-employment to explore and test their ideas, write plans and start their own businesses or achieve alternative outcomes in education, training, and volunteering. During the course, young people are offered practical advice, mentoring support, and financial assistance (where necessary) to set up in business.

The program is for young people who have a business idea they want help to explore, are aged 18–30, are unemployed or working less than 16 hours a week, and live in England, Scotland, Wales, or Northern Ireland. The program offers support to apply for a low-interest loan to help start a business, one-to-one support to help them test their idea and realize it, training to teach them what they need to know to start their business and mentoring to develop their business or access other opportunities in education or work.

The key performance indicators (KPIs)

Since 1976, The Prince of Wales's charity has helped 750,000 young people and supports over 100 more each day. Three in four young people supported by The Prince's Trust move into work, education or training.

This program specifically has helped more than 80,000 young people set up their business since 1983. Over the past 30 years, the program has created more than GBP 49.1 million in social value. For every GBP 1 invested in the program, an estimated GBP 4.31 of social value is created in return. Of the estimated GBP 4.31 social value created by the program, GBP 3.24 is the value created as a result of the young people's increased skills and their progression into self-employment, work or training. The remaining GBP 1.07 is the social value created for the state, as a result of the program. This value is largely in terms of additional tax levied on business profits and young people's income from employment, as well as savings from reduced benefit payments and reductions in offending behavior. Nine out of ten young people who started their business through the program were confident that they would be able to support themselves in the future thanks to this program.

Learnings and recommendations

The Prince's Trust has more than 30 years of success in helping unemployed young people to set up a business. One of the key elements of the program is mentoring—young entrepreneurs are matched with volunteer business mentors to provide ongoing support and advice throughout the start-up process. There's also a four-day "Explore Enterprise" course which helps young people develop their business ideas, start writing a business plan and learn about business basics such as accounting and marketing. Once young people have written their business plans they attend a panel meeting to discuss their ideas. If their business plans are viable they are offered low-interest loans (for those who require financial support and grants where available). This combined package of practical support, financial assistance and mentoring is what makes The Prince's Trust Enterprise Programme so successful.

7.4   Public-Private Partnerships

– This section is written in collaboration with Denis Pennel, Ciett Managing Director –

> The International Confederation of Private Employment Services (Ciett) works hard to promote public-private cooperation as a solution to youth unemployment. However, we see that it is extremely challenging to set up such collaborations provided that the communication between the parties is hampered by misunderstandings or prejudice. Success stories often involve a focus on common goals, with respect for each other's different starting points. Our activities promoting public-private partnership therefore mostly include sharing of best practices, and sharing information about the private employment services industry. (Denis Pennel, Managing Director Ciett)

Youth unemployment is a complex issue and there is no one single best-practice solution to the problem. As highlighted throughout this book, tackling youth unemployment requires a multi-stakeholder approach. While individual stakeholder groups may be able to handle some parts of the equation, other initiatives require the specific interaction of these various stakeholders. Public-private partnership (PPP) among public and private employment services is an emerging trend around the world. It can prove particularly effective in addressing unemployment among specific segments of the population, such as young people, who may require a dedicated and tailored approach, which governmental agencies oftentimes cannot provide alone. PPPs allow governments to get a hold of the core problem and create solutions tailored to the different groups of unemployed youth ranging from highly educated university graduates to poorly educated kids and NEETs (see Chapter 1).

By working together in a planned and coordinated manner, public and private employment services have the opportunity to address youth unemployment holistically. They can assess the challenges and opportunities and then pool resources and know-how to identify openings in the labor market. Successful public-private partnerships acknowledge where the relative strengths and weaknesses of the two employment services lie and allow each party to focus on their areas of expertise and play to their strengths.

PPPs can take a number of forms. Some are driven at a national level with governments implementing active labor market policies (ALMPs), which encourage an open dialogue and cooperation between the two employment services. Others are formed on a more regional or local level.

The nature of the partnership will vary in different parts of the world, too. Europe is probably the continent where public-private partnership between employment services is most developed. It has proven extremely beneficial in improving market access and in fostering job creation. What follows are a few selected international and national initiatives that have been established to foster public-private partnership in the employment sector.

7.4.1   EU PARES Initiative

The EU has played an important role through its PARES (Partnerships in Employment Services) initiative, which showcases best practices in public-private cooperation and provides inspiration for fostering closer ties. The goal is to encourage EU-level dialogue to improve the cooperation between the different stakeholders, both public and private.

7.4.2   Selected National Initiatives to Foster PPPs

France: In France for example, in 2008 at the start of the economic crisis, the public employment services transferred 320,000 long-term unemployed people to the private employment services sector and charged it with finding jobs for them. It recognized that these people needed the specialist approach that private employment services could deliver in identifying opportunities, training for skills, and transitioning people into work.

UK and the Netherlands: Both the UK and the Netherlands have established public-private partnerships with regards to the provision of services to unemployed youth. In a project in the Netherlands, young individuals who find themselves newly unemployed are immediately sent to private employment services that help them find employment. If after six months their job search continues they will be transferred to public services. In the UK, the situation is reversed. Newly unemployed young people are initially supported by the public employment services and if after six months they are still looking, they will be transferred to the private employment services sector.

Japan: Japan has taken a different approach. Here, public and private employment services collaborate to temporarily place unemployed individuals as staff into government and public offices and government-affiliated corporations.

A variety of jobs are now contracted under these arrangements with private companies. This includes continuous jobs such as reception staff in museums, attendants at exhibitions and data processors in schools. Temporary contracts are also used to handle temporary peaks in workload such as the administrative work associated with issuing local government resident cards, which need to be circulated at the start of each fiscal year.

The streamlining of operations within government-affiliated corporations has also made them more open to embracing temporary staffing as a solution to meeting their need for flexibility in line with economic fluctuations. It has driven an ongoing cooperation between public and private employment services in meeting the needs of governments.

Australia: The Australian government has taken a market approach to public-private partnerships in the employment sector. Public services are primarily focused on the long-term unemployed and disadvantaged groups and the delivery of welfare services, while private employment services are used as intermediaries with the mandate to reduce unemployment and improve access to the labor market. Comprehensive legal protection for workers ensures that they are not exploited by agencies. More specifically, these legislations position workers as "clients" of private employment agencies thus urging agencies to treat them properly with long-term plans (STS, 2014).

USA: Government-funded state- and regional-level centers operate towards increasing employment, retention, earnings and occupational skill attainment. This in turn will improve the quality of the workforce, its productivity and competitiveness and will simultaneously reduce overall welfare dependency. The private employment sector plays a key role in helping these centers meet one of their primary goals: placing individuals in jobs with private employers. Private companies help the centers by screening job applicants or placing them in positions with their customers. In some regions of the USA, these private firms account for the majority of all placements that are made by job centers. In some cases, the staffing firms actually operate from inside job centers.

The result is a win-win situation: (1) the public center meets its placement targets and secures its funding; (2) the private staffing firm enjoys a valuable source of job candidates; (3) employers have an easy and reliable way to reach out to the best matching candidates with the skills they need; and (4) job seekers find employment.

Private employment service firms in the US are also part of a network of businesses called the National Business Partnership, which is affiliated to 'America's Job Bank', an online labor exchange portal that operates at a national level and connects employers and job seekers. Those seeking work post their resumé in the database and are able to search for job openings across 50 states. Employers can create customized job orders and automatically search the resumés of workers who have the skills they are looking for.

7.4.2.1 Public-Private Partnerships Optimize the Match between Supply and Demand

Matching supply with demand in the labor market will be a growing challenge in the decades ahead. Companies on the one hand find it difficult to recruit people with the skills profiles they need, while workers often feel overwhelmed at the prospect of finding a job. They feel cast adrift in a vast jobs market amid the constantly shifting fortunes of companies and economic sectors with which they are often unfamiliar. Young people in particular are not well equipped for job search. Finding employment requires a dedicated approach and youngsters themselves are ill prepared. Meanwhile the public employment services have neither the resources nor the structure for such a search and are likely to already be stretched to capacity. Speaking to the *Financial Times* in 2013, José Dolado, a professor of economics at Carlos III University in Madrid, argued that Spain's public employment services were too thinly staffed to find work for the six million unemployed.

Hence, by strengthening the cooperation between public and private employment services one can improve the match between supply and demand in the labor market. This facilitates the support provided to workers in transitioning from unemployment to work, and from shrinking sectors to growing sectors.

In today's fast-moving economic environment, jobs are constantly
being created and destroyed resulting in individuals having to be
on a constant job hunt. However, the labor market environment lacks intermediaries that can successfully support
individuals in this process by identifying opportunities to
transition from old jobs to new opportunities.

Private employment services that act as agencies can ease some of this pressure. In many ways they are ideally suited for this type of challenge given that
they closely work with employers and therefore have a good understanding
of their needs, emerging new job opportunities, and the types of skills and
training workers will need to be suited for these positions. Consequently,
these private employment services perform a critical function in bridging the
gap and provide a stepping-stone for young people into the world of work.
The agencies' work is essential to also help young people (specifically those
coming out of unemployment) stay close to the labor market, gain some
work experience—even if just part-time—and as such increase their skills and
employability. Roughly 40% of agency workers are under the age of 25 years
and for many of them, employment agencies represent their first exposure to
the world of work.

To avoid a Generation Jobless, we need to reduce inequalities between young,
employed individuals and those who are left outside the labor market, potentially working in the informal sector (a growing concern in many European
countries, such as Italy: cf. BBC, 2013b). Employment agencies have proven
to be an effective way to help young people transition from informal to
formal employment including social protection through the government. It is
noteworthy that those countries with the highest penetration of agency work
(including Germany, France, Ireland, the Netherlands, and the UK) are also
those countries with the lowest levels of undeclared work.

7.5   More National ALMPs

Many more countries around the world have implemented Active Labor
Market Policies (ALMPs) that are designed to tackle youth unemployment.
A recent OECD report entitled "Off to a Good Start?" reviews ALMPs from
16 countries that are targeted at young people in transition from education to
employment OECD, 2010). Bell & Benes (2012) provide an extensive overview
of earlier studies as well, categorizing them as outlined in Table 7.2.

TABLE 7.2 Categories and literature of programs for youth in transition programs

Category	Description	References
Proactive, early-intervention career development strategy	Helping young people reflect about their career intentions early on during education to ensure that education is targeted towards that specific outcome.	Bell & O'Reilly, 2008; Hooley et al., 2011; OECD & ILO, 2011; OECD, 2010
Direct outreach	Making the outreach of career guidance services more pro-active instead of waiting for youth to approach them.	Archer, 2004; OECD, 2010
Work experience while learning strategies	Actively connecting with the labor market during education will shorten the school-to-work transition period. This strategy focuses on the promotion of gaining work experience (summer jobs, internships, volunteering, etc.).	Hango, 2010; OECD & ILO, 2011; OECD, 2010
Job-search assistance strategies	Job search programs are very effective at helping young people transition into the world of work.	OECD, 2010
Demand-side strategies	Graduate databases, employer partnerships in education, wage subsidies, outreach to employers to participate in work experience and education, and subsidies to accommodate apprentices.	Betcherman et al., 2007; OECD & ILO, 2011
Specific youth population strategies	There are various specific sub-groups of young people that all need to be accounted for through specific programs, including young women, indigenous youth, youth with disabilities.	
Enhanced employment insurance programs for unemployed new graduates	Offering new graduate employment insurance schemes that accounts for their longer transition periods.	OECD & ILO, 2011
Visibility and promotion of various career pathways, including VET	Countries with dual education systems and apprenticeship systems have among the lowest youth unemployment rates. Countries should focus more on building similar dual education systems.	OECD, 2010; Taylor, 2007; Versnel et al., 2011.

(continued)

TABLE 7.2   Continued

Category	Description	References
Promotion of entrepreneurship and self-employment	Entrepreneurship is increasingly regarded as an alternative to integrating more youth into the labor market.	OECD, 2010
School-to-work transition service policy framework	These programs should be coordinated in order to enhance their overall effectiveness.	
Evaluation and monitoring	Very few programs evaluate and monitor their effectiveness and efficiency. It is critical that this is being done on a regular basis to ensure that young people are getting the school-to-work transition support they need	Bezanson, 2008

Source: Adopted from Bell & Benes (2012)

In the following I would like to present some selected national ALMPs, including the "flexicurity" model, the Peruvian action plan for youth, and some more programs from Germany, the UK, South Africa, and the Arab world.

7.5.1   The Flexicurity Model

The Nordic flexicurity model positions itself at the tension between labor market flexibility (which is important for employers to stay competitive, thus impacting job creation) and social security (which is important for employees and the overall population), offering the "best of both worlds." The majority of policies either increase flexibility for employers or security for workers, compromising the other (European Commission, 2007). However, some countries such as Denmark and the Netherlands found a way to combine both (Viebrock & Clasen, 2009).

While the flexicurity model cannot easily be replicated in other European countries due to structural differences, it may still serve as a role model when implementing similar customized Active Labor Market Policies (European Commission, 2014i).

The European Commission is advocating the flexicurity model across the EU in that it helps countries implement (1) flexible and reliable contractual arrangements, (2) comprehensive lifelong learning strategies, (3) effective active labor market policies, and (4) modern social security systems.

7.5.2   Peruvian Action Plan for Youth Employment

Similar to other South American countries, Peru has experienced a significant economic expansion between 2000 and 2010. Nonetheless, more than 60% of all unemployed individuals were young people, roughly 80% of employed young individuals worked in precarious jobs, and more than 50% of the total Peruvian youth population had considered leaving the country if they were given the chance (ILO, 2013).

These challenges require bold policy initiatives to gain control. The Peruvian government has therefore developed a national employment policy (2010–2014) with priority on youth employment—through the youth employment action plan. The goals of this action plan are to create employment opportunities, foster the employability of young people prior to entering the world of work, and boost youth entrepreneurship. The initiative is overseen by an independent committee, which monitors the success of the implementation.

The following reforms were introduced as part of this action plan: (1) a facilitated application process through the introduction of a free-of-charge certificate (CERTIJoven), (2) skills training programs (Jóvenes a la obra), (3) the modernization of career guidance services at universities, (4) a dedicated training program for young entrepreneurs (ProJoven Emprendedor), (5) an information system for market assessments, and (6) an information and orientation service for young people working abroad (Infomigra).

The program is a huge success and might serve as a role model for other Latin American countries. Up until the end of 2012, close to 400,000 young people were supported through this action plan.

7.5.3 The German "Integration durch Austausch (IdA)" Program

Germany is known for its excellent labor market policies, as reflected in the below-average overall unemployment rate, youth unemployment rate, and youth-to-adult unemployment ratio.

One interesting program that was launched in 2008 (with a duration until 2015) is called "Integration durch Austausch" (Integration through Exchange). The program aims at supporting the vocational integration of disadvantaged young people, with IdA I focusing on young people and unemployed young adults, and IdA II focusing on people with disabilities. More specifically, it fosters transnational mobility and exchange projects.

7.5.4 Sanssi-card (Finland)

The Sanssi-card[1] enhances the employability of young people who have difficulties in finding jobs on their own, offering wage subsidies to employers who recruit young graduates. If a young person has the card, it tells the employer that it is possible to get a wage subsidy for hiring that young person. The maximum amount of salary support is about EUR 650 a month in a full-time job and the employer can get the support for up to ten months. The Sanssi-card can be used by private companies, organizations, foundations, associations or local authorities but not by state institutions.

7.5.5 The UK Youth Contract Program

The UK Youth Contract Program was launched in 2012 with the aim of reducing youth unemployment through a range of support initiatives. The government expects GBP 1 billion to provide 500,000 new opportunities for youth. The funding is meant to enable businesses to create job opportunities for young people in that it helps employers financially if they take on a young person for more than 26 weeks (using a wage incentive program). Moreover, it helps the most disengaged and disadvantaged 16- to 17-year-olds by supporting them to get back into education or start an apprenticeship. Also, the program offers young people the opportunity to spend more time with job center advisors, thus enhancing their odds of figuring out what they can and want to do next (Youth Contract Program, 2014).

7.5.6 Selected South African Youth ALMPs

– This section is written in collaboration with Mpho Nosizinzo Pearl Mahanyele, Crawford & Company Ltd –

> Thirty-eight years ago, South Africa's youth took to the streets
> in a fight against an unfair education system. Today, nearly

half of the nation's young people take to the streets to look for jobs.

Mpho Mahanyele

According to the World Economic Forum (WEF) Global Risk 2014 report (World Economic Forum Global Risk Report 2014), South Africa has the third-highest unemployment rate in the world for people between the ages of 15 and 24. The report estimates that more than 50% of young South Africans between 15 and 24 are unemployed, most are women who have never held a job in their lives. Youth unemployment constitutes 73% of the total unemployment in the country. Therefore the ratio of youth-to-adult unemployment is about three (i.e. for every unemployed adult there are three unemployed youth). Only Greece and Spain have higher unemployment in this age range. Gainful employment rates for youth are way below the average of emerging countries (12.5% as compared to 36%). Likewise, the labor market participation rate of young people in South Africa is below average (24.4% as compared to the emerging market average of 42%).

By any conventional standard, unemployment in South Africa, and especially youth unemployment, is extreme, requiring bold initiatives to help resolve (or at least lower) rates. Yet, due to below-average GDP growth rates (as compared to the other BRICS countries), it is particularly challenging to succeed in such endeavors.

South Africa is faced with the complex challenge of the poor economic participation of young people, which inhibits the country's economic development and imposes a larger burden on the state to provide social assistance. The salient features of this stunted participation are high persistent youth unemployment and low entrepreneurial activities among young people.

We need to acknowledge that there are no easy fixes, and that everyone has to be part of the solution. Government, of course, has an urgent responsibility to address unemployment in general and youth unemployment in particular. However, the responsibility extends to businesses and individuals too. Only a collective effort will make a difference.

Given the scale and complexity of South Africa's unemployment problem, and especially of youth unemployment, no single or easy policy solution exists. Stimulating faster growth in general, and employment creation in particular, requires the determined adoption of a broad package of long-term measures to address and resolve both supply-side and demand-side constraints.

Since South Africa became a constitutional democracy in 1994, it has had a long history of institutional, policy, and legislative instruments that have contributed to youth enterprise development and economic participation. South Africa is one of the few countries in Africa that has grappled with, changed, and refined its institutional, policy, and legislative frameworks to address the needs of its youth.

The National Development Plan set forth by the South African government focuses on how political emancipation can be translated into social and economic benefits for all South Africans, but particularly for young people; it targets an ambitious goal of reducing unemployment to as low as 7.7% by 2030. The current level sits at 25.2% (Department of Statistics South Africa 2013 Report).

The National Youth Policy 2009–2014 notes that South Africa's democracy and its social development approach to public policy need to create and enable an environment in which the lives, work, and prosperity of young people are placed at the center of the country's growth and development. Through the National Treasury and Department of Labour, government has introduced youth unemployment policy options for South Africa with the aim of incentivizing entities to employ young people. The Department of Economic Development (EDD) has introduced a short-to-medium term multi-pronged strategy that aims to propose interventions that provide young people with income and opportunities, and encourages community service and engagements around targeted programs to enable entry into the economic mainstream. The National Youth Development Agency (NYDA) has provided the Integrated Youth Development Strategy (IYDS) with the key mandate of implementing the following interventions geared towards the economic participation of young people, namely youth work, national youth services, and education and skills relevant to economic empowerment.

- *The National Skills Development Strategy (NSDS)*, a five-year strategy started in 2011, promotes partnerships between employers, public education institutions, private training providers and the Sector Education and Training Authorities (SETAs), to ensure that cross-sector and inter-sector needs are addressed. The key driving force of this strategy is improving the effectiveness and efficiency of the skills development system. This strategy represents an explicit commitment to encouraging the linking of skills development to career paths, career development, and promoting sustainable employment and in-work progression. The emphasis is particularly on those who do not have relevant technical skills or adequate reading, writing, and numeracy skills to enable them to access employment.
- The *Itukise (Get yourself ready) program*, promoted by the Ministry of Trade and Industry in 2014, presents an opportunity to develop and market the profile of the manufacturing sector to young people by the provision of decent work and increasing opportunities for learning on and off the job.
- The *Youth Enterprise Development Strategy (YEDS)*, a ten-year plan started in 2013, aims at fostering youth economic participation through

entrepreneurship. It focuses on the acceleration and growth of youth-owned and youth-managed enterprises that are capable of contributing to the country's GDP growth rate. The policy instrument offers mentoring and coaching, youth business incubation, business infrastructure support, links to procurement opportunities, youth entrepreneurship awards, youth entrepreneurship promotion and awareness, youth special projects and sector-specific enterprise creation, and the youth entrepreneurship collateral fund. The youth entrepreneurship data system and research program will assist with the monitoring and evaluation of this strategy and will reveal whether targets are being met; it will also suggest recommendations to close gaps.

- *Employment Tax Incentive*: The government has also implemented the Employment Tax Incentive, which subsidizes businesses that hire young (19–29) workers. It is a two-year program and the amount provided to the business in the form of tax reductions depends on the salary of the employee.

Employment creation is key to eradicating poverty and reducing inequality. Accelerated economic growth and investment are required to reduce unemployment. South Africa's economic growth improved dramatically with the transition to democracy and has been reasonably robust and stable throughout the democratic era. The South African economy grew at 3.2 percent per year on average from 1994 to 2012. Despite these positive signals, South Africa still has a long way to go, particularly with regard to education and youth employment. Disproportionately high rates of youth unemployment, and simultaneous shortages of sufficiently qualified workers, clearly illustrate the dilemma.

7.5.7   The Arab Stabilization Plan

– The Arab Stabilization Plan is provided by Farida Kamel, Program Manager at Flat6Labs Cairo –

A number of intra-regional government loans and donations were put in place after the first wave of uprisings in the region. Although a tempting and easy fix to stop the fiscal hemorrhage in politically volatile countries for a while, they are not conducive to more competitive and vibrant regional economies. Indeed, these loans are more often synonymous with deepening problems in an already economically fragmented region with disparate rates of economic growth. This fragmentation is a burden to the region, and most importantly to its youths, as millions of job opportunities are gambled with to provide short-term fiscal relief. By focusing on building public-private regional investment opportunities in key sectors such as infrastructure, healthcare, education, and renewable energy, the region could create significant job opportunities for the region's youths. According to the Arab Stabilization Plan put forth by Majid H. Jafaar, CEO of Crescent Petroleum, the oldest oil & gas company in MENA, a regional fund should be put in place to orchestrate and implement strategic investments to speed-start job creation at impressive and sustainable rates. Should regional governments commit fully to a USD 30 billion regional fund, up to 3,300,000 infrastructure-related jobs in oil-importing countries and up to 1,470,000 jobs in developing oil-exporting countries could be created in the region over a period of five to seven years. The Arab Stabilization Plan is but one of the many local, regional, and international studies and plans that have been put forward in recent years to spur massive job creation in the region. However, politics continues to shape regional relationships in a strikingly ambiguous and complex manner, contributing to the region's failure to create intra-regional economic initiatives targeting job creation and the empowerment of the region's youths.

7.6 Conclusion

If the recent financial crisis and the resulting youth unemployment crisis has taught us one thing, then it is that we need better early warning mechanisms that allow us to anticipate major labor market crises, built on metrics—such as the skills mismatch in the case of the youth unemployment crisis—that indicate whether or not we are moving in the right direction.

Through multi-stakeholder involvement, orchestrated and facilitated by policymakers, we may be able to avoid repeating what we have seen lately. Policymakers have implemented an armamentarium of programs to reduce youth unemployment around the world. However, these measures came very late and it remains unclear whether the burnt soil will become fertile again or whether we indeed have turned today's youth into a Generation Jobless. What is clear already is that all the programs that policymakers have agreed upon need to be executed effectively and efficiently to cut losses. Both short-term operationalization of these policies and long-term sustainable stabilization strategies with adequate monitoring and evaluation mechanisms are needed.

It is clear that the operationalization of these strategies needs to be driven by all stakeholders, including employers, educators, entrepreneurs, international organizations, and youth. Only then do we have a chance to get a hold of the problem. Public policy has the means and the power to lay the foundation for change—but this needs to be done in the form of facilitation and not regulation. Policymakers need to lay aside their own political agendas and devote themselves fully to solving this dilemma—in the best interests of the generations to come. If policymakers accept this challenge and take on this major challenge, I am confident that we can collaboratively tackle youth unemployment and move forward in a constructive manner.

8

More Solutions

The best ideas are born if they grow on the fertile ground of other ideas. It is through the collision of multiple ideas that we find break-through solutions to some of the biggest problems.

Peter Vogel

Chapters 4 to 7 focused on the different core stakeholder groups and associated proven solutions to tackle youth unemployment. The purpose of this chapter is to showcase even more solutions and solution ideas that have been suggested or implemented at a variety of related events I attended or networks I am involved with, including the Global Economic Symposium, the World Economic Forum Global Shapers community, the Skoll World Forum, the World Economic Forum Global Agenda Council on youth unemployment, solutions proposed by youth for youth, among others. In the following I will briefly share these solutions and solution ideas.

8.1 Solutions Proposed at the Global Economic Symposium

The Global Economic Symposium (GES) is a global solution-oriented symposium that brings together multiple stakeholders to develop and discuss research-based and long-term solutions to some of the biggest problems of our time. It is an outstanding event that I truly enjoy attending and contributing to. One of the many topics that have been extensively discussed at recent

GES events is youth unemployment. In the following I present a few selected ideas that are featured in the GES knowledge database (http://www.global-economic-symposium.org/knowledgebase/knowledgebase).[1]

8.1.1 A Dual Approach to Training for Educated and Uneducated Young People (Proposed by Sailesh Iyer)

The current youth unemployment crisis affects both, the well educated and the uneducated young population. Both groups require different solutions. By looking at these two groups separately, policymakers could build more customized programs with greater impact.

- *Educated youth:* The increasing rates of well-educated young people exert pressure on the labor market, because they oftentimes lack employment experience when entering the labor market. One approach to tackle this issue could be compulsory on-the-job training that takes place during education. This scheme would be based on a mandatory intake of trainees/interns based on the company's size, age, geography, and profitability. Such an approach would result in a win-win situation with (1) young people gaining hands-on work experience, (2) educational institutions benefiting from more intensive collaboration with industry and ideally a reduction of the gap between the education system and the labor market, and (3) employers benefiting from the novel skills and capabilities of young and dynamic talents (see for example Chapter 6 on reverse mentoring). These programs could be cross-subsidized by government funding to ensure that all employers can participate.
- *Uneducated youth*: Vocational training programs (to focus on job-specific skills and capabilities) could prove to be optimal for uneducated youth. "Provided by government-funded institutions and non-governmental organizations with local experience, they could be better calibrated to the needs of the participants and local employers." (GES knowledge database.

8.1.2 Concerted Efforts to Tackle Youth Unemployment (Proposed by László Andor)

Because there is no one-size-fits-all solution to youth unemployment and because of the complexity of orchestrating a combination of short-term and long-term solutions, it is critical that efforts are coordinated. First, any effort needs to involve a comprehensive policy strategy with clear guiding principles (e.g., the ILO resolution on youth employment or the Europe 2020 resolution for the EU). Second, while a strategy is nice, it is the implementation that proves whether or not the policy measure works. Hence, any resolution needs to be clearly communicated towards youths and their parents to make sure that they understand when and where they can tap sources of support in case they do not manage the school-to-work transition on their own. Third, policy implementation can only be successful if all actors contribute. That said, governments need to join forces with the private sector, social organizations, labor market services, the education sector, and civil society organizations, among many others.

8.1.3   A System of Graded Job Security (Proposed by Juan Dolado and Colleagues)

Many countries have regulations in place that force employers to pay high severance packages when they lay off permanent employees whereas severance payments are much lower for temporary workers. Consequently, many companies avoid hiring people on permanent contracts, given the high costs they would incur in times of recession. Instead, those companies focus on rotating those employees with fixed-term temporary contracts that have to be renewed. The resulting higher employee turnover rate ends up lowering productivity and causing temporary jobs to become dead-ends rather than stepping-stones. By introducing a system in which temporary work contracts are replaced by contracts under which employment protection gradually increases over time, this extremely detrimental rotation system could be replaced by a more fruitful one, resulting in less of a "sharp edge" between temporary and permanent employment. "To foster the labor mobility of young workers, the system could incorporate the creation of a worker-specific fund. Under this so-called Austrian model, the firms anticipate a small fraction of any redundancy payments by making annual payments into the fund" (Bentolila et al., 2008).

8.1.4   Reducing the Minimum Wage (By Assar Lindbeck)

"In countries with high minimum wage, the employment prospects for young and inexperienced workers would be enhanced if the minimum wage were reduced." This is based on the assumptions (1) that employers would be able to hire more people at a similar total cost and (2) that it is better to have a low-paid job than no job at all.

8.1.5 Promoting Junior-Senior Teams (By Dennis Görlich)

Both young and old workers are faced with higher unemployment rates as compared to mid-age groups. Despite this similarity, the reasons are somewhat different. While young unemployed are confronted with the problem because of lacking work experience, their older counterparts are either too expensive for their jobs or have lost out in terms of productivity. Building complementary junior-senior teams could counteract challenges that both groups face. As outlined in Chapter 6, both mentoring and reverse mentoring programs have an added value given that if younger and older workers team up they can transfer their expertise towards the other party. The on-the-job expertise can be transferred from the older worker to the younger worker. In turn, the younger worker can help the older worker to sustain productivity and to train him or her in certain skills (e.g., IT-related skills or language skills). Such a task-force of one younger and one older person may lead to a lower salary for each of the two individuals as compared to a stand-alone job. However this is always better than being unemployed. Moreover, such programs could kill two birds with one stone and allow policymakers to move away from target-group specific programs to implementing multi-group programs.

8.2 Grassroots Initiatives by the Next Generation

During recent years we have observed a sharp increase in youth-driven solutions to youth unemployment. This illustrates the level of frustration among young people and an attitude of "if you don't help us get out of this dilemma we will have to take care of it ourselves."

This is not that surprising and it makes a lot of sense that we see so many youth-driven initiatives. I would even argue, alongside many others (e.g., Huffington Post, 2014), that youth themselves are the best source of solutions to their own problems, given that they are the ones most affected by the crisis and being most savvy of what the world will look like in 10 to 20 years—the world that they will be shaping with their knowledge, competencies, interests and lifestyles. In the following I would like to depict a few of these youth-driven solutions to youth unemployment, some of which have been implemented already while others are currently being implemented.

8.2.1   Solutions Suggested by the WEF Global Shapers

A few years ago, the World Economic Forum launched a community of leaders under the age of 30 called the Global Shapers. I joined this international group of people three years ago and through this made a large variety of extremely valuable acquaintances. Given that this community is exclusively comprised of members of the generations we are discussing in this book—that is to say the Millennials and the Digital Natives—I felt it would make sense to dedicate a part of this book to this community and to share some of their ideas. In the following I will feature selected projects that have been developed by Shapers.

This global community of thinkers and doers launched an event series called Shape Europe in which Global Shapers from around the world gather for a few days and develop solutions for some of the most pressing issues mankind is currently facing. In Fall 2013, Madrid Global Shapers organized the first Shape Europe event in Madrid (Spain) around the topic of youth unemployment. Here are some short descriptions of ideas that were generated during this event and that are currently being implemented.

8.2.1.1   *Code Nation*

Programming is becoming one of the "golden jobs." Nowadays almost everyone's work relies on software and behind that software there is always a programmer. The employment market has not yet matched the technological boom the world has been seeing in past decades. With a little bit of perspective, we can be sure that the importance of coding will grow exponentially as technology develops at the speed it is doing right now. Therefore, to prepare future generations to meet this gap, this project aims to teach children (ages 9 to 16) to write software the same way they learn math, literature or science, enabling them to acquire the skills that the market requires and, more importantly, that the future job market will require as well. The idea is to prepare young Europeans for an unavoidable trend for technology related activities in which programming skills will be needed. The project will help bring the existing code club partnership into three local communities within the upcoming half-year.

LEARN MORE

Earlier in this book (Chapter 5) I described the case of Coderise, an already functioning initiative from Latin America that teaches kids the art of coding. Many more such programs are needed which is why the Global Shapers initiative comes at the right time.

8.2.1.2   School of Makers

Entrepreneurship is gradually becoming one of the most valued skills the market demands, and it is not just a matter of fashion or trend, it is because companies and employers have realized that entrepreneurship is linked to many other useful skills. To build and promote entrepreneurship at a basic level, this projects aims to foster that entrepreneurial attitude within high school students (ages 15 to 18). To do so, the Global Shapers will engage students in a series of workshops in class. These workshops will be developed and monitored by trained mentors who will help students along the way. At the end of the trimester (or the period of time that the school establishes), all the projects will be presented in public, rated, and all the teams will compete against each other in a final round of judging. That way students will not only learn to create and be part of a project of their interest but they will also develop management and teamwork abilities.

> ### LEARN MORE
>
> Similar programs that are already running (see Chapter 4) include those organized by Junior Achievement. They organize high-school level startup competitions on a national level. One excellently functioning example is Young Enterprise Switzerland (YES).

8.2.1.3   Turning Recruitment Processes into Learning Experiences

Current recruitment processes focus exclusively on selecting the most suitable candidate for a pre-defined job. These processes normally lack any feedback or outcome for the candidates who are not selected so they gradually become demotivated and this may, in some cases, lead job seekers to give up on pursuing a specific position they have aimed for. However, it might be that there are only a few skills missing that the applicant could easily learn (for example through an internship elsewhere or in a self-study setting) and thereafter be a perfect match for this employer. Yet, the majority of employers do not successfully nurture their future talent pool amongst young job market entrants. This project aims to transform the traditional recruitment processes into learning experiences for job seekers while at the same time offering the company a valuable and efficient screening tool. The project will help companies to organize contests and business games in which job seekers will face real-life challenges so that the recruiting process turns into a training program. Candidates will test their skills in a practical manner enabling employers to hire the most suitable candidate. The candidates who are not finally hired will at least have acquired some experience and will be better prepared for their next recruiting process. At the end of the process, the company will give all candidates a certificate to recognize the training.

8.2.1.4   Pay it Forward—Peer-to-Peer Career Support

This project aims to generate commitment within society. We live in a highly connected world and we should benefit from that to help one another, especially in terms of employment. The idea is to create an online platform where each user can ask for help while helping others at the same time, leading to a snowball effect based on a "pay it forward" strategy (possibly linked to some "virtual credits" that each user receives for helping someone—credit that he or she can then spend on seeking someone else's advice). A simple example to illustrate this project is the following: I'm a translator looking for a job at the UN but I'm not familiar with the UN's internal hiring process. Another user has worked for the UN and explains to me how the hiring process goes and gives me some tips. At the same time, I help another user who is looking for someone to translate his CV. This way, everyone gives and gets something in return using the means within their reach and creating value and job opportunities. There is always something you can give that others will value and find helpful.

8.2.1.5   What Do YOU Want to Do with Your Life?

Up until a few years ago, young people in Western countries were seen as a generation of self-focused individuals who have nothing to worry about and sit around being comfortable at their parent's home. However, recent years have proven that this view was wrong. Today's youth grew up at the transition from an analogue to a digital world, the rise of a world that fears terrorism, in a world that has experienced one of the greatest economic crises in history of mankind, a world where popular rebellions pop up almost on a daily basis, a world where political, economic, and educational systems are being questioned, and a world where the individual's privacy is being replaced by mass surveillance. In fact, no previous generation has experienced such a great amount of change in such a short period of time, as has today's youth.

As a consequence, the world also needs to be shaped by today's youth and not exclusively by previous generations. The wisdom of those previous generations is partly outdated whereas today's youth can bring extraordinarily valuable things to the table.

Given that governments, universities and other agents are not able to successfully lead this change in the short term, this initiative aims to encourage youth to define their identity and take the lead; to be passionate about their ideas; to have strong and informed opinions; to be optimists in spite of it all; to take on responsibility; to be doers instead of talkers; to attempt impossible things and to achieve them. Like John F. Kennedy said: "We have the power to make this the best generation of mankind in the history of the world … or to make it the last one."

To achieve this goal, Global Shapers in Spain have launched the project "What do YOU want to do with your life?" This project collects and shares the stories of as many young people from Spain as possible and, through in-depth interview-based research, comes up with crowdsourced solutions and recommendations as to how the state of youth can be improved. Similar to the US-based ten-year old Road Trip Nation project, a team of young individuals will travel the country interviewing Spanish youth to build a database of collective wisdom from which these recommendations can be deduced. Based on the information in the database, key stakeholders will be approached to provide strategic recommendations for novel policy instruments and initiatives, maybe even setting up a venture with the mission to deploy these solutions.

LEARN MORE

Take an in-depth view on the generational characteristics and differences between current and previous generations (see Chapter 2).

8.2.1.6 Leadcap

According to McKinsey (2013), only one-third of employers think that current graduates are ready for employment with the skill gap being the strongest driver of youth unemployment. Leadcap provides a platform that enables networking between young people and employers in India, and provides intensive future defining opportunities that prepare them for fast track careers. The flagship program "CEO Shadowing" offers students the possibility to spend quality time with a CEO. The goal is to inspire them to pursue bigger goals, thereby enabling them to become future role models themselves.

In 2012, the government of Karnataka piloted the fellowship program with 1,000 students chosen from eight higher education institutions. Almost one-third of these students were able to find employment (compared to current employability of merely 10 percent) and another 50% enrolled for continuing education. The program was recently included into the Karnataka budget session of 2013–2014 to improve the employability of 20,000 students by 2015. This program was chosen by the Global Agenda Council 2012 in Dubai as one of the most important initiatives in youth empowerment. The program is currently being expanded to other geographic locations.

In order to replicate the success of Leadcap, three things are recommended. First, true skill development can only occur if the industry drives the initiative with students. Second, to be truly transformational, adult learning should be based on Andragogy—self-exploratory, problem-centered learning, with student's active involvement. Third, skill building is not a one-off, but a continuous process. Hence, even after program completion, students should be made part of an alumni network and career management center, which updates them with employment opportunities and skill enhancement tools and lessons.

This program is easily replicable and expandable to other countries as the model itself is based on the public-private partnership. For implementing this model in Africa or anywhere else, essential partnerships between educators, government, and employers need to be established. Once these partnerships are formalized, the programs can be delivered in three simple steps—fellowships, CEO shadowing, and self-actualization teams.

8.2.2   More Nextgen Solutions

8.2.2.1   *Edupass: Gateway to International Opportunities*

– This section is provided by Luis David Sena, Founder –

> Bridging the unemployment gap by connecting and placing
> students with job opportunities and educational resources.
> *Luis David Sena, Founder Edupass*

Despite its growth in the past ten years, the Dominican Republic faces several obstacles to achieving better opportunities for its young citizens. Among these obstacles, youth unemployment is one of the most problematic, having peaked at over 30% (IMF Statistics). Moreover, precarious workplace conditions and low salaries threaten the development of the young population. In particular, there is a lack of decent work opportunities for youth.

Edupass, founded in 2014, empowers and supports Dominican students to pursue international education and training programs as well as internships in order to become globally competitive. Edupass helps them select the right high-quality academic programs, offers financial support, operates a talent network of outstanding young people, serves as change agents when it comes to designing new policies for higher education and the labor market, contributes to the modernization of the higher education sector in the country, and places students in internships and short-term programs that can bridge the unemployment gap through the Youth Employment Practical Training (YEPT) program that is tailored to small- and medium-sized enterprises (SMEs).

The YEPT program offers work permits of up to 12-month duration to work in temporary employment with a specified company to gain necessary experience as a stepping-stone to permanent employment. The YEPT addresses three issues that lead to youth unemployment:

- Skills mismatch: The skills mismatch is one of the biggest problems in the youth unemployment crisis. Both employers and young people are unhappy with the overly formal and theoretical education system that leaves students feeling ill prepared and lacking the necessary practical skills for the labor market. According to the World Youth Report 2011, "many young people … questioned the quality of education they and their peers receive: whether or not it is relevant to available jobs [and] how their knowledge and skills will serve them in the long-term" (United Nations, 2011). The YEPT offers students hands-on practical experience that will strengthen their skills.
- Eliminate the stigma of "no experience, no job": Many young job applicants are often discouraged to search and even apply for jobs because they are afraid the "no experience" component of their resume would make employers immediately discard their application. For companies, hiring a student without practical experience represents a risk because the newly hired employee may not be able to perform his or her duties adequately. The YEPT offers participants at least one full year of professional experience during which students will develop the necessary skills for that specific job or industry which allows prospective future employers to better assess their abilities.
- Incentivize companies to create jobs for youth: The YEPT incentivizes the creation of youth-specific jobs by partnering with employers, both public and private. Similar to apprenticeship systems in Germany, Austria, and Switzerland, companies can train young people on the job and tailor-educate them on specific tasks they need to handle. Ultimately, the companies can help in building a relevant pool of motivated future talents.

For the YEPT to be implemented successfully, government, private sector and youth must be united as a strong voice to advocate and promote the inclusion of youth as a key player to solve issues that affect youth the most. "I believe that strong public-private partnerships are needed for effective solutions' success. In particular, I would argue that the collaboration of the private sector is a key pillar for the provision of opportunities to youth, especially, to those that went to college" (Luis Sena).

strong public-private partnerships are needed for effective solutions

8.2.2.2 Leaders of Tomorrow: Bringing Leadership Skills Programs into School

– This section is provided by Mohammad Nibras, Initiator –

Despite the grand optimism inspired by India's economic growth the alarming numbers of youth unemployment (also underemployment and informality) are a reminder of how much ground the country has yet to cover. The country's story of growth still skips a beat on very fundamental questions of food and education. Nevertheless, India is a reservoir of huge potential, particularly with regards to youths, of which there are many in the country.

The Leaders of Tomorrow (LOT) initiative links with schools and colleges to create a leadership curriculum that forms part of their daily routines, focusing on leadership as a practice rather than a theory. LOT is a 12-month youth empowerment and leadership program aimed at bringing world-class education and life skills to children from marginalized communities in India. It combines virtual mentoring (global mentors) with on-site training (local trainers). As part of the program students participate in internships at local employers.

Despite being a novel initiative (2014), LOT has already received great national and international recognition. In a first pilot project, LOT partnered with local employers in remote areas in South India, offering 150 students the opportunity to gain relevant leadership experience before entering the job market by the end of 2015. The project's short-term goal is to develop at least 10,000 young leaders by implementing hubs all across India.

LOT is a low-cost youth empowerment model with the goal of building a bootstrapped and globally scalable model. To scale LOT and replicate new projects elsewhere, there are two critical components: (1) a team of local trainers and volunteers and international advisors; and (2) a hub (e.g., a local school or civic organization) where trainings take place and which needs to offer space and adequate IT infrastructure to operate the program. The collaborative effort between educational institutes, civic organizations, public policy, and corporate entities is essential in solving the youth unemployment (and underemployment) crisis. However, the implementation of such a multi-stakeholder solution requires a well-coordinated and conscious effort and it cannot be expected to happen overnight.

8.2.2.3 enke: Youth Development South Africa

– This section is provided by Pip Wheaton, CEO and co-founder of enke –

> enke gives the youth of our country a platform to be change agents in their own communities. They encourage the youth

to be entrepreneurially minded, finding solutions to problems and becoming active citizens in our country.

Pip Wheaton

The South African education system is not equipping young people with the skills and experiences to overcome challenges and create their own opportunities. However, contrary to the general narrative about youth in South Africa, enke, a South African youth development organization, sees a generation that is eager to change the world. The organization inspires, trains, and supports young people to take action on the most pressing social issues in their local communities. Through the programs, young people develop skills that lead to future employment success—practical skills like project design and management, and social and emotional skills like resilience, confidence, social awareness, and problem solving ability.

Two programs are run by enke: the Trailblazer Program for high school learners, and the Ignition Program for students and young professionals. Both programs develop leadership, giving young people the opportunity to lead meaningful social change in their communities.

Since 2009 enke has worked with over 1,250 young people; people such as Meghan who is running a social enterprise in Khayelitsha, training young photojournalists; like Katleho who was recognized by the *Mail & Guardian*'s Top 200 Young South Africans for reducing risk-taking behavior amongst primary school learners in QwaQwa; like Sky who raised ZAR 14,000 for his rural Limpopo school.

In January 2014, enke followed up with 35% of their alumni to study the correlation between project completion and development of four non-cognitive competencies (otherwise known as social and emotional skills): grit, growth mindset, self-efficacy, and social awareness. They found a positive trend linking higher levels of grit and growth mindset in alumni who had run projects during their involvement with enke. When looking at "life destination," they found that 91% of those surveyed are in employment, education or training, compared to a national average of 69%. In addition, 16.5% of alumni had started a business or social venture beyond their involvement with enke.

Of course there are limitations to these insights; for example a potential selection bias of program participants a well as the lack of a control group. The majority of learners who apply for enke will have a level of proactivity that perhaps their peers do not have. Yet, the participants reflect the socio-economic diversity of South Africa with 80–85% coming from under-resourced schools. Nonetheless, these first findings are promising and indicative that training is not enough and that young people need to apply their knowledge in the real world.

8.2.2.4   *Spark Inside: Life Coaching for the Hardest-to-Employ Youth*

– This section is provided by Baillie Aaron, Executive Director of Spark Inside –

> Unemployment is not exclusively an economic problem but also the result of cultural and social factors, particularly in deprived communities where barriers to employment are greater and where there is a deep pessimism over job prospects.
>
> *Baillie Aaron*

Youth unemployment is often greatest in disadvantaged areas with a high rate of broken families, drug use, and criminal records. Within these communities, there are fewer legitimate employment opportunities, as well as reduced access to knowledge and skills relevant to work. Young people from disadvantaged backgrounds often lack clarity on what they want to do. Some feel unmotivated to apply for jobs; others are limited by low self-confidence from repeated rejection. A minority of them decides to pursue work in the underground economy. These issues tend to reinforce each other, leading to increased difficulties for young people from disadvantaged backgrounds in securing legitimate employment.

Addressing the behavioral causes of youth unemployment is more complex than simply creating more jobs, encouraging entrepreneurship or providing training opportunities. It requires the use of professional techniques to support a change in attitude for young people, such that they are motivated to want to pursue work, and understand that employment can be meaningful and fulfilling. Specialized support for young people from the most highly disadvantaged backgrounds maximizes the impact of employability programs.

The UK charity Spark Inside tackles the cultural and social causes of unemployment among the hardest-to-employ young people through professional life coaching. Life coaching supports these young people to think and take action on their own by enhancing strengths, rather than by "fixing" problems. Coaches do not mentor, advise, or offer treatment; instead, they help clients devise their own solutions to problems by asking powerful questions that engage the young people in guided self-reflection around values, motivations, and goals, and that encourage them to identify passions for specific skills, jobs, or activities that they would be interested in pursuing as a career. In this way, Spark Inside empowers 15 to 25 year-olds involved in the criminal justice system to proactively pursue fulfilling education, employment, or training opportunities.

In 2013, Spark Inside piloted its one-to-one, through-the-gates coaching program with eight teenage boys nearing release from young offenders institutions Feltham and Cookham Wood. An independent evaluation of the pilot, conducted by the University of Cambridge's Institute of Criminology, shows early signs of promise for coaching as a rehabilitative intervention: one year after the boys had been released from prison, all who completed the coaching program were actively pursuing or engaged in education, employment or training. This is in line with other studies that attest to the effectiveness of coaching in supporting vulnerable young people into better life outcomes — increased goal attainment, enhanced resilience, ameliorated depression and stress, and increased well-being (USC, 2011; Foyer Health Programme, 2013).

Building on the success of its first program with teenagers in prison, Spark Inside is expanding its coaching services to include bespoke programs for young men and women who are in prison, serving probation sanctions, or otherwise considered to be at high risk of offending.

8.2.2.5   Socionext: Entrepreneurship Education with Social Impact

– This section is provided by Ian Choo, Chief coach and facilitator on the pilot program in Copenhagen Business School in 2013 –

The Socionext program consists of the Social Entrepreneurship and Social Responsibility Challenge—an innovative and practical skills development course for final-year university students. Students complete their projects within four months of initiation, which consists of designing and implementing a campaign or project that generates actual income. All income generated goes towards scholarships for talented South African students from disadvantaged communities, who might otherwise not get a chance to study (local partners are Studietrust and The Tertiary School in Business Administration (TSiBA)).

By integrating entrepreneurial projects into the academic curriculum, and focusing on the personal development of students, Socionext helps to create a solid foundation of practical skills and self-awareness for the successful development of social impact projects.

The course has run successfully since 2010 at the University of Amsterdam, the Copenhagen Business School, TSiBA, and The University of Cape Town. The programs increase employability, helping disadvantaged communities and young talents in South Africa, and offering the possibility for students to create projects with real impact.

• Employability: To date, nearly 300 students have participated in Socionext programs, many of them going on to great careers in industry and/or further education. Private sector sponsors have taken a particular interest in the participants as they have noticed that the mindset and skills acquired during the program are of great value.

• Helping disadvantaged communities: In the first years Socionext classroom projects generated enough income to fund two scholarships that have been awarded to students through partners in South Africa. These partners carefully select the young scholars for whom this scholarship serves as a springboard to a great career.

• Creating projects with real impact: Students going through the Socionext course are required not just to acquire theories but also to actually implement and generate revenue within a 14-week period, so the results for the communities in which the program operates are visible and immediate. An overview of the projects can be found on the Socionext website.

The actual execution of practice-focused, mentor-enabled, facilitated courses is (by design) much more resource-intensive for our educational partners; nevertheless, the results have been motivating and meaningful. On an ongoing basis, the transformative power that young people possess can be humbling when they are able to harness the best of their abilities toward something greater than themselves, if only we allow them to.

In building the community, the ethos of the Socionext course and its use of mentors is a great platform to let real life into the classroom. The ambitious requirement to generate actual revenue in a limited time frame has been noted to be a key accelerator in enabling active learning—as the feedback from the marketplace is real and often quite immediate.

8.2.2.6 *Ze-Ze: Community Approach for Incubating Social Ventures*

– This section is provided by Narkis Alon, Co-founder of Ze-Ze –

> We engage youth to utilize and develop their skills for creating jobs for communities in need. By doing this, they create job opportunities for themselves.
>
> *Narkis Alon*

Ze-Ze is a youth-driven social organization that promotes the creation of community social enterprises. All profits are reinvested into the social enterprise or used to launch other social enterprises. The core activities of Ze-Ze are the organization of events (e.g., exhibition of art pieces created by blind artists), the operation of an orchestra comprised of street musicians, the operation of a night bar that integrates social causes in its content and hosts social entrepreneurs during the day, and the operation of our printing factory Zot-Zot.

Ze-Ze tackles youth unemployment in that the majority of employees and community members are young people, all benefiting from either paid employment or volunteering opportunities in one of the social ventures and projects. Many of these volunteering positions are then converted into paid employment as soon as the social venture is financially self-sustaining. Moreover, besides directly employing young people in all the projects Ze-Ze encourages young people to initiate social projects and utilize their skills for creating jobs.

Launched in 2011, Ze-Ze's social ventures collectively employ 60 people (more than half being young people) and engage over 400 volunteers (mostly young people). These people get to work in an enterprise that has a social mission and that offers them the opportunity to initiate their own project within the framework of Ze-Ze. The volunteers benefit because they gain professional experience, connections and entrepreneurial inspiration.

What other organizations can learn from Ze-Ze is the combination of impact, fun, self-fulfillment, and the creation of financially sustainable businesses. Young people want to advance in their careers while having fun. By offering them a space where they can develop themselves, learn, have fun, and do meaningful work, they will join the cause without asking for any (or a high) salary. Over time, they will increase their employability and each of the projects will become financially sustainable so they can be hired on a full-time basis.

8.3 Even More Ideas

8.3.1 Tradability of Tasks and the Global Distribution of Jobs

– This section is provided by Dr. Dennis Görlich, Kiel Institute for the World Economy –

> Jobs are essentially bundles of separate tasks. Some of these tasks are tradable in the sense that their output can be delivered via the Internet. Online platforms matching job seekers and employers on such tasks could be a mechanism to alleviate youth unemployment in the short run, while at the same time limiting brain drain caused by potential out-migration.
>
> *Dennis Görlich, Kiel Institute for the World Economy*

Statisticians typically classify occupations by means of an elaborated coding system, for example the International Standard Classification of Occupations (ISCO). Yet, looking inside these occupations, we can see that the tasks carried out by workers in their individual jobs can vary considerably. Table 8.1

shows—based on the examples of teachers and IT experts—the share of workers performing a particular task. Teachers uniformly carry out "teaching, training," "collecting data, documenting," and "consulting, advising," forming the characterizing set of primary works tasks of a teacher. A large fraction also combines these tasks with other tasks, for example organizing and coordinating tasks (87%). Yet, all the other tasks also belong to the task bundles of at least some teachers in the sample. Doing the same exercise for IT experts, we find that "collecting data and documenting" and "consulting and advising" are the characterizing primary work tasks of IT experts. Yet, a large fraction also reports carrying out programming, measuring and testing, or research and engineering tasks. These two examples illustrate that, apart from some occupation-specific core tasks, jobs are rather individual bundles of tasks.

In principle, it should be possible to divide single tasks between different workers, even if significant transaction costs for communication and coordination may be incurred and, in some cases, productivity may decline if complementary tasks are separated. Some of the work tasks may in fact be inseparable from the job, in the sense that they have to be carried out at the location of delivery: think of nursing, treating, and healing others. There are a number of tasks, however, that may be separable from the job's geographic location because they are tradable via the internet without any degradation in quality; think of programming or marketing and PR tasks (e.g., social media representative). A task can be considered tradable if it (1) requires little face-to-face contact with customers or colleagues, or if it requires little proximity to the object being processed, (2) requires intensive use of computers, (3) can be codified (i.e. entails clearly defined work processes), and (4) is based on a routine (i.e. entails repeating work steps).

Using survey data, it is almost impossible to devise whether a specific task is tradable because this would require knowledge about the context in which a task is carried out. Deciding on the necessity of face-to-face contact is therefore always subjective. Moreover, evolving technologies may render non-tradable tasks tradable. Despite such limitations, it is possible to reveal tendencies. Evaluating the tasks listed in Table 8.1: on the four tradability criteria mentioned above, it turns out that collecting data and documenting; organizing, planning and coordinating; marketing, PR and advertising; research and engineering; and programming are the most tradable tasks.

8.3.1.1   *How Can Tradable Tasks Help in Tackling Youth Unemployment?*

At first thought, it appears that even more jobs are at risk because tradable tasks may be sent offshore. Yet, being skilled in tradable tasks may also offer

TABLE 8.1   The share of workers performing each task in two exemplary occupations (Görlich, Kiel Institute for the World Economy)

Description of task	Teachers		IT Experts	
	Share	Freq.	Share	Freq.
Installing, constructing, manufacturing	0.078	20	0.214	136
Measuring, testing, quality control	0.824	210	0.785	499
Operating, monitoring machines/processes	0.176	45	0.619	394
Repairing, reconstructing	0.369	94	0.561	357
Selling, buying	0.490	125	0.426	271
Transporting, packing, shipping	0.310	79	0.278	177
Marketing, PR, advertising	0.635	162	0.376	239
Organizing, planning, coordinating	0.875	223	0.789	502
Research, engineering	0.710	181	0.818	520
Teaching, training other	1.000	255	0.601	382
Collecting data, documenting	1.000	255	0.978	622
Consulting, advising, informing	0.992	253	0.954	607
Serving, accommodating, cooking	0.184	47	0.047	30
Nursing, treating, healing others	0.459	117	0.101	64
Securing, guarding	0.545	139	0.291	185
Cleaning, recycling	0.376	96	0.131	83
Programing	0.071	18	0.769	489
Number of observations	255		636	

an opportunity if the right technologies are in place. There are numerous online platforms, which are matching freelancers and employers, for example oDesk.com or Amazon's Mechanical Turk. Job seekers—or rather "task seekers" as they should be called in this context—can sign up to the website listing their skills and expertise. Similarly, employers can sign up, posting descriptions of tasks they need to get done. Once a match is made, the resulting job output can be delivered to the client online. Both freelancer and employer will have the chance to rate each other after completing the task.

Given that some European countries (e.g., Germany) are facing skill shortages, while others (e.g., Spain or Greece), are facing high youth unemployment rates, online platforms may do a modest but good job in getting young people from these places to work, at least in the short run. This is true especially for young workers who are very adept with computers, have little work experience, and receive low unemployment benefits. Offering their skills on online platforms may allow them to earn a small wage, obtain documented work experience, and prevent skills obsolescence, while at the same time they continue to contribute to their own country's economy and offer their skills to the local labor market (at least in the mid-term if not immediately) and thereby limit brain drain, one of the most daunting factors for many European economies. Apart from this, there may be knowledge transfer, which is associated with innovation and growth.

8.3.1.2   Some Limitations of This Solution

First and foremost, these assignments are not real jobs and the approach is thus unfit to offer any viable long-term prospects to young people, even though a positive track record may allow the job seeker to secure more and better paying assignments. Yet, it is unlikely that the assignments turn out to be stepping-stones to lasting employment relationships on a large scale. Besides this, trade unions fear that employers may increasingly rely on these platforms, and thereby reduce employment in regular jobs. They also warn not to become too dependent on an employer who has some additional power by rating workers publicly. Moreover, a technological solution such as online platforms for trading tasks can of course only cover a limited range of tasks and, hence, only a limited range of jobs. There is hardly any job that is entirely tradable since most jobs also involve some face-to-face contact to customers or colleagues. Migration, therefore, is an inevitable strategy in the majority of cases, as long as local labor demand is weak.

8.3.2   Creating Opportunities for Youth in a Microglobal Age

– This section is provided by Simón Levy-Dabbah, author of *The Microglobal Age* –

We are living in an era in which the enormous amount of information and experiences available makes us want to live at a frenetic pace, as we try to absorb everything and decide what is best for us. This amazing array of options has also created a new generation of human beings who are lost within this ocean of data and will not, or cannot, take a clear direction in their lives. Some of our younger kin have reached a point at which they refuse to follow the traditional path chosen by their predecessors; that of school, higher education, and work. Yet, in this refusal, they have also lost their own identity and are now moving without any objective, thus walking into a downward spiral of negativity and lack of feasible opportunities.

These younger generations are part of a huge transition, a moment of profound change in human history, where ideas and emotions are changing completely all of our rules of coexistence in society, but where we have also lost the capacity to analyze and understanding our surroundings. So much wealth of knowledge, so readily available, has created a new kind of person, one that is moved by its senses and emotions; but it has also created scores of people who are overwhelmed by the power this represents. The lack of opportunities for this new breed within traditional enterprises has turned many away, leaving them without a real option within established corporations. Even more, the recent economic crisis has reduced dramatically the opportunities for our younger generations, making them the victims of our past and present economic decisions.

Yet, within all this turmoil and the apparently negative panorama, some of these folks have been pushing forward looking for a different way to fit into the economic model. We are looking at a continuous stream of persons trying to enter a thinning job market, people who need opportunities, who have desires and goals that they can't achieve where the older workforce did. So they create, they develop their own businesses, small units that provide them with work and which satisfy their expectations, becoming micro-entrepreneurs, giving life to their own new system. This is now a trend, where more and more young people take the road towards a freelance model, one that fits with the times in which they are immersed.

This can also be an opportunity to innovate and to create a whole new economic system, one in which creativity and independence become the reigning values for businesses. The huge challenge for the older folks, who have desensitized themselves to these changing environments and especially to the needs of young people, is to change their mindset and gear themselves towards a new paradigm, one in which traditional enterprises, as well as purchase and sales operations, are no longer the rule. This is now an era of microcompany networks providing experiences that solve a need permanently. Leaders of industry and politics need to encourage those young people who now seem lost into this new paradigm and excite them with future possibilities under a new economic model. It is our responsibility to evolve and incorporate the next generations into a positive cycle, showing them that the massive amounts of information and knowledge available to them can work in their favor.

This is the great challenge we face as humankind: we need to adapt to the new circumstances, face the changes, and provide a solution for the young, one in which they feel included and can exploit the full potential of their capacities through a new model; a model in which timing, value solutions that solve needs, open exchange of experiences, and affinities will rule business—a new microglobal age.

8.3.3   Ideas from the Skoll World Forum

- Governments as catalysts for entrepreneurship: Governments can play a central role in fostering youth entrepreneurship.[2] Not by directly investing in young people's startups but instead by serving as a catalyst to entrepreneurship by purposefully purchasing from startups created by young individuals.

Moreover, governments could incentivize larger companies to purchase from startups that have been created by young people. Again, the government would serve as a catalyst to help young companies get off the ground.

- Networks of community services: Given that today's youth has a strong global mindset with a desire to improve the state of the world, governments alongside other key stakeholders could build networks of community services that utilize young unemployed individuals, and so generating a win-win solution for both the youth and society. Young people who have previously been unemployed get access to work and the communities get things done that would otherwise remain untouched for months or years.

8.3.4   Ideas from the WEF Global Agenda Council

In 2012, the World Economic Forum created a Global Agenda Council (GAC) that seeks to develop and promote bold and radically new ideas to tackle youth unemployment.[3] The council has committed to advance solutions on three dimensions: (1) innovation that is scalable, (2) implementation that takes place on a national level and (3) inspiration through global campaigns. These are some of the initiatives.

- TEN Youth Mentoring and Apprenticeship Program: Apprenticeship systems that are being combined with mentoring programs have proven to be highly effective at helping young people entering the world of work. For that purpose, GAC has developed a program called the Ten Youth Mentoring and Apprenticeship Program, which encourages companies to invest in "M&A" (Mentoring and Apprenticeship) support for at least ten first-time hires.
- National youth employment strategies: To build effective labor market policies, it is critical that countries develop strategies that allow for a nationally synchronized and harmonized implementation of programs based on a shared vision as well as clear objectives and metrics. The Global Agenda Council on Youth Unemployment has committed itself to developing national youth employment strategies in a variety of countries, starting off with Cambodia and several countries in Africa.
- EYE opener—a global campaign: It is of critical importance that decision-makers take coordinated, comprehensive and inspired steps to tackling youth unemployment. To ensure that all relevant stakeholders are on the same page, a campaign is needed to disseminate the strategies systematically. For this purpose, the Global Agenda Council has launched the Eye on Youth Employment campaign, which will bring policy recommendations and proven solutions to the attention of business, government, and civil society leaders, suggesting coordinated implementation to generate the biggest possible impact.

9

Building Multi-Stakeholder Solutions for Youth Unemployment

Coming together is a beginning; keeping together is progress; working together is success.

Henry Ford

Youth unemployment does not have to end in a catastrophe. But if we want to avoid a Generation Jobless we need to act quickly and implement both short-term solutions for today's youth and long-term solutions to avoid repeating what we are seeing today. In a recent contribution I made for the 2014 Global Economic Symposium (GES), I suggested that we have to tackle the world's most pressing issues with a multi-stakeholder approach.

> The world we live in is becoming increasingly complex and interdependent. Traditional institutions are having difficulties keeping up with the pace of change that we are facing and as a consequence solving global problems. In order to solve the world's most pressing issues, we need to implement multi-stakeholder solutions that span across sectors, geographies, philosophies, languages, races, religions and all other potentially imaginable barriers. (Vogel, 2014)

This is exactly the approach I took in the second part of this book with the overall ambition to offer transparent and well-reflected insights into the phenomenon of youth unemployment and to showcase "ready-to-implement" and proven solutions from various stakeholders around the world. In doing so this book hopefully serves as guidance for policymakers, educators, entrepreneurs, parents, employers, international organizations, and, of course, for young people to get active and start doing something about youth unemployment. It should serve as a call to action because only those who get active can actually achieve something. I would like to conclude with a few recommendations for implementing multi-stakeholder solutions (MSS).

9.1   Six Guidelines for Building Multi-Stakeholder Solutions

9.1.1   Guideline #1: Define the Problem You Are Trying to Solve and Clearly Articulate Your Solution

The problem that you (and I) are trying to solve in this context appears obvious at first: High rates of youth unemployment around the world. However, as discussed in Chapter 1, the problem itself is composed of a variety of factors that collectively drive youth unemployment, including both supply- and demand-side factors as well as a mismatch between both.

Consequently, the problem of youth unemployment can be sub-divided into an array of smaller problems all of which require the action and interaction of different stakeholders. The mismatch between the education system and the labor market, for example, requires the action of educators (to change the curriculum), employers (to get involved in the classroom to ensure the curriculum is relevant to the world of work), public policy (to facilitate the process of curriculum re-design) and youth itself (they need to participate and benefit from the new programs). As another example, the overall lack of youth-compatible jobs (low aggregate demand) requires the combined efforts of a different set of stakeholders—primarily policymakers and employers.

The array of different sub-problems related to youth unemployment makes it difficult, if not impossible, to clearly and concisely articulate the problem we are trying to solve—I had a hard time outlining it in its full complexity within the 80,000 words of this book.

Nonetheless, it is of utmost importance not to get lost in words and get to action quickly. This is everything but a trivial challenge given the complexity and inter-relatedness of both the origins of and the solutions to youth unemployment. As Einstein said: "We can't solve problems by using the same kind of thinking we used when we created them." It requires bold action and entrepreneurial forward thinking to collaboratively bring more young people into the labor market. It is likely that the most successful ideas will emerge from youth itself.

9.1.2 Guideline #2: Determine Your Success Metrics to Ensure that You're Doing It Right

Once you have clearly articulated the problem that you are trying to address and the specific solutions you propose, you should define the Key Performance Indicators (KPIs) based on which you will track the performance of your solutions. Just like there is no one-size-fits-all solution to youth unemployment there is also no one-size-fits-all KPI.

Depending on the problem you're trying to solve, the KPIs will vary considerably. Some relevant ones in the context of youth unemployment include the number jobs created for young people, reduction of youth unemployment, reduction of the NEET rate, reduction of the youth-to-adult unemployment ratio, ensuring that a certain percentage of one's company is composed of young workers, or an increase in the number of young people starting their own companies upon graduation.

The most suitable KPI also depends on the stakeholders and those to whom they need to report. All case studies described in this book indicated their KPIs, offering you deep insights into the feasibility and success of each solution.

9.1.3 Guideline #3: Define the Relevant Stakeholders that Need to Be Involved

For it to be a MSS, your solution needs to involve at least two stakeholder groups. Each of these stakeholders either affects or is affected by the solution to the problem you are trying to solve. Figure 9.1 illustrates the most important stakeholders in the fight against youth unemployment, namely policymakers, NGOs/NPOs, employers, entrepreneurs, educators, parents and family as well as young people themselves.

As illustrated previously, the mismatch between the education system and the labor market asks for a coordinated approach between at least educators, employers, public policy, and youth, whereby generational change and modified attitudes towards the labor market require action from parents' and from youths as well as the labor market's reaction.

9.1.4 Guideline #4: Involve all the Relevant Stakeholders from the Beginning

Once you know who the most relevant stakeholders for your solution are, it is important that you bring all of them to the table early on. This will increase the odds that your solution will be relevant to all of them. By openly

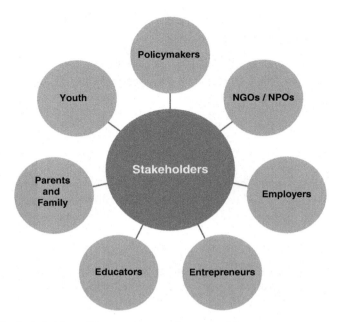

FIG 9.1   Stakeholders of the youth unemployment crisis

discussing needs, constraints, resources, capabilities, and KPIs for each of the different stakeholder groups, the most effective strategy can be identified and implemented.

9.1.5   Guideline #5: Coordination and Supervision, not Regulation

Depending on the type of solution, the MSS will require the interplay between two or more of these stakeholder groups, asking for a varying degree of coordination and supervision. To ensure the successful implementation of an MSS you need to have one central coordinating unit (person or organization). This unit will need to ensure that all involved stakeholders fulfill their promises, that frequent meet-ups are held and assessments made and that the group is working in the right direction. Such a multi-stakeholder coordinating unit must act as a facilitator rather than a regulator.

9.1.6   Guideline #6: Focus on the Heroes and Share the Learnings

Just like I am doing in this book, it is important to showcase best practice examples of how organizations, individuals, or governmental bodies have taken bold action to solve the youth unemployment crisis. By offering a platform to share their successes, challenges, and failures we can ensure that more people are incentivized to get active themselves and launch similar or even better solutions. To have a scalable impact beyond the boundaries of one's own organization it is important that one shares key insights and learnings with other similar organizations.

9.2 Conclusion

To have a large and lasting impact in the fight against youth unemployment, we must jump over our own shadows and start collaborating, sharing knowledge and best practices. This is not the time for egocentrism but one for a more balanced stance including altruism and collectivism—in the interest of our children. We must engage in an open dialogue to come up with and share the most suitable solutions to help today's and tomorrow's youth. We must act in a collaborative manner if we want to tackle youth unemployment. We must leverage the wisdom of the crowd and include as many individuals in the dialogue as possible. We must be ready to help others implementing similar solutions.

Ultimately, we must take full responsibility for what is happening now and drive forward solutions as effectively and efficiently as possible to make sure that the world of tomorrow, the world we are leaving to our children, remains a pleasant place to live in. As a widely used Native American saying goes: We do not inherit the Earth from our Ancestors, we borrow it from our Children.

Afterword

"Books are good enough in their own way, but they are a mighty bloodless substitute for living"

Robert Louis Stevenson

Thank you very much for reading my book "Generation Jobless?" You had to invest both time and money to read it and I hope that, in return, you have gained some valuable insights into how we can all make a difference in solving youth unemployment around the world.

I would be most delighted to meet you someday and see how you have worked with the book, whether you have implemented projects yourself, consulted policymakers, educators, or businesses based on the case studies discussed in this book, whether it has helped you raise your own children in a 21st century style to prepare them for the labor market of the future or whether you simply read it to get a better understanding of the youth unemployment crisis and the related causes and effects. Please tell me. I would love to hear from you.

In any case, I would be most delighted to see that my book has been of value to you and your team and that my time preparing the book, the contributors' time preparing their cases and chapters, your time and your money to buy and read the book were all well spent.

Please make sure to frequently visit www.generationjobless.eu because I will be uploading news, new case studies and projects from around the world. Also, if you are aware of a project that creatively tackles youth unemployment that I did not feature in this book, please reach out to me or submit it on the website.

Please also do not forget to share this book with your network as we can only achieve our goal if we collaboratively tackle youth unemployment.

Twitter: *"Can we avoid a #generationjobless? I just joined @pevogel's #movement to tackle #youthunemployment: www.generationjobless.eu."*

- **Facebook:** I have joined the movement to tackle youth unemployment. Are you going to join too? www.generationjobless.eu.
- **Embed in your website/blog:** Share the book cover page which you can find on www.generationjobless.eu/media and add a hyperlink to the page www.generationjobless.eu.
- **Short Media/Blog Release:** If you have your own blog I would be thankful if you publish a short media release about *"Generation Jobless?"* I am happy to send you a customized template for a blog article. Contact me at info@petervogel.org.

Now you've read plenty of my stuff and I kept you away from action long enough. Now put your thoughts to action and help me tackle youth unemployment.

Dr. Peter Vogel
Switzerland
Info@petervogel.org
@pevogel

Notes

1 The Youth Unemployment Crisis and the Threat of a "Generation Jobless"

1. Others also use the term "Lost Generation." However, I purposefully decided not to go with that term given its connotation with young people growing up in the time of World War I.
2. A more refined regional assessment of the education system includes whether there is compulsory education and if yes until what age. (The average duration of compulsory education in South and West Asia is 5.7 years whereas it is 10.6 years in North America and Western Europe). Moreover, we need to account for the net enrolment rates (NER) for basic education as this indicates how many young people might actually engage in work activities even prior to the end of compulsory education. According to the UNESCO Institute for Statistics, the global average of NER has reached roughly 90%. Yet, Sub-Saharan Africa is still below 80% (UNESCO, 2012).
3. Sometimes youth is further divided into teenagers (15–19 years old) and young adults (20–24 years old) in order to further customize support measures to the specific age groups.
4. Statement made by Assar Lindbeck at the Global Economic Symposium: http://www.global-economic-symposium.org/knowledgebase/the-global-society/tackling-youth-unemployment/proposals/youth-unemployment.
5. Definition adopted from the website of the International Labour Organization (ILO): http://www.ilo.org/public/english/employment/yen/whatwedo/projects/indicators/2.htm.
6. To make these assessments I took both the youth and the adult unemployment rates provided by the OECD from 2004 to 2014 (OECD StatExtracts: http://stats.oecd.org).
7. In this regional assessment I focus on the EU28 member states + Switzerland, Norway, Iceland and non-EU Balkan countries.

3 Trends and Outlook

1. That study had been commissioned by the Department for Business, Innovation and Skills.

4 Entrepreneurship: Turning Job Seekers into Job Creators

1. Statement at the Global Economic Symposium 2013 in Kiel.

6 Employers' Contribution to Tackling Youth Unemployment

1. A project by Credit Suisse Diversity and Inclusion Switzerland.

7 Designing Active Labor Market Policies to Tackle Youth Unemployment

1. Adopted from Bell & Benes (2012).

8 More Solutions

1. These solutions have been adopted from the GES knowledge database where they have been published by the respective individuals: http://www.global-economic-symposium.org/knowledgebase/knowledgebase.
2. Ideas adopted from http://skollworldforum.org/2013/09/18/tackling-youth-unemployment-is-the-most-important-issue/?series=whats-not-being-discussed-during-un-week-this-year-about-the-post-2015-development-framework-but-should-be.
3. The WEF Global Agenda Council on tackling youth unemployment: http://www.weforum.org/community/global-agenda-councils/youth-unemployment-visualization-2013%20.

Bibliography

Acs, Z. 2006. How Is Entrepreneurship Good for Economic Growth? *Innovations: Technology, Governance, Globalization*, 1(1): 97–107.

AIHW (Authoritative Information and Statistics to promote better health and wellbeing). 2012. What about Indigenous Australians? http://www.aihw.gov.au/australias-welfare/2013/indigenous-australians/ (accessed June 2014).

Apple. 2014. Apple Classrooms of Tomorrow – ACOT². http://ali.apple.com/acot2/principles/ (accessed June 2014).

Archer, C. 2004. University Students' Perceptions of their Readiness to Enter the Workforce upon Graduation. University of Lethbridge.

Arulampalam, W. 2001. Is Unemployment Really Scarring? Effects of Unemployment Experiences on Wages. *Economic Journal*, 111(475): 585–606.

Audretsch, D. B. 2002. The Dynamic Role of Small Firms: Evidence from the US. *Small Business Economics*, 18(1): 13–40.

Ayers, S. 2013. *The High Cost of Youth Unemployment*. Washington, DC: Center for American Progress.

Barclays. 2013. Barclays to recruit a further 1,000 apprentices and announce groundbreaking new programme to support 10,000 young people into work. http://www.newsroom.barclays.co.uk/Press-releases/Barclays-to-recruit-a-further-1-000-apprentices-and-announce-groundbreaking-new-programme-to-support-9ef.aspx

BBC. 2013a. How to live with your parents when you are an adult. http://www.bbc.com/news/business-25356377 (accessed July 2014).

BBC. 2013b. Jobless young Italians face life on the black market. http://www.bbc.com/news/business-24734058.

Belbin, M. 1981. *Management Teams: Why They Succeed or Fail*. Elsevier, Burlington, MA.

Bell, D. N. F. & Blanchflower, D. G. 2011. Young people and the great recession, IZA Discussion Paper No. 5674 (Bonn).

Bell, D. & Benes, K. 2012. Transitioning Graduates to Work: Improving the Labor Market Success of Poorly Integrated New Entrants (PINEs) in Canada. CCDF.

Bell, D. & O'Reilly, E. 2008. Making Bridges Visible: An Inventory of Innovative, Effective or Promising Canadian School-to-Work Transition Practices, Programs and Policies. Canadian Council on Learning.

Bentolila, S., Dolado, J. J., & Jimeno, J. F. 2008. Two-tier employment protection reforms: The Spanish experience. CESifo DICE Report.

Betcherman, G., Godfrey, M., Puerto, S., Rother, F. & Stavreska A. 2007. A Review of Interventions to Support Young Workers: Findings of the Youth Employment Inventory. SP Discussion Paper No. 0715. The World Bank.

Bezanson, L. 2008. Career Development: From Under-Represented to Inclusive: Opening Doors to Post-Secondary Participation. The Canada Millennium Scholarship Foundation.

Biavaschi, C., W., Eichhorst, C., Giulietti, M. J., Kendzia, A., Muravyev, J., Pieters, N., Rodríguez-Planas, R., Schmidl, & K. F., Zimmermann. 2012. Youth unemployment and vocational training. Background report for the World Development Report 2013.

Blanchflower, D. G. & Oswald, A. J. 1998. Entrepreneurship and the youth labour market problem: a report for the OECD. Report to OECD, Paris. November.

Blanchflower, D. & Street, T. 2004. Self-employment: More may not be better. NBER Working paper No w10286 Cambridge, MA.

Broomhall, H. S. & Winefield, A. H. 1990. A Comparison of the Affective Well-Being of Young and Middle-aged Unemployed Men Matched for Length of Unemployment. *British Journal of Medical Psychology* 63, 43–52.

Brüderl, J., Preisendörfer, P. & Ziegler, R. 1992. Survival Chances of Newly Founded Business Organizations. *American Sociological Review*, 57(2): 227–242.

CACEE. 2014. Five Characteristics New Grads Should Not Talk About When Applying for Jobs.

Card, D., Kluve, J. & Weber, A. 2010. Active Labour Market Policy Evaluations: A Meta-Analysis. *The Economic Journal*, Wiley Online Library.

Carree, M. A. & Thurik, A. R. 2010. The impact of entrepreneurship on economic growth. In Z. J. Acs & D. B. Audretsch (eds) *Handbook of Entrepreneurship Research*: 557–594. New York: Springer.

Center for Native American Youth. 2014. http://www.cnay.org/WhyWeAreHere.html (accessed June 2014).

Chigunta, F. 2002. *Youth Entrepreneurship: Meeting the Key Policy Challenges.* Wolfson College, Oxford University, England.

CIPD. 2012. Learning to work: Survey Report. London.

Clancy, C. 2013. Shocking Number of Youth Jobless, Not in School. The Huffington Post. http://www.huffingtonpost.ca/2013/06/20/youth-unemployment-canada-cibc_n_3473194.html?just_reloaded=1 (accessed July 2014).

Coenjaerts, C., Ernst, C., Fortuny, M., Rei, D. & Pilgrim, M. 2009. Youth Unemployment. In: *OECD, Promoting Pro-poor Growth: Employment.* OECD, Paris.

Cominetti, N., Sissons, P., & Jones, K. 2013. *Beyond the Business Case: The Employer's Role in Tackling Youth Unemployment.* The Work Foundation.

Committee of the Regions of the European Union. 2012. Rethinking skills in the context of Europe 2020.

Cooper, A. C., Gimeno-Gascon, F. J. & Woo, C. Y. 1994. Initial Human and Financial Capital as Predictors of New Venture Performance. *Journal of Business Venturing*, 9(5): 371–395.

Curtain, R. 2000. Towards a Youth Employment Strategy. Report to the United Nations on Youth Employment.

DA Denmark. 2012. Flexicurity 2nd Gen: Effort Against Youth Unemployment.

Deloitte. 2014. Global Human Capital Trends: Engaging the 21st Century Workforce. Deloitte University Press.

Demidova, O. & Signorelli, M. 2011. The Impact of Crises on Youth Unemployment of Russian Regions: An Empirical Analysis. *China-USA Business Review*, 10(7): 471–507.

Dencker, J. C., Gruber, M. & Shah, S. K. 2009a. Pre-Entry Knowledge, Learning, and the Survival of New Firms. *Organization Science* 20(3): 516–537.

Dencker, J.C., Gruber, M. & Shah, S. K. 2009b. Individual and Opportunity Factors Influencing Job Creation in New Firms. *Academy of Management Journal* 52(6): 1125–1147.

Dencker, J. C. & Gruber, M. 2014. The Effects of Opportunities and Founder Experience on New Firm Performance. *Strategic Management Journal*. Chicago.

Deo, M. 2013. Doctor Population Ratio for India – The Reality. *Indian Journal of Medical Research*, 137(4): 632–635.

Désiage, L., Duhautois, R., & Redor, D. 2010. Do Public Subsidies Have an Impact on New Firm Survival? An Empirical Study with French Data. TEPP Working Paper, No 2010 – 4. ISSN 2110-5472.

Die Chance. 2013. Zahlen und Erfolg 2013. Foundation "Die Chance."

Erikson, E. H. 1959. Identity and the Life Cycle. *Psychological Issues*, 1, 50–100.

ETUC (European Trade Union Confederation). 2013. Framework of Actions on Youth Employment.

Eurofound. 2011. Young people and NEETs in Europe: First findings (résumé) European Foundation for the Improvement of Living and Working Conditions (EFILWC). Dublin, Ireland.

Eurofound. 2012. NEETs – Young people not in employment, education or training: Characteristics, costs and policy responses in Europe. European Foundation for the Improvement of Living and Working Conditions (EFILWC). Dublin, Ireland.

Eurofound. 2013. Young people and temporary employment in Europe. European Foundation for the Improvement of Living and Working Conditions (EFILWC). Dublin, Ireland.

European Commission. 2007. Towards Common Principles of Flexicurity: More and Better Jobs through Flexibility and Security.

European Commission. 2008. Expert Group: Entrepreneurship in higher education.

European Commission. 2011. Statement by President Barroso at the "Youth on the Move – Make it Happen" event.

European Commission. 2012a. EU Employment and Social Situation Review.

European Commission. 2012b. Effects and impact of entrepreneurship programmes in higher education.

European Commission. 2014a. Youth Guarantee. European Commission: http://ec.europa.eu/social/main.jsp?catId=1079 (accessed June 2014).

European Commission. 2014b. Youth on the Move. http://ec.europa.eu/youthonthe
move/ (accessed June 2014).

European Commission. 2014c. Erasmus+. http://ec.europa.eu/programmes/erasmus-
plus (accessed June 2014).

European Commission. 2014d. Action Teams. http://ec.europa.eu/europe2020/pdf/
barroso/report_en.pdf (accessed June 2014).

European Commission. 2014e. Quality Frameworks for Traineeship. http://www.
consilium.europa.eu/homepage/showfocus?focusName=quality-framework-for-
traineeships-adopted&lang=en (accessed June 2014).

European Commission. 2014f. European Alliance for Apprenticeships. http://
ec.europa.eu/education/policy/vocational-policy/alliance_en.htm (accessed June
2014).

European Commission. 2014g. EU Skills Panorama. http://euskillspanorama.cedefop.
europa.eu/ (accessed June 2014).

European Commission. 2014h. Youth Employment Initiative(YEI): http://europa.eu/
rapid/press-release_IP-14-784_en.htm (accessed May 2014).

European Commission. 2014i. Flexicurity: http://ec.europa.eu/social/main.jsp?catId=
102 (accessed June, 2014).

Eurostat. 2014. Harmonized unemployment rate by sex – age group 15-24. http://
epp.eurostat.ec.europa.eu/tgm/table.do?tab=table&init=1&language=en&pcode
=teilm021&plugin=1 (accessed July 2014).

Fast Future. 2008. Designing your Future: Key Trends, Challenges, and Choices Facing
Associations and Nonprofit Leaders. ASAE Publishing.

Fayolle, A., Gailly, B. T., & Lassas-Clerc, N. 2006. Assessing the Impact of Entrepreneurship Education Programmes: A New Methodology. *Journal of European
Industrial Training*, 30(8/9): 701–720.

Foyer Health Programme. 2013. Take a positive step for your well-being.

Furlong, A. 2007. The Zone of Precariety and Discourses of Vulnerability: NEET in
the UK. *Journal of Social Sciences and Humanities*, 381, 101–121.

FutureWork Forum. 2010. Employing the Next Generation. A report by Generation
Europe Foundation and The FutureWork Forum.

GES (Global Economic Symposium). 2013. Empowering Workforce: 4-Generations
Demography Management. http://www.global-economic-symposium.org/
knowledgebase/empowering-workforce-demography-management-with-four-
generations (accessed June, 2014).

Görlich, D., Stepanok, I. & Al-Hussami, F. 2013. Youth unemployment in Europe and
the World: Causes, Consequences and Solutions.

Gough, K. V., Langevang, T., Owusu, G. 2013. Youth Employment in a Globalising
World. *International Development Planning Review*, 35(2), 91–102.

Green European Journal. 2013. Brain Drain or Just Mobility? http://www.
greeneuropeanjournal.eu/brain-drain-or-just-mobility (accessed July 2014).

Gregg, P. & Tominey, E. 2004. The Wage Scar from Youth Unemployment. CMPO
Working Paper Series No. 04/097.

Gunderson, S., Jones, R. & Scanland, K. 2004. The Jobs Revolution: Changing How America Works. Copywriters Inc.

Gurney, R. M. 1980. The Effects of Unemployment on the Psychosocial Development of School Leavers. *Journal of Occupational Psychology*, 53, 205–213.

Haas, M., & Vogel, P. 2015. Supporting the Transition from Unemployment to Self-employment – A Comparison of Governmental Support Programs across Europe, in: J. Brewer, S. W. Gibson (eds) *Necessity Entrepreneurship: An Institutional Review*, Edward Elgar, Northampton, MA.

Haltiwanger, J., Jarmin, R. & Miranda, J. 2009. Who Creates Jobs? Small vs. Large vs. Young: University of Maryland, U.S. Census Bureau.

Hango, D. 2010. Labour Market Experiences of Youth After Leaving School: Exploring the Effect of Educational Pathways Over Time. Statistics Canada.

Hasluck, C. 2012. Why businesses should recruit young people. Briefing Paper. UKCES.

Herald Scotland. 2014. Drinks giant Diageo launches £5m youth unemployment programme. http://www.heraldscotland.com/business/company-news/drinks-giant-diageo-launches-5m-youth-unemployment-programme.23471471.

High Level Group on the Modernisation of Higher Education. 2013. Improving the quality of teaching and learning in Europe's higher education institutions. http://ec.europa.eu/education/library/reports/modernisation_en.pdf (accessed June 2014).

Hooley, T., Marriott, J. & Sampson, J. 2011. Fostering College and Career Readiness: How Career Development Activities in Schools Impact on Graduation Rates and Students' Life Success. University of Derby, International Centre for Guidance Studies.

House of Lords. 2014. Youth Unemployment in the EU: A Scarred Generation? 12th Report of Session 2013–2014 – European Union Committee.

Huffington Post. 2014. The Solution to Youth Unemployment Lies with Young People Themselves: www.huffingtonpost.com/maria-fanjul/the-solution-to-youth-unemployment_b_4640517.html (accessed June 2014).

Hussainat, M. M., Ghnimat, Q. M. & Al-Dlaeen, M. A. 2012. The Impact of Unemployment on Young People in the Jordanian Community: A Case Study from Unemployed Perspective. *Asian Social Science*, 9(1).

IBIS Capital Report. 2013. Global e-Learning Investment Review. United Kingdom.

ILO (International Labor Organization). 2010. Trabajo decente y juventud en América Latina. Lima, Peru.

ILO (International Labor Organization). 2011. Migrants Return to India.

ILO (International Labor Organization). 2012a. World of Work Report: Better Jobs for a Better Economy. Geneva, Switzerland.

ILO (International Labor Organization). 2012b. Eurozone Job Crisis: Trends and Policy Responses. Geneva, Switzerland.

ILO (International Labor Organization). 2013. Global Employment Trends for Youth. Geneva, Switzerland.

ILO (International Labor Organization). 2014a. Ban Ki-moon: Decent jobs for youth are essential to the future we want. http://www.ilo.org/global/about-the-ilo/newsroom/news/WCMS_247414/lang--en/index.htm

ILO (International Labor Organization). 2014b. Youth employment in Africa. http://www.ilo.org/addisababa/media-centre/news/WCMS_234712/lang--en/index.htm Geneva, Switzerland.

IOE (Institute of Education – University of London). 2009. Tackling the NEETs problem. Supporting local authorities in reducing young people not in employment, education and training. www.ioe.ac.uk/tacklingneets.pdf (accessed April 2014).

IOM (International Organization for Migration). 2013. World Migration Report.

Istance, D., Rees, G. & Williamson, H. 1994, Young people not in education, training or employment in South Glamorgan, South Glamorgan Training and Enterprise Council, Cardiff.

Jacobs, E. 2014. Twelve Ways to Fix the Youth Unemployment Crisis. Brookings Institution.

Johnson Controls. 2009. The Smart Workplace in 2030 – Summary. Global Workplace Innovation.

Johnson, B. C., Manyika, J. M. & Yee L. A. 2005. The next revolution in interactions. McKinsey Quarterly.

Johnson, M. 2014. *The Worldwide Workplace – Solving the Global Talent Equation.* Palgrave Macmillan.

Katz, J. A. 2008. Fully Mature but Not Fully Legitimate: A Different Perspective on the State of Entrepreneurship Education. *Journal of Small Business Management,* 46(4): 550–566.

Kotloff, K. L. 2004. Re-structuring of Educational System: A Panacea for Youth Unemployment in Africa. *Journal of Education and Practice,* 5(6).

Lazear, E. P. 2005. Entrepreneurship. *Journal of Labor Economics,* 23(4): 649–680.

Lemonade Stories. 2004. www.lemonadestories.com.

Lewis, K. & Massey, C. 2003. Youth Entrepreneurship. In: A. De Bruin, & A. Dupuis (eds) *Entrepreneurship: New Perspectives in a Global Age*: 206–226. Ashgate Publishing Limited. London, UK.

Lipnach, J. & Stamps, J. 2000. *Virtual Teams: People Working Across Boundaries with Technology.* John Wiley & Sons Inc.

Lund, S., Manyika, J. M. & Ramaswamy, S. 2012. *Preparing for a New Era of Work.* McKinsey Quarterly.

Manaconda, M. & Petrongolo, B. 1999. Skill Mismatch and Unemployment in OECD Countries. *Economica* 66: 181–207.

Manpower. 2012. Youth Unemployment Challenge and Solutions.

Manpower. 2013. Talent Shortage Survey: Research Results.

Martin, G. 2009. A Portrait of the Youth Labor Market in 13 Countries, 1980–2007. *Monthly Labor Review*: 3–21.

McKee-Ryan, F., Song, Z., Wanberg, C. & Kinicki, A. 2005. Psychological and Physical Well-Being during Unemployment: A Meta-Analytic Study. *Journal of Applied Psychology,* 90(1): 53–75.

McKinsey. 2012. The world at work: Jobs, pay, and skills for 3.5 billion people.

Mourshed, M., Patel, J. & Suder, K. 2014. *Education to employment: Getting Europe's Youth into Work.* McKinsey.

Meager, N., Bates, P. & Cowling, M. 2003. An Evaluation of Business Start-Up Support for Young People. *National Institute Economic Review*, 186(1): 59–72.

Monitor Company Group. 2009. *Paths to Prosperity – Promoting Entrepreneurship in the 21st Century.* Cambridge, MA: Monitor Company Group.

Morsy, H. 2012. Scarred Generation. *Finance and Development*, 49(1).

Nordström Skans, O. 2004. Scarring effects of the first labour market experience: A sibling based analysis. IFAU Working Paper Series 2004:14. IFAU, Uppsala.

NY Times. 2013. Migration to Mexico. http://www.nytimes.com/interactive/2013/09/22/world/americas/migration-to-mexico.html?ref=americas&_r=0 (accessed July 2014).

O'Higgins, N. 2001. Youth unemployment and employment policy: a global perspective. MPRA Paper 23698. University Library of Munich.

O'Sullivan, R., Mugglestone, K. & Allison, T. 2014. In This Together: The Hidden Cost of Young Adult Unemployment. Young Invincibles.

OECD. 2000. Employment Outlook – Chapter 5: The partial renaissance of self-employment.

OECD. 2001. Putting the Young in Business: Policy Challenges for Youth Entrepreneurship. The LEED Programme.

OECD. 2010. *Off to a Good Start? Jobs for Youth,* OECD Publishing.

OECD & ILO. 2011. Giving Youth a Better Start: A Policy Note for the G20 Meeting of Labour and Employment Ministers.

OECD. 2013. Skills Strategy. http://skills.oecd.org/documents/oecdskillsstrategy.html (accessed June 2014).

OECD. 2014. Employment and labor markets: Key tables from OECD. http://www.oecd-ilibrary.org/employment/employment-and-labour-markets-key-tables-from-oecd_20752342 (accessed June 2014).

Palfrey, J. & Gasser, U. 2008. *Born Digitals*. Basic Books.

Pfeiffer, F. & Reize, F. 2000. Business Start-ups by the Unemployed: An Econometric Analysis Based on Firm Data. *Labour Economics* 7(5): 629–663.

Platt, W. 1984. Unemployment and Suicidal Behaviour: Review of the Literature. *Social Science and Medicine* 19, 93–115.

Prensky, M. 2001. Digital Natives, Digital Immigrants. In *"On the Horizon,"* NCB University Press.

Rosen. A. 2013. The Entrepreneurship Answer to Youth Unemployment. Forbes Magazine. http://www.forbes.com/sites/amyrosen/2013/11/18/the-entrepreneurship-answer-to-youth-unemployment/ (accessed June 2014).

Rowley, K. M. & Feather, N. T. 1987. The Impact of Unemployment in Relation to Age and Length of Unemployment. *Journal of Occupational Psychology* 60, 323–332.

Ryan, P. 2001. The School-to-Work Transition: A Cross-National Perspective. *Journal of Economic Literature*, 39(1): 34–92.

Schoof, U. 2006. Stimulating youth entrepreneurship: Barriers and incentives to enterprise start-ups by young people, International Labour Office.

Selingo, J. J. 2012. On Students' Paths to College, Some Detours Are Desirable? The Chronicle of Higher Education. http://chronicle.com/article/On-the-Path-to-College-Some/135910/ (accessed June 2014)

Shanghai Bureau of Human Resources and Social Security. 2014. 1000 Plan. http://1000plan.safea.gov.cn (access June, 2014).

Shepherd, D., Wiklund, J. & Haynie, J. 2009. Moving Forward: Balancing the Financial and Emotional Costs of Business Failure. *Journal of Business Venturing*, 24(2): 134–148.

Sieger, P., Fueglistaller, U. & Zellweger, T. 2011. Entrepreneurial intentions and activities of students across the world. International report of the GUESSS Project.

Simpson, J. & Christensen, J. 2009. Youth Entrepreneurship and the ILO, Note on practices and lessons learned, Small Enterprise Programme, International Labour Office, Geneva.

Solman, P. 2013. The Youth Unemployment Crisis: A Fix that Works and Pays for Itself. http://www.pbs.org/newshour/making-sense/the-youth-unemployment-crisis/ (accessed June 2014).

Stanford. 2005. You've got to find what you love. Commencement Speech by Steve Jobs: http://news.stanford.edu/news/2005/june15/jobs-061505.html (accessed August 10, 2014).

Stangler, D. 2009. The Economic Future Just Happened: Ewing Marion Kauffman Foundation.

Statistics Sweden 1998. New started enterprises in Sweden 1996 and 1997, Statistika meddelanden, SCB, Örebro.

STS (State Training Service). 2014. Jobs program supports young unemployed people. Office of Education. https://www.training.nsw.gov.au/news/rtes_partnering. html (accessed July 2014).

Swiss Education. 2014. Vocational education and training. https://swisseducation. educa.ch/en/node/126897 (accessed June 2014).

Talwer, R. & Hancock, T. 2010. The Shape of Jobs to Come: Possible New Careers Emerging from Advances in Science and Technology (2010 – 2030). Fast Future Research Report.

Taylor, A. 2007. Pathways for Youth to the Labour Market: An Overview of High School Initiatives. Canadian Policy Research Networks and the Canadian Council on Learning.

Taylor, P. & Keeter, S. 2010. Millenials: A Portrait of Generation Next – Confident. Connected. Open to Change. Pew Research Center.

Techcrunch. 2012. Apple: 20,000 Education iPad Apps Developed; 1.5 Million Devices In Use At Schools. http://techcrunch.com/2012/01/19/apple-20000-education-ipad-apps-developed-1-5-million-devices-in-use-at-schools/ (accessed June 2014).

TEDx. 2010. Cameron Herold: Let's raise kids to be entrepreneurs. http://www.ted. com/talks/cameron_herold_let_s_raise_kids_to_be_entrepreneurs.

TEDx. 2013. Peter Vogel. Empowering tomorrow's leaders to re-invent the labor market. https://www.youtube.com/watch?v=C6TRnLoYdtA.

The Economist. 2013. Youth Unemployment: Generation Jobless. http://www.economist.com/news/international/21576657-around-world-almost-300m-15-24-year-olds-are-not-working-what-has-caused.

The Prince's Trust. 2014. Mental Health Warning for Jobless Young. The Youth Index 2014.

Thornberry, T. P. & Christenson, R. L. 1984. Unemployment and Criminal Involvement: An Investigation of Reciprocal Causal Structures. *American Sociological Review* 49, 398–411.

Timmons, J. A. 1990. *New Business Opportunities: Getting to the Right Place at the Right Time*, Brick House Pub Co.

Tirapani. A.N. 2012. *Youth Attitude to the Job Market. Overcoming the Skills Mismatch*. ThinkYoung.

Toffler, A. 1970. *Future Shock*. Random House.

UNESCO Institute for Statistics. 2012. Global Education Digest: Opportunities lost – the impact of grade repetition and early school leaving. Montreal, Canada.

UNESCO. 2014. What do we mean by youth. http://www.unesco.org/new/en/social-and-human-sciences/themes/youth/youth-definition.

United Nations. 2011. Youth Employment: Youth Perspectives on the Pursuit of Decent Work in Changing Times. World Youth Report. Geneva, Switzerland.

United Nations. 2012. Secretary-General. http://www.un.org/News/Press/docs/2012/sgsm14451.doc.htm (accessed September 2014).

United Nations. 2013a. The future of employment: the world of work in 2030. Special Joint Meeting, NY.

United Nations. 2013b. Challenges and hope for world's indigenous youth. http://undesadspd.org/IndigenousPeoples/NewsandMedia/tabid/1615/news/329/Default.aspx (accessed June 2014).

US Census Bureau. 2012. Table 232. Mean Earnings by Highest Degree Earned: 2009. http://www.census.gov/compendia/statab/2012/tables/12s0232.pdf (accessed July 2014).

US Department of Labor. 1999. Trends and Challenges for Work in the 21st Century. http://www.dol.gov/oasam/programs/history/herman/reports/futurework/report.htm.

USC (Unique Story Coaching). 2011. Pilot Outcome Report.

Van Praag, C. M. & Versloot, P. H. 2007. What Is the Value of Entrepreneurship? A Review of Recent Research. *Small Business Economics*, 29(4): 351–382.

Versnel, J., DeLuca, C., Hutchinson, N., Hill, A. & Chin, P. 2011. International and National Factors Affecting School-to-Work Transitions for At-Risk Youth in Canada: An Integrative Review. *The Canadian Journal of Career Development*, 10(1): 22–31.

Victor Pinchuk Foundation, 2013.

Viebrock, E., & Clasen, J. 2009. Flexicurity – a state-of-the-art review. REC Working Paper.

Vogel. 2010. Entrepreneurs: The Creators of Tomorrow's Jobs. An Essay for the St. Gallen Symposium: http://papers.ssrn.com/sol3/papers.cfm?abstract_id= 2478742 (accessed June 2014).

Vogel, P. 2013a. Intra(Entre)preneurial Solutions to Recruit and Retain Tomorrow's Leaders. ZfU Leadership Training. http://www.slideshare.net/pevogel/intra entrepreneurial-solutions-to-recruit-and-retain-tomorrows-leaders (accessed May 2014).

Vogel, P. 2013b. The Employment Outlook for Youth: Building Entrepreneurial Ecosystems as a Way Forward. Paper for the G20 Youth Forum 2013, St. Petersburg, Russia.

Vogel, P. & Fischler-Strasak, U. 2014. *Fostering Sustainable Innovation within Organizations: Building Intrapreneurship Innovation Ecosystems*. Springer Publishing.

Vogel, P. 2014. Guidance for Generating Multi-Stakeholder Solutions to Global Problems. Contribution for the 2014 Global Economic Symposium.

Wallstreet Journal. 2011. Generation Jobless: Young Men Suffer Worst as Economy Staggers. http://online.wsj.com/news/articles/SB1000142405297020450530457 7000380740614776.

Wentworth, L. & Bertelsmann-Scott, T. 2013. SA-EU Summit 2013: Investment and Jobs in South Africa and SADC: http://www.saiia.org.za/opinion-analysis/sa-eu-summit-2013-investment-and-jobs-in-south-africa-and-sadc.

White, S. & Kenyon, P. 2001. Enterprise-based youth employment policies, strategies and programmes. Initiatives for the development of enterprise action and strategies, Working Paper, InFocus Programme on Skills, Knowledge and Employability, ILO, Geneva.

Winefield, A. H. 1997. Editorial: Introduction to the Psychological Effects of Youth Unemployment: International Perspectives. *Journal of Adolescence,* 20(3): 237–241.

WMFC (West Midland Family Center). 2014. Generational Differences Chart.

Wolbers, MHJ, 2003. Job Mismatches and their Labour Market Effects among School Leavers in Europe. *European Sociological Review*, 19(3): 249–266.

World Bank. 2011. *Migration and Remittances Factbook,* 2nd Edition.

Youth Contract Program. 2014. http://www.dwp.gov.uk/youth-contract.

Index

Printed by Printforce, the Netherlands